PLANTAGENET
QUEENS AND
CONSORTS

Dr Steven J. Corvi has presented papers at West Point, to the War Studies Society, King's College London and Fort Hays State University. He researches and teaches the late English medieval period with a special emphasis on the Wars of the Roses and English queenship. He regularly teaches graduate courses in British and European History, and has created seminar courses on English queenship from Matilda to Elizabeth I. He is the author of three books and has been an advisor and commentator for documentaries produced for The History Channel.

PLANTAGENET QUEENS AND CONSORTS

FAMILY, DUTY AND POWER

STEVEN J. CORVI

AMBERLEY

In loving memory of my Queen Mother, Elizabeth B. Corvi; and
for my daughter, Katherine E. Corvi; and Malisa A. Morais

First published 2018
This edition publshed 2020

Amberley Publishing
The Hill, Stroud
Gloucestershire, GL5 4EP

www.amberley-books.com

Copyright © Steven J. Corvi, 2018, 2020

The right of Steven J. Corvi to be
identified as the Author of this work
has been asserted in accordance with
the Copyrights, Designs and Patents Act
1988.

ISBN 978 1 4456 9915 8 (paperback)
ISBN 978 1 4456 6960 1 (ebook)

British Library Cataloguing in Publication
Data.
A catalogue record for this book is
available from the British Library.

Typesetting and Origination by Amberley
Publishing
Printed in the UK.

CONTENTS

INTRODUCTION

The period of 1236-1485 in English history was one of immense socio-economic change, which transformed the medieval world into the Early Modern era. The monarchy, and more specifically the roles of royal consorts, evolved during this period. *Plantagenet Queens and Consorts* identifies Eleanor of Aquitaine, Queen Consort of Henry II, as the blueprint for English queenship. Prior to Eleanor, England had been scarred by the dynastic conflict known as 'The Anarchy', in which Matilda, heir of Henry I, and her cousin, King Stephen, vied for the crown. As the wife of Matilda's son, politically astute Eleanor redefined and rehabilitated the role of consorts in English government.

Compared to women in other European countries, women in medieval and Early Modern England were fairly liberated, and were routinely active in local and national government, apprenticed to trades, ran their own businesses, and were both influential patrons of and participants in the arts. Through their leadership, our subjects created a climate that made it possible for England to have its first queen crowned in her own right, Mary I, in 1553. Mary was followed by Elizabeth I and two centuries later Victoria, the latter two widely considered to be among the most successful British monarchs of all. The figures that followed in Eleanor's footsteps earned the confidence of the English people, and created a tradition that enabled Margaret Thatcher to be elected Prime Minister three times over. In contrast, the United States is more traditional, and some could argue, more repressed, in its attitude toward women in government. The United States has a poor presence of women in local and national government, and has yet to elect a female president or even vice-president.

There have been several recent publications that have garnered an interest in women's roles during this evolutionary period in English history. However, unlike these other works, I do not consider this book as a 'women's history'. To separate men's and women's roles is limiting, in that it ignores their symbiotic relationship, where their actions influence both one another and their environment. The historian Allen J. Frantzen sums it up nicely: 'Gender is a tool for reconceptualizing male as well as female roles, reconfiguring the power struggle between sexes, and merging sexual distinction founded on reproductive differences.'[1] There is a wealth of primary source information and recent scholarship on some of our subjects, like Margaret of Anjou and Elizabeth Woodville. Other subjects require more digging for source material, from which we must make educated inferences. For example, Katherine of Valois' documentation is lacking, due in part to the attitude of medieval France toward women's inheritance, which resulted in Salic law.

Eleanor of Provence is the first in our study to follow in the shadow of Eleanor of Aquitaine. Her lineage was through Eleanor

---

1 Allen J. Frantzen, 'When Women Aren't Enough' in *Studying Medieval Women*, ed. Nancy F. Partner (Cambridge, USA, Medieval Academy of America, 1993), p. 143.

of Aquitaine's youngest son King John (of *Magna Charta* fame), whose son Henry III married Eleanor of Provence. She was married at twelve and became queen to Henry III. Her impact on the evolution of queenship has been overlooked. There has been an excellent modern biography by Margaret Howell, *Eleanor of Provence: Queenship in the Thirteenth-Century England* (1998). Eleanor of Provence's important influence upon Henry III's reign, especially in strengthening the monarchy against a belligerent baronage, helped orchestrate the overthrow of Simon de Montfort, and ultimately led to the coronation of her son Edward I.[2] She will start off this study with a good foundation for the evolution of queenship in England.

There is a significant amount of primary source information on Isabella of France, most of which concerns her successful rebellion and deposition of her husband, Edward II, and her regency on behalf of her son. The Gascon Rolls in the UK National Archives remain unpublished in their entirety. They are valuable in that they document government in the Late Medieval era, and more specifically the relationship of English kings with their subjects in Gascony. Isabella and the activities of her household feature prominently in the Rolls. Helen Castor recently featured Isabella in a chapter in her study on a selection of English queens, and Alison Weir provided a biography in 2009. Weir's work has attracted criticism in some quarters for portraying Isabella in an overly positive light, and for attempting to absolve her of any blame in her husband's mysterious death. But Isabella, like all of our subjects, was a complex figure, and we aim to examine her more objectively.

---

2   Margaret Howell, *Eleanor of Provence: Queenship in the Thirteenth-Century England* (Blackwell Publishing, 1998), pp. xvii-xviii.

Kathryn Warner also produced an interesting biography of Isabella in 2017 that perhaps achieved this goal.

While the men surrounding Philippa of Hainault have been extensively studied, she herself has not. The reason is unclear, since her political, military and dynastic contributions are well documented. The personal accounts of the queen's household survive, as well as some of her correspondences. Some of Philippa's personal belongings have also survived, such as the Harley Manuscript Collection, which includes her psalter. The works of Jean Froissart are an invaluable resource for studying fourteenth-century events involving England and France. Froissart was in the service of Queen Philippa of Hainault, and was present at many of the political and military events taking place during the first half of the Hundred Years War. He likely knew and frequently interacted with many of the members of the royal family that are included in his chronicles, though some of his accounts were lifted from other sources. What is problematic about works that are funded by a royal patron, of course, like Froissart's, is that they can be biased. Therefore, we have counter-balanced them with other contemporary sources.

Joan of Kent, Princess of Wales, never became queen owing to the death of her husband, Edward the Black Prince, just one year before his own father. But she wielded influence over her husband and her son, and had ties to the Lollard movement. With the exception of a few journal articles and the erudite biography by Penny Lawne (2015), Joan and her role in English society has not been thoroughly examined in the past thirty years. Most of what has been published on her concerns her complicated marital history. Edward overlooked his cousin's sordid past, which played out in the courts, and forfeited a foreign political marriage to wed her. A letter written by Edward to Joan after the battle of Najera in 1367 gives us clues that their marriage was one of great affection; he addressed her as 'My dearest and truest sweetheart and beloved companion'. According to Froissart, the daughter-in-law of his patroness was 'la plus belle de tout le royaume d'Engleterre et la plus amoureuse' – 'the most beautiful woman in all the realm of England, and the most loving'. The Chandos Herald also gave her praise.

Like her sister-in-law Joan of Kent, Katherine Swynford never wore a crown but was allied with a man who wielded immense political power in England and abroad. Unlike our other subjects, she began her career as a royal mistress, eventually being raised up to become the wife of her lover. Katherine's childhood and first marriage are shrouded in mystery; her ancestry and even the number of her children are the subject of debate for historians. In contrast, we have no shortage of sources for Katherine once she became allied with the Duke of Lancaster. Since the chroniclers of the period, like Thomas Walsingham, were ecclesiastical, they typically condemned Katherine and the duke's relationship. Criticism against Katherine subsided somewhat when she finally became the duke's wife, and she earned praise as a patron of the arts and religious houses, especially Lincoln Cathedral. Since no letters written by Katherine Swynford survive, nor her own will, the Duchy of Lancaster records are some of the best contemporary sources available to learn about her life. Other valuable sources include John of Gaunt's Register, the civic and clerical records from Lincoln and Leicester, and the Calendar of Patent Rolls. None of these entries, however, tell us anything about Katherine's personality or feelings.

The biggest challenge in researching Katherine is that the romance surrounding her life must first be deconstructed. Anya Seton's historical novel *Katherine* has been reprinted for each new generation and has thus captivated countless readers. Though the plot of the novel was well researched at the time by Seton, it has not held up to further scholarship on Katherine, which has corrected many of the errors within the novel. *Katherine* does its largest disservice, however, by applying notions of romantic love and modern sensibilities to a medieval woman. Jeanette Lucraft's biography on Katherine, which evolved from her dissertation, has had a significant role in rescuing the real Katherine from Seton's legend. Alison Weir has also made Swynford the subject of a biography.

Joanna of Navarre had a successful political career before she came to England. She competently governed Brittany after the death of her first husband, and it was there that she met Henry Bolingbroke while he was abroad. Their union was the second marriage for both. With the exception of a few chronicles written during the reign of her husband, Henry IV, most of our source material for Joanna's life concerns her trial in England during the reign of her stepson, Henry V. Joanna was the only English queen ever to be tried for witchcraft. A. R. Myers' 'The Captivity of a Royal Witch: The Household Accounts of Queen Joan of Navarre, 1419–21' in the John Rylands Library is currently the definitive work on the topic.

Katherine of Valois is our most challenging subject, and most of what we know of her life in France and her marriage to Henry V is conjecture based on sources where she warrants only a brief mention. Volume 9 of the *Foedera* covers the period of March 1413 to July 1420, almost the entire reign of Henry V. Included within are documents concerning the preparations for the invasion of France, Henry's military successes there, and negotiations concerning his strategic marriage to Katherine of Valois. Volume 10 of the *Foedera* covers the period from July 1420 to October 1441, discussing the end of the reign of Henry V and the minority of his son, Henry VI. The details of Katherine's clandestine marriage to Owen Tudor are even more mysterious than her first marriage. Interestingly, Katherine is one of the few women in our study for whom personal goods survive; her bed is on display in Leeds Castle.

There has been a resurgence of interest in the final three ladies in our study, Margaret of Anjou, Elizabeth Wydeville and her daughter, Elizabeth of York. This is no doubt due in part to the publication of several popular histories and novels which have been adapted into miniseries, but also to the discovery of the remains of Richard III. Due to the intricacies of this period, Margaret and the two Elizabeths often overlap in the primary source material. Historians like J. L. Chamberlayne, A. R. Myers and J. L. Laynesmith have published journal articles on all three. *Hardyng's Chronicle* is a prime example of source material being shared by all three. It was revised several times in order to satisfy the ruling monarch at the time, and his family. The original version of the text, ending in 1437, demonstrated a Lancastrian bias, whereas a later edition favoured Edward IV and Elizabeth Wydeville.

Margaret of Anjou wielded considerable influence over her husband, Henry VI, during his bouts of madness, and therefore was often in control of the government. Most of the contemporary sources, like *The Great Chronicle of London*, are critical of Margaret's policies and the unruly behaviour of her troops during the dynastic struggle that has become known as the Wars of the Roses. Since Margaret ran the court under the guise of a regency during her husband's many episodes of irrationality, her queenship can be considered a dry-run for how future English queens crowned in their own right would rule. Helen Maurer recently published the definitive biography of Margaret of Anjou.

We see the women of this period as power brokers through their respective ability to produce heirs and to project the power of the monarchy in their own persons, which could be tenuous. Female authority was judged through the lens of military leadership.

Elizabeth Wydeville has been the subject of recent biographies by David Baldwin and Arlene Ockerlund, both of which examine her ancestry, social connections, clandestine marriage and contributions as queen and widow. We have an abundance of rolls, wills, household accounts and records of patronage for Elizabeth, among them *Hall's Chronicle, Hardyng's Chronicle, The Coventry Leet Book* and *The Hastings Papers*, to name just a few. There is also a significant amount of Italian source material concerning Elizabeth in the archives of Milan, among them Raffaelo de Negra's letter to the Duchess of Milan, a report to the Duke of Milan, and a letter from Luchino Dallaghiexia, a supporter of the Earl of Warwick, to Duke Galeazzo Maria Sforza of Milan. A. F. Sutton and L. Visser-Fuchs' scholarship has done much to rehabilitate the undeserved reputation of Elizabeth Wydeville. Sutton and Fuchs proved Elizabeth was pious and a promoter of culture in the English court. They also refute the claim that Elizabeth Wydeville had any involvement in the demise of the Earl of Desmond, as claimed by his grandson during the reign of Henry VIII, in what became known as 'the Desmond affair'. They also confirmed the claim that the 'Hours of the Guardian Angel' belonged to Elizabeth Wydeville. A. R. Myers proved in his article on the queen's household that Elizabeth Wydeville was a careful manager of money who spent less on household and personal expenses than any of her predecessors. J. R. Lander disproved the theory that Elizabeth Wydeville sought undeserved prestige and money for her family through arranging improper marriages for her siblings.

Along with her husband and her mother, Elizabeth of York has enjoyed renewed interest from historians. Arlene Ockerlund, Alison Weir and Amy Licence have all published recent biographies on the first Tudor queen. The challenge with studying Elizabeth of York as queen consort is that the historian must first sift through the Ricardian propaganda that villainises her family. The *Titulus Regius*, for example, proclaimed the offspring of Elizabeth Wydeville and Edward IV illegitimate, based on the claims of his pre-contract to another woman. There is also the problem of a mysterious letter 'discovered' by George Buck. In his account of Richard III's reign, Buck reproduced the contents of this controversial letter, which Buck claims was written by Princess Elizabeth of York to the Duke of Norfolk, asking for his help in arranging her marriage to her uncle, Richard III. The letter supposedly resided in the private papers of Thomas, Earl of Arundel and Surrey. Only Buck, an apologist for Richard III, mentions the letter. The original (if there ever was one) has long since disappeared. Alison Hanham and Arthur Kincaid have both weighed in on the authenticity of this letter. A recent dramatic miniseries, *The White Princess*, has floated the idea of Elizabeth York having an incestuous relationship with her uncle Richard III. No doubt the Buck letter fuelled this modern myth. It makes for good storytelling, but is far from historical fact.

Despite the unique challenges of studying medieval and Early Modern history, I hope I have been able to unearth these fascinating people, each of whom walked in the shadow of Eleanor of Aquitaine, the prototype for the English queen consort. I have reconstructed their lives to the best of my ability, aiming to inform readers on their contributions to the rule of England during the formative period of 1236–1485.

In the Beginning...

Henry I was a considered a 'great ruling king' and was noted by Orderic Vitalis in his *Historia Ecclesiastica*. He usurped the throne of England by quick thinking and cunning plans after the 'accidental' death of his elder brother William II. He was able to keep his older brother Robert from the throne through determination and pure will. This created some tension, but Henry was able to secure his kingdom and defeated Robert in battle at Tinchebray in 1106; a rather unorthodox succession, but Henry proved to be the superior monarch and reflected the warrior-king persona that started with his father, William the Conqueror.

Nonetheless, this was not the ideal atmosphere for succession. Henry I's reign was successful in the typical medieval manner: the king had his lords pay fealty to him in service and in return he rewarded his barons within the manorial system; he was the warrior-king and was a capable leader of men in battle. However, reigns don't last forever and the succession would become a problem later in Henry's reign. This comes to light after the death of his eldest son in the sinking of the *White Ship* in 1120. This left Henry with a female successor, Matilda, after the premature death of her husband Heinrich V of the Holy Roman Empire in 1125. Henry presented his daughter as successor-magnate in 1126 to the baronage at Westminster. Henry secured an oath of fealty to abide by the succession of his daughter and her heirs as the next monarchs of England. This was not the time for such innovation in thought. Medieval society in England at this time was not completely backward, but was principally ruled by a feudal order cemented by monastic and Christian patriarchal ideals. This precluded women from participating in any real political or societal positions of power, especially if it were over men of the same class. This was further reinforced by the wholesale belief that Eve tempted Adam out of the Garden of Eden.

Matilda's struggle for the throne of England was a perfect example of female power and how it was perceived during this period; and Eleanor of Aquitaine witnessed it firsthand. The 'Anarchy' displayed some of the elemental problems with a woman ruling during this period, since the capacity to lead men in battle was one of the key elements a being a monarch. Since women did not have chivalric and military training and subsequently could not elicit the confidence of soldiers and knights, they were considered inferior to a man in the position of monarch. Matilda's father did, however, try to secure his daughter's validity as a monarch by having the leading barons and knights swear fealty to her.

It also did not help that her second husband, Geoffrey Plantagenet, was disliked by many of the English barons. The marriage was one of convenience and not love, as was usually the case for the Middle Ages. However, it was particularly stormy and Geoffrey was a womanizer and had little respect for his wife. The contemporary accounts of Henry of Huntingdon talk of Matilda's 'masculine firmness', and this was of course a pejorative description. Her already fragile claim to the throne was challenged by Stephen of Blois, who seized it through speed and guile, recalling Henry I's grab for power earlier in the twelfth century. However, Stephen was a weak and vacillating king who did not command the respect that Henry I had won from the peerage. Matilda asserted her claim, and the 'Anarchy' began; England's aristocrats warred and perpetuated private feuds to further their own interests. There was no leadership to bring England under control, and this period saw a return to something like the chaotic Anglo-Saxon period before the Norman Conquest.

Matilda was supported by her half-brother Robert of Gloucester. She made little headway at first, but was able to secure a victory at Lincoln in 1141 and captured King Stephen. Unfortunately, Matilda was not able to garner direct support to rule as monarch. She was viewed by the barons as imperious and haughty and did not fully comprehend the intricacies of the feudal system. Matilda could not simply rule by decree, which she felt was her God-given right as a Holy Roman Empress. Instead she reached out to Henry of Blois, Stephen's brother, who was also papal legate and the Bishop of Winchester, to garner support. Henry conferred on her the title 'Lady of England' and promised to be loyal to her, but this was essentially a personal agreement. It did not embody the fealty system that was in play at the time.[3] Matilda realised now that she would not be able to have direct rule over England and that her best option would be to employ her son Henry Plantagenet as heir apparent. At this juncture, Stephen's son Eustace became an impediment to that goal.

It was clear that Matilda could not maintain order in England with the current barons in power. On the other side of the Channel, Matilda's husband Geoffrey secured Normandy, which was a vital blow against Stephen. Stephen could not secure the fealty of his most powerful baronage and even at times endured revolts. Matilda, meanwhile, had her son knighted by her uncle King David of Scotland. This made the young Henry Plantagenet (aged sixteen) a viable baron for future consideration as the King of England. King David then secured a marriage alliance between himself and the powerful baron Earl Ranulf.

King Stephen wanted to eliminate Henry Plantagenet as a rival to his son Eustace and hoped to capture him, but Henry was able

---

3   R. H. C. Davis, *King Stephen* (Longman, 1967), p. 56.

to escape and harass many northern counties with the help of Ranulf and others. This was a constant thorn in Stephen's side. Henry wisely retreated to Normandy to consolidate his power and raise a large army, realising his presence in England would only result in sieges and a scorched-earth policy against any castle that harboured him. From Normandy he was able to form a new opposition to Stephen.

Stephen's reign was tenuous at best and the barons were not prepared to accept his son Eustace as successor. This presented Matilda with the opportunity to offer her son Henry Plantagenet as a viable candidate. It was a major compromise on her part in the face of reality. The vassalage system of England in the twelfth century was one where fealty of the landed aristocrats was a martial agreement in which a woman could not participate. Matilda garnered support for her son, and when Eustace died in August of 1153 the agreement was made with Stephen that he would rule until his death and would name Henry Plantagenet as his heir to the throne. So here we have undeniable female influence over the succession and the monarchy itself. Matilda may have failed to secure the throne for herself, but in her vigour and determination she was able to secure the throne for her bloodline and expel an existing familial dynastic claim. This watershed event had a lasting impact on the English monarchy and English queenship in the future.

Matilda's exceptional example did have a more immediate impact on Henry II's reign, as his wife Eleanor of Aquitaine was a critical component in his vassal estates and the power pyramid of Henry's Angevin dynasty. There are no records of Matilda's approval or disapproval of her son's choice of queen but there is no doubt that this union created a powerful monarchy and that Eleanor did have a significant influence over Henry's Angevin empire.[4]

The Shadow Falls...

Eleanor of Aquitaine, daughter-in-law of Mathilde, was a proprietorial understudy of queenship and witnessed the realities of a woman ruling in her own right during the High Middle Ages. Eleanor had the duchy of Aquitaine, the most powerful province in France, and could wield significant authority and influence since it was not lost to her if her husband died or divorced her – it was tied into the dowry that belonged to the household, and if that was dissolved it would revert back to Eleanor. This fact alone was what kept Henry and Eleanor as husband and wife, king and queen. In many ways, Eleanor exerted royal authority and power through this duchy in her own right.

The myth of Eleanor has grown since her death and has sparked much speculation. The scant sources and historical records have led to many misleading interpretations: 'A pseudo-Eleanor of historiography has been created, owing little to the historical record, as writers have felt free to pile conjecture upon conjecture.'[5] Nevertheless, we do know the considerable influence Eleanor had upon two kings by marriage, and of her further influence as the mother of two more, Richard and John. The realities of queenship could not have been made clearer to her than they were during the 'Anarchy' as Matilda pressed her claim as queen regnant, and demonstrated that a ruling monarch had to have martial skills and

---

4   Marjorie Chibnall, *The Empress Mathilda: Queen Consort, Queen Mother, and Lady of the English* (Blackwell, 1991), pp. 204-206.

5   Michael Evans, *Inventing Eleanor: The Medieval and Post-Medieval Image of Eleanor of Aquitaine* (London: Bloomsbury, 2014), p. 3.

the ability to inspire and lead men into battle. These were not skills engendered in females and Eleanor would have been painfully aware of this. This is not to say that Eleanor could not wield power; she did, albeit in an indirect manner through patronage and offering effective counsel. Eleanor was queen consort, queen mother and queen regent, but never a queen in her own right as a ruling monarch; in this role she created the blueprint for future English queen consorts.

A successful monarchy during the period in question, 1200–1485, was usually constituted of king and queen operating in a familial ruling dynastic system based on the feudal manorial model. As a result, we don't have pink history for women and blue history for men, as is the current trend in much historical research. To separate the genders in this bi-archy loses the coherency of medieval monarchy in England. The most obvious point is that succession was a vital component of monarchy and this was dependent upon a queen.

Eleanor's queenship in England came during a period of relative prosperity and security thanks to her husband King Henry II. The Angevin empire that defined Henry II's reign was a product of his marriage to Eleanor. She had already displayed her forthrightness and self-belief while she was married to Louis VII in her decision to go on crusade with her French king. From the scant historical record we can deduce that Eleanor was imbued with considerable political skill and worldly sophistication. Compared to Louis VII she was by far the bolder personality and exerted influence through her powerful Duchy of Aquitaine over Louis and his court. She disliked many of Louis' advisors (the feeling was mutual) and displayed an independence which would ultimately lead her away from Louis, but not before she produced two daughters, Marie and Alix. Since Salic law in France banned female succession to the throne, Louis was burdened with a succession crisis.

Eleanor's supposed proclivity for sexual behaviour could make Louis jealous, and when she cast her eye upon young Henry Plantagenet, son of Matilda, there would be a lustful union. All warnings to both Eleanor and Henry were ignored. According to Giraldus Cambrensis Henry was forewarned by his father Geoffrey, 'forbidding him in any wise to touch her, both because she was the wife of his lord and he had known her himself'. Eleanor was bold enough to make a cuckold out her husband, who was a ruling monarch. She realised a union with Henry could produce a more enduring legacy. This behaviour was considered outrageous and immoral for a woman, but Eleanor was no ordinary woman and her husband had shown weakness in controlling her and her duchy. When the chance of a more stable partner presented itself to her she seized it, which would be considered the norm for a king. Louis could condemn her to death for adultery, which was a capital crime on the part of a queen, but Eleanor knew this would create problems with her vassals, who loved her, or perhaps provoke a reaction from Henry himself. In these manoeuvrings Eleanor displayed considerable political skill and social sophistication in the precarious environment of the Middle Ages. In the end, Louis VII was faced with a succession crisis and a duchy he could not control. His need for a male heir outweighed the need to keep Aquitaine. An annulment was granted in 1152 on the grounds of consanguinity, and rumour had it Eleanor was already pregnant with Henry's first child, unbeknownst to Louis.

Eleanor immediately denounced all of Louis's claims to Aquitaine, secured the alliance of her chief vassals and attained approval for her marriage to Henry Plantagenet. This in itself showed great political acumen and independence for a woman. Eleanor married

Henry in May of 1152 at St Pierre in Poitiers in a quiet ceremony. Her future was now secured. Henry was a formidable partner and a match for her ambition. The couple had shared interests and were a good match, though Henry was the dominant partner. It seems that for the first ten to fifteen years of their marriage Henry was attentive to Eleanor while she produced him many male heirs; the historical record is unclear on Henry's fidelity in this honeymoon stage of their marriage, but it is clear he spent much time with his wife when he was not away on the business of the realm. The marriage did provoke Louis, who in time went to war with Henry, Normandy and Aquitaine with the support of some of his barons. Henry of Huntingdon wrote that 'this marriage brought about great enmity and discord between the French king and the duke [Henry Plantagenet]'.[6] Later the marriage began to fail; by 1166, Henry's infidelity was common knowledge.

Eleanor showed her remarkable independence and defiance in 1173 by staging a revolt against Henry with her sons. This revolt was the product of discontent among their sons over his obsession with personal control of his vast Angevin kingdom. He did not relinquish any real control to his sons and he alienated Eleanor from her beloved duchy of Aquitaine. This cocktail of resentment led to a tumultuous time for Henry II that included the death of Thomas Beckett. The strife between Henry and Thomas Beckett began in a close friendship that turned sour when Henry expected Thomas to be his yes-man as the Archbishop of Canterbury, particularly in relation to the monarch's sway over canon law. Thomas Beckett had been Henry's right-hand man as Chancellor of England, and

---

6   Henry of Huntingdon [trans. Diana Greenway], *The History of the English People 1000-1154* (Oxford: Oxford University Press, 1996), p. 88.

when he appointed him archbishop Henry assumed this would continue. What was particularly interesting was that both Matilda and Eleanor advised Henry not to make Beckett archishop. This showed profound political insight from both Matilda, Henry's mother, and Eleanor, Henry's queen. Beckett's murder in 1170 was a gateway event that enabled Eleanor to stage a rebellion with her sons through the discontent generated by Henry's apparent involvement in the archbishop's grisly end.

Eleanor saw her homeland of Aquitaine as belonging to her, and when she saw that Henry had subjugated it to his rule she sought to defy this perceived tyranny. She named her son Richard as heir apparent to Aquitaine and united him with her other son, Henry, the crown prince and heir apparent to the Angevin kingdom. Young Henry felt he was only a puppet of his father's whims. Eleanor planned her revolt with her sons and former husband Louis VII of France. When it erupted into full-blown rebellion, King Henry was able to turn the tide through shrewd political manipulation and martial prowess. He paid penance for the murder of Thomas Beckett in 1173 with a public display of humility at Canterbury by walking barefoot to the cathedral and having the monks whip him. This action engendered fierce devotion to Henry II and was the underlying cause of the failure of Eleanor's revolt.

Eleanor was kept under house arrest after the rebellion until Henry II's death in 1189. She did make her son Richard the Duke of Aquitaine, even though Henry II tried to pass the duchy to his favourite son John. Eleanor bided her time and maintained relations with Richard after the death of her eldest boy, young Henry. Eleanor, always defiant, kept control of the succession. During his lifetime Henry II was able to contain his wife, but time was on her side and she displayed perseverance in the succession. Eleanor was quite aware that the Duchy of Aquitaine was loyal to her and that Henry could not supersede her rights owing to the dowry and the unrest such an action would unleash.

Richard would fiercely defend his and his mother's rights to the duchy. Before his death Henry attempted, with Eleanor's reluctant help, to allay the feuds between his sons. He asked Eleanor, as the Duchess of Aquitaine, to name John as Duke of Aquitaine and Poitou. Eleanor of course refused, and, realising that she would garner support against him from King Philip of France, Henry II retracted his request. These events displayed Eleanor's strength and her ability to exert power through her duchy and the succession. Even the great Henry II could not overrule Eleanor's will. This is further illustrated in the *Gesta Henrici Secundi*:

> He sent instructions to his son Richard that he should without delay surrender the whole of Poitou with its appurtenances to his mother Queen Eleanor, because it was her heritage ... and Richard surrendered all Poitou to his mother.[7]

The powers of a medieval queen were being defined in Eleanor's persona. Her ability to navigate the political waters with Henry II, Philip of France and her sons displayed an acumen for queenship and expanded its role in the feudal system of England. Eleanor was able to orchestrate control through Philip and her son Richard by the fact they united against Henry II when he refused King Philip's request for the return of the dowry of his sister Alix after Henry

---

7 *Gesta Henrici Secundi: The Deeds of Henry II [in English Historical Documents 1042-1189*, trans. and ed. D. C. Douglas & G. W. Greenway (London, 1953), p. 46.

delayed her marriage to his son Richard. This encouraged war with the King of France and Richard allied against Henry, but Richard was called to the cross and thus was preoccupied with a crusade to the Levant.

Henry was forced by Philip to leave England to Richard and was to pay homage to King Philip for all his Continental domains. Philip also made Henry surrender Alix to him and arranged for Richard to marry her. Near to death, Henry accepted all the terms laid down by Philip. As had been imposed on Philip earlier, he forced Henry II to give the kiss of peace to his son Richard. Henry, as a fighter, did have some last words for his son Richard, according to Giraldus Cambrensis: 'God grant that I may not die until I have had a fitting revenge on you.' Henry died shortly threreafter whereupon Richard had Eleanor released and, more importantly, made Eleanor effectively Queen Regent of England when he went on crusade. Even at the age of sixty-seven Eleanor exerted an enormous influence over the Angevin empire that Richard had inherited. In many ways, Eleanor was the queen Matilda always wanted to be a generation earlier, in actual authority if not in name.

She had direct influence over Richard's choice of bride. A marriage to Alix seemed out of the question for she had had a previous sexual relationship with his father Henry II, which would always cast a shadow over the legitimacy of any children they would produce. It is also arguable that this previous relationship was particularly hurtful to Eleanor and that she wanted to erase that painful memory. Evidence suggests that Eleanor revived interest in Berengaria, sister of Sancho VII, King of Navarre, the southern province in the Pyrenees. This was a good political match since a marriage into the Navarre royal family could secure the southern borders of Aquitaine. Eleanor might have exerted influence over Richard's decision when he eventually married Berengaria. She would have approved of this marriage for both personal and political reasons. Furthermore, the province of Navarre would have been closer to the troubadour culture of Aquitaine in Eleanor's eyes.

Richard was going on crusade, and to secure his Angevin empire Berengaria was used to form a political alliance with Sancho VII against Raymond VI of Toulouse to protect Richard's southern borders. This idea falls into line with Eleanor's attitude towards marriages and political alliances and, coupled with her personal feeling toward Alix, would make the most sense.

Eleanor had her other son, John, go to England to secure the rest of the Angevin empire, another example of her political savvy after Richard's coronation. Eleanor favoured the succession of John upon Richard's death at the siege at Chalus in 1199. She was at Richard's deathbed and comforted him until the end. This was a ghastly blow to Eleanor – she had lost her 'little lamb' and favourite son. The future of the Angevin empire lay with John and Eleanor knew this and realised she had to secure John's succession with her presence. In her twilight years Eleanor offered full support to John against Philip II of France and Arthur, Duke of Brittany, who claimed the throne. The disappearance and presumed death – perhaps at the hands of John himself – of Arthur, Duke of Brittany, created a more stable throne for John. The *Annales of Margam* says that John, having returned from Molineux in a small boat, ordered his nephew in the boat and then rowed out of sight and stabbed him with a sword, disposing of the body in the Seine with rocks to weigh it down. This news was relayed to Eleanor but King John insisted Arthur died of natural causes.

John could not save Normandy; he lost the province to King Philip of France and would not recover it. The town of Poitou shifted allegiance to the King of France after the passing of Eleanor, the townspeople mourning that they had lost their beloved duchess. Despite King John's ineptitude, Eleanor's legacy for the English monarchy was Aquitaine, which remained under English rule until the end of the Hundred Years War (1337–1453).

Eleanor knew a woman could not rule England outright – Matilda's failure was a clear example of that – but she was able to exert power as a queen consort through her offspring. She knew that Henry needed his sons for the succession of his dynasty and survival of his empire and knew that control of them therefore meant control over Henry. Furthermore, Eleanor was able to exert direct influence through her dowry of Aquitaine, a cornerstone of Henry II's Angevin empire. The shadow of Eleanor was created with her strong will and assertion of her independence by any means necessary. She provided wise counsel to kings and she was even able to oversee the Angevin empire in the absence of Richard. In the game of chess (which reached England more or less with the Norman Conquest), the queen is the most powerful piece on the board...

ELEANOR OF PROVENCE

Eleanor of Provence's story is part of the Eleanor legacy in that Henry III, her husband, was the Duke of Aquitaine, an inheritance from his grandmother Eleanor of Aquitaine. Both Eleanors were duchesses of Aquitaine and no doubt Eleanor of Provence was familiar with Eleanor of Aquitaine's life and resounding impact on queenship and dowagership. Eleanor of Provence would be married to a weak king whose power lay prostrate before the barons and Magna Charta and its later clauses of 1225,[8] and the Provisions of Oxford (1258).

When Henry III ascended to the throne in 1216, he was only nine years old and was to rule by consent of the barons rather than ruling over them. William Marshal was the regent until his death in 1219. Marshal reluctantly took control as regent through the urging of his fellow barons, especially the leading baron Lord Ranulf:

---

8   King Henry III issued in 1225 what became the final and authoritative version of Magna Charta. It is clauses of the 1225 charter, not the charter of 1215, which are on the Statute Book of the United Kingdom today.

You are so good a knight, so fine a man, so feared, so loved, and so wise that you are considered one of the first knights in the world. I say to you in all loyalty that you must be chosen. I will serve you, and I will carry out to the best of my power all the tasks you may assigne me.[9]

Thus began a very successful regency. Marshal and his barons were able to oust the French Prince Louis and restore order in England from 1216 to 1219. The 1217 treaty brokered by Marshal after the defeat of Louis's army reinstated the authority of the minor King Henry III. Marshal worked through the treasury to ensure equanimity amongst the barons. When he died in 1219 the regency continued, and from about this time it became the case that a king would always need the consent of his barons to reign. The Charter of Liberties, Magna Charta, had changed the environment of government and put restraints on royal authority, especially in the area of raising taxes. This meant that a strong personality would be required – and one with martial skills – to win the barons' respect, or at least grudging acquiescence. These were not personality traits Henry III possessed, and this would create a tumultuous reign. He was crowned in 1220 for the second time; his first coronation was hastily done without the Archbishop of Canterbury or even a crown, though it was legal through acclamation. Henry III was the first king since 1066 to grow up and spend most of his life in England, a change in the French pedigree. It seems that he spoke some English, which of course was not the language of the court.

---

9 Sidney Painter, *William Marshal: Knight-errant, Baron, and Regent of England* (Baltimore: The Johns Hopkins Press, 1933 [1967]), p. 195.

Henry III was driven to get back the lands in France that were lost during his father's reign, but since many of the Norman castles in England were forfeited to his leading barons, they were not keen on seeing the campaigns in France succeed, since they would have to return the granted land in England to the former Norman lords. This baronial conflict needed a strong military leader to unite the cause. Henry III was not that leader and floundered, losing the campaign in France in 1230. The French knight Simon de Montfort soon came on the scene and he seemed to Henry to be a useful conduit through which to project power. Henry III's great confidence in Simon de Montfort and his friendship may stem from the fact that his kingship started – successfully – with the wise William Marshal as regent, so Henry felt, perhaps even unconsciously, that a strong advisor was vital to a successful kingship. Unfortunately, Simon was lacking one important virtue that the great Marshal was imbued with – loyalty.

Henry III also used the Jewish banking system to his benefit to extract money from his barons if they defaulted on their loans. This of course created resentment among the nobles and would later bring persecution to the Jewish community. He personally drained money from the Jewish bankers at the same time. However, Henry's attention was drawn away from this struggle for money to his next big decision, for him personally and the realm: choosing a wife.

Henry III had been in negotiations to marry Joan of Ponthieu before Eleanor of Provence was suggested. Both unions had political advantages, and the course of politics and Henry's personality would decide the matter. The King of France was against the marriage to Joan and was scheming in Rome to block the dispensation that Henry III sought. This was to prevent an alliance with Brittany, which the French Capetian dynasty did not want. Since another conflict with the King of France would not be supported by his barons, the disadvantages of such a union outweighed the advantages. Henry thus turned his attention to Eleanor of Provence.

A medieval aristocratic marriage always involved some sort of property transaction. Henry III offered a settlement to Eleanor of Provence at the moment of their marriage, which amounted notionally to a third part of his property. If he died before her she would then enjoy this property, although she could not dispose of this dower. Eleanor of Provence's dower included cities, lands and tenements which had by custom been designed for previous queens of England. It was a very generous offer.

From what we know of Eleanor's mother, Beatrice of Savoy, all of whose four daughters married kings, one imagines that she would have been well prepared for her marriage and would therefore have experienced no sense of shock that her future husband was a man of twenty-eight, her senior by sixteen years. Despite the slight defect of drooping eyes there is no reason to think that Henry was other than personable, but he had no chivalric glory to stimulate the imagination of a medieval aristocratic girl. He was a man with a fine sense of style for a royal court and he extended every courtesy to make the young Eleanor comfortable and happy. He was generous and warmhearted and was prepared to lavish upon her love and affection, even though under the laws of God and marriage it was a wife's duty to please her husband.

The royal bethrothal at the church door with a full nuptial mass in the cathedral was followed by the blessing of the marriage bed. Six days later the coronation of Eleanor of Provence occurred. It was a glorious state occasion. Henry made sure that his queen's coronation rivalled his own and was witnessed by the great barons of the realm; their presence was taken to represent their assent to her authority as Queen of England. The coronation of a queen followed that of an anointed king by way of the official royal instrument represented in the Latin phrase *regina Dei gratia*, 'Queen by the grace of God'.

In 1238 there was an assassination attempt on the king; fortunately for him he was not in his bedchamber but in Eleanor's. This suggests he was an attentive husband and spent intimate time with the queen. The would-be assassin was executed for his crimes but the dramatic attempt does reveal a disillusionment with Henry's reign. At sixteen Eleanor produced a son, an heir for Henry – the future Edward I. Henry was elated both for personal and political reasons and he gave thanks to God and his queen. Henry showed great compassion for his wife during her first experience of childbearing at such a tender age. Eleanor now had her own stake in the future dynasty in the person of her young son. The birth put Eleanor in a higher state of royal favour.

Henry was gracious toward Eleanor's family members. In recognition of his abilities, Henry gave Eleanor's uncle William of Savoy the position of chief counsellor. This move would obviously create tension among the barons, who were angry that an outsider could usurp their authority with the king. In fact, William of Savoy's career was brief, since he died in Viterbo in 1239. Henry's patronage of his in-laws did not end with William; he subsequently gave Eleanor's uncle Peter of Savoy many grants of land and titleage in Richmond, Surrey and Sussex. This put Peter on the same level as many of the English barons and created resentment from 1240 onward. Another black mark on Henry's reign was his loss in Poitou and the end of the Poitevin revolt in 1242 following the Battle of Taillebourg.

The preferential treatment of Eleanor's family members further alienated Henry and Eleanor from the English peerage. One of the leading barons, Richard of Cornwall, brother to Henry III, was to be married to Eleanor's sister Sanchia of Provence as Henry was trying to align the interests of his family with Eleanor's. The marriage did bring the two families closer, and provided the groundwork for the Treaty of Paris, but it also sowed yet more seeds of resentment among Henry's English barons. One last appointment in 1241 that further alienated Henry was that of Boniface of Savoy as the Archbishop of Canterbury. This was opposed but ultimately approved by the monks and Rome. Henry did not understand the importance of fair dealing and balance – or at least the appearance of it – to his barons and seemed to surround himself with Savoyards in an attempt to insulate himself from English politics. Eleanor of course supported these decisions and was automatically thought to be the cause of this foreign influence. On occasion she served as a mellowing influence upon the king when it came to tough political decisions regarding appointments, and she also tried to be loyal both to the Savoyards and her husband.

Henry's relationship with Simon de Montfort had created resentment, but when he banished Simon and his sister Eleanor from the kingdom after Simon had arranged a loan in the king's name without permission he did not accrue much credit from the barons. Henry was even more furious because he had granted de Montfort the title of Earl of Leicester, which meant land and wealth. However, Henry had kept his sister's dowry for the crown, which sparked deep resentment in de Montfort. There would ultimately be a showdown between the two. Henry dispatched de Montfort to Gascony in 1248 to solve the dispute with the Gascon lords and smooth over relations with France. At this juncture it seems that Henry and Simon were entwined in a symbiotic power relationship where the need lay more on Henry's side, owing to his mismanagement of government. After Simon de Montfort succeeded in his remit in Gascony he returned to the court with a suspicious eye on Henry. He wanted recompense for the money he had spent to fortify Gascony to secure its safety. Henry III refused to pay and the queen became involved along with her sister-in-law; she reminded her husband that those castles would one day be Edward's. Subsequently Henry III agreed to establish a commission to count up the costs but refused to let Simon return until he heard from his accusers.

Eleanor was in the middle of Henry's conflicts with his barons, and especially with Simon, but her worst disagreement with her husband came when he granted power to the Lusignans in 1252 in order to counter the growing power of de Montfort and the barons. Eleanor never trusted the Lusignans, who were expelled from France because of their brutal tactics and overbearing greed. They were effective but left much bitterness in their wake. Henry only saw them as a counterbalance to the power of the English barons, who were constantly whittling away at his authority. Eleanor confronted the king, believing the Lusignans' tactics were destroying his credibility. When Henry and Eleanor reconciled in 1253 they had their last child, Katherine, born in November 1253. This event was marked with great celebration as the previous child, Edmund, had been born eight years previously.

In the spring of 1254, Eleanor and Henry were planning the marriage of Lord Edward to Eleanor of Castile, daughter of the King of Castile. This marriage was also in the shadow of

Eleanor of Aquitaine: that Eleanor, as we have seen, had made her duchy part of the Angevin possessions when she married Henry II. During this period, Eleanor of Aquitaine's daughter Leonor became Queen of Castile and her husband, Alfonso VIII, asserted that Leonor's dowry was the province of Gascony. This was not confirmed by Eleanor or Henry II but it was the pretext for the invasion of Gascony in 1206, during King John's reign. This old claim re-emerged, but Henry was quick to aid Alfonso X to suppress a rebellion in Gascony and the marriage of Lord Edward and Eleanor of Castile cemented a truce and lifted the threat of Alfonso's claim to the province. Eleanor of Provence and Henry III were able to visit Gascony, a pleasurable visit at a time of peace. They were able to reconnect and nurture their marriage with a trip through the province and a stroll down memory lane recalling their courtship and marriage, and their loyalty to each other. This was in stark contrast to the relationship between Eleanor of Aquitaine and Henry II, who never reconciled.

One theory might help to explain some of the vitriol that was heaped upon Eleanor during her reign as queen. A passage from Madeline Caviness describes the attitudes that were common in the thirteenth century about a woman's role, especially as queen:

The female was regarded as the sexual aggressor in Christian theology – whether as Eve, who handed the fruit to Adam; Salome, whose wiles and erotic dance destroyed John the Baptist (as imagined on the eleventh-century Hildesheim column); or in the form of Luxuria. One of the few female grotesques in the Hours blows her own horn; bare-breasted with flowing hair, she is like the personification of Lust in the early twelfth-century porch sculpture at Moissac.[10]

Eleanor of Provence was another strong-willed woman who displayed qualities that were not appreciated by her contemporaries, but her husband did benefit from those qualities and in some cases they even saved him from his own weakness in making decisions. Overall, she did provide the major qualities a queen needed to secure the succession, and in her case with a more suitable king than Eleanor of Aquitaine did.

In the summer of 1253 Eleanor was given the regency of England while Henry was away quelling the Gascon rebellion. This was another watershed event, since Eleanor was ruling the kingdom through her husband's will. She was entrusted with the great seal and power to execute authority as she saw fit. It was a limited role but it displayed the confidence Henry had in his queen and her administrative abilities. Eleanor handled the finance – a vital and complex task, of course – with help from the leading magnates. That she could work with them showed a political awareness, and her careful funding of the Gascon campaign is impressive. She displayed regal discretion and kept the realm in order and most importantly garnered the funds needed for Henry's campaign. We see an able executrice who was capable of making sound decisions in a tumultuous period and keeping her personal feelings out of the decision-making process. A steady hand was what was needed and she provided

10   Madeline H. Caviness, 'Patron or Matron? A Capetian Bride and a Vade Mecum for Her Marriage Bed' in Nancy Partner, ed., *Studying Medieval Women: Sex, Gender and Feminism* (Cambridge, MA: The Medieval Academy of America, 1993), p. 38.

it during the regency. Eleanor showed notable restraint and she handled the political process with considerable poise – something which her contemporaries don't seem to have given her credit for because she was a woman.

Eleanor enjoyed more independence than her predecessors; Eleanor of Aquitaine only had direct management of her dower lands as a widow. This can be seen as positive progress in queenship powers. Eleanor could control her lands through grants, she could bequeath them and ultimately she could serve writs in her own name. This was a progression of the queen's power which was independent from the power of the king. Of course, Eleanor projected this power with consent from her husband. It is important to remember this tacit consent to the management of the estate as being in the background, since qualities that would be considered prudent in a man would be viewed as an unfeminine or 'unnatural' in a woman of the Middle Ages.

The Oxford provisions of 1258[11] represented a severe diminution of sovereign power. They required the king and queen to be overseen by a council of fifteen, and Parliament would have three annual meetings with or without the king's calling. Further, wardship in the monarch's 'gift' would be decided by another council of five. This affected Eleanor personally as she felt that it was an attack on royal appanage. The palace revolt that gave rise to these provisions involved three factions. First there was Simon de Montfort and his alliance with the powerful English barons, then Eleanor's Savoyard

---

11   The Provisions of Oxford of 1258 proved to be a significant reform to Magna Charta and stripped Henry III of most of his powers and set a precedent that was more binding than Magna Charta itself. This would ultimately lead to the Barons' War of 1264–67. It would add new dimensions to English Parliament with the inclusion of knights, burghers and merchants and freemen to the 'Common' element of the bicameral legislature body.

faction, and finally Henry III's faction, allied with the much-hated Lusignans. To further complicate things, Eleanor's oldest son Edward was waging a war in Wales and was pushing for funding in Parliament. Since the result of all this factionalism would of course fall upon the king, the revolt in 1258 was mostly focused on him and the Lusignans. Henry caved in and agreed to all the terms, hoping to get funding for a Sicilian campaign he had promised the Pope – but this was not to happen.

The Oxford provisions changed English constitutional history and really shifted the rule of the sovereign away to a system of rule with and by consent of Parliament. This is not to say the monarch had to rely on Parliament for everything that involved taxation, since we will see that circumventing the consent policy could be done when the barons' desires were in accord with the king's, as illustrated in the reigns of Edward I, Edward III and Henry V.

Eleanor of Provence was seen as an integral part of this conflict by some outside the close-knit court circle. She had secured baronial appointments and marriages for her Savoyard family within some of the highest ranks of English society and in the process alienated many of the native English barons. She was definitely seen as a political player at court and a power to be reckoned with. This will be seen most clearly during the tumultuous and controversial period to come, as the problems of 1258 festered for six years and broke into armed, open conflict between de Montfort and the king, almost bringing Henry's reign to an end.

The period of 1260–64 saw consolidation of both sides into coalitions, with the king, Eleanor and Edward on one side and Simon de Montfort and the English barons on the other. Family feuds were put to one side in light of the growing external threat to the crown. Eleanor gave her full support to Henry; her first loyalty had always been to her family and this was the case here. The main avenues through which she supported her husband were the papacy, her Savoyard family and her French connections; her family could provide mercenaries in Henry's defence. Eleanor was quite aware of the animosity between her husband and Simon de Montfort and understood the kind of man de Montfort was: ruthless and ambitious and prepared to steamroll Henry III if it served his purpose. Simon had harboured much hatred for Henry and his policies and was implacable in his pursuit of the king and especially the favourites he held at court.

The conflict came to a head with a bloody battle at Lewes in 1264. Simon de Montfort was steady in his resolve and received a blessing from bishops for the forthcoming action. It was viewed as a crusade against the perceived tyranny of the king, as was illustrated by the white cross displayed on the garments covering his forces' armour. Simon did have a flair for the dramatic, and thoughtfully played it to the hilt to validate his cause in the eyes of the English people. This political theatre was important and in many ways Simon understood the use of propaganda better than Henry III and Eleanor, who were always working under the assumption that monarchy was anointed and divinely ordained. Henry had his son Edward with him; a consummate warrior and great knight, he nonetheless had a little of the Plantagenet boisterousness about him and it was rumoured he was carousing the night before the battle. Henry, on the other hand, made sure his debts were in order, especially regarding his support of the crusades; he wanted his crusader vow to be fulfilled if he fell in battle.

The battle began on the morning of 14 May 1264. The tactical initiative was surrendered to de Montfort by Henry's son with his impetuous charge on the London rabble (irregular soldiers without armour or adequate weapons), which was premature. The motivation for this attack by Edward seems to have been the threat of harm to his mother. Emotion had overruled tactical expediency – though it does illustrate the importance of Eleanor as an inspiration to her subjects and family. De Montfort had carefully baited the young knight into attacking and he kept his forces in reserve to attack Henry's main force. This was a battlefield lesson that Edward would remember when he became king. De Montfort of course had much more actual battlefield experience, with his many wars in France and his experience while on crusade. He understood the use of subterfuge and feint in the melee that ensued at Lewes.

As Edward was drawn off in a fruitless pursuit, Simon moved his forces downhill toward Henry's forces as they advanced up the hill. It was of course a major tactical blunder to allow one's enemy to choose the ground on which to fight, and in this case the ground chosen by de Montfort was superior for missiles as well as providing the impetus for a mounted shock attack moving downhill. Simon's forces were able to gain the initiative and trap Henry's retreating army in the castle. Simon reformed his mounted contingent and foot soldiers for a concentrated attack on the castle. This effectively cut off Henry's forces from Edward's mounted arm. During the Middle Ages the mounted arm was used primarily as a shock weapon to break lines and cause disarray; in this case the initiative was no longer available to Henry. Furthermore, the line of supply and communication was also cut off once Henry tried to fortify his forces in the castle.

Since this was not intended to be a battle of annihilation – de Montfort wanted to capture Henry and his son Edward as political hostages – the battle was over by noon and Simon had sent in a peace envoy to accept Henry's surrender. The Mise of Lewes was agreed upon. Henry formally surrendered to Gilbert de Clare to spite de Montfort and was then taken hostage along with his son. Henry and Edward were then separated and Henry was led to St Paul's while Edward was placed under house arrest at Wallingford Castle. Henry was kept under supervision throughout the summer in London and away from Westminster. Henry had agreed to all the provisions in the Oxford agreement of 1258, but Simon de Montfort realised that Henry would be likely to go back on his word if he regained power. He called three parliaments and drafted stricter provisions. There was another council set up to oversee these provisions and to make appointments and run the routine offices of the crown.

Eleanor now realised the gravity of the situation and travelled to the French court in Paris. She steadily gained support and gathered her resources. Simon had also been busy in his efforts to disinherit Prince Edward and make Henry a king in name only. England fell into discord as de Monfort's rule became more brutal and his press for more power began to disturb even his most ardent supporters. One of de Montfort's supporters, Thomas de Clare, and his brother Gilbert de Clare, Earl of Gloucester, lost confidence in Simon, and the rebellion and its motivations. This loss of confidence stemmed from de Montfort's promotion of himself and his family, his reluctance to release Edward, and the employment of foreign mercenaries, which caused the same discontent as when Henry III had done it.

In late May 1265 Prince Edward escaped with the help of Thomas de Clare. The scheme was simple; Edward playfully raced his guards on horseback, and when their horses were tired he mounted a secretly prepared fresh horse and rode away. He rendezvoused with royalists led by Roger Mortimer and escaped to the stronghold of Wigmore.

Edward then started to plan a campaign against de Montfort, promising to follow the ancient customs and laws and expel all foreign influence from England. Eleanor would not have approved of this, of course, but she did understand the reality of the situation and that the future of the crown was at stake. Concessions had to be made to keep her husband on the throne and her son as his heir. Eleanor was displaying her loyalty by maintaining the authority of her husband and son in Gascony and securing whatever aid she could to help her son, who had planned a methodical campaign which would encircle and trap Simon de Montfort.

Edward was able to cut off de Montfort from his forces at Kenilworth. Battle was joined at Evesham on 4 August 1264. De Montfort was desperate and dressed Henry in de Monfort's colours, intending to have Henry go down with him if the battle turned against him. In the ensuing melee de Montfort was killed and his body was mutilated – his head, hands, feet and testicles were cut off. This was a vengeful recourse, but example had to be made and the royalists had the defeat at Lewes fresh in their minds. Luckily for Henry, he was recognised before he could be cut down.

The dramatic and brutal end came fast but then a peace had to be hammered out. A new leader was on the scene in the form of Henry's son Edward, and this would help in the transition. After the battle, Henry was exhausted. His recuperation was accelerated by the arrival of his wife. Eleanor can be seen here as Henry's essential emotional support. He wanted his family back to consolidate the power of the monarchy, and Eleanor was the linchpin. She returned to England in 1265. Her son Edward was busy quelling the last of the rebellions after de Montfort's death.

Eleanor returned but Peter of Savoy and other close relatives who had served as council to the queen did not. Henry's court was no longer racked with factional in-fighting between the Savoyards, Lusignans and de Montfort's followers. Different factions would evolve under the new king, but for the moment the Second Barons' War was over.

Eleanor was also eager to provide for her younger son Edmund, and was instrumental in securing his future. Her attention to her family and the monarchy had a steely consistency throughout her queenship. Edward continued to mop up resistance through 1266 and 1267, which allowed Eleanor and Henry to go to France to settle the business of the realm. The King of France specifically asked Henry to bring Eleanor, which showed the respect in which she was held. Eleanor was seen as the oil to lubricate the wheels of progress in relations between France and England, which made her indispensable to Henry at this critical juncture after such upheaval.

Eleanor turned her attention to the question of property and estates, since the losses during the rebellion were considerable. She recovered the lands that had been taken from her, which included eight major estates with a considerable annual value, enough to run her court. In 1268 Peter of Savoy died and left his Richmond estate to Eleanor, which may have caused a degree of uneasiness for Edward – he was awarded the rest of Peter of Savoy's English estates, an appropriate allocation for the heir apparent. The Richmond estate would revert to the crown upon Eleanor's death, so Edward could accept its temporary loss to pay for the running of Eleanor's court and her daily expenses. This was sensible forward planning. She wanted to smooth the transactions so turmoil could be avoided and make the eventual succession of Edward as trouble-free as possible.

Eleanor was determined not to risk any rifts between herself and Edward. She effectively created an environment of accord and peace. She was able to acquire the earldoms of Derby, Leicester and Lancaster for Edmund. This balanced approach paved the way to a good relationship between Eleanor and her son Edward when he became king.

Marriage during the medieval era was an instrument of family ennoblement and international politics, so Eleanor set her sights on getting her son Edmund a good marriage. The woman that Eleanor had secured, with Edmund's approval, was Avelina, daughter of Isabelle de Forz, the heiress to the Aumale and Devon earldoms. The dower settlement was high, and Eleanor secured it. The outlay for the nuptials came from Eleanor's Richmond estate. Edmund was married in 1269 at Westminster in the presence of the king, Eleanor and Prince Edward. This was an advantageous marriage for Edward, as his brother would be a leading member of the baronage in the kingdom. It is important to understand that it was Eleanor who brokered this marriage as it related directly to the future security of the throne. Eleanor was exercising her power as queen in a distinctly new way. She used her position to take a direct role in the succession. In this she offered a blueprint for future queens and how they would operate over the next two centuries.

The last five years of Henry III's reign show two different dynamics for Eleanor in her relationships with the ruling monarch and the heir to the throne. It is important to look at the differences between the reigns of Henry III and Edward I, since they are diametrically opposed styles of monarchy. Edward was a typical Plantagenet warrior-king who found comfort in the tournament and saw international conflict as a way to elicit loyalty. Henry, on the other hand, was not a successful warrior but a political animal through and through from the beginning of his reign; he had to be, since he relied on the baronage through the regency. He relied on others to fight wars.

The ageing king wanted peace and was still a prisoner of his own barons. Edward inspired the barons through his leadership and desire to expand the realm through military success. Eleanor admired both men and sat between the two kingships. From attitudes engendered by her background and family in Provence, Edward's chivalric ambitions were attractive to her. Edward was more decisive and active and he was what England needed after the turmoil of Henry's reign. The Plantagenet 'spirit' was the driving force behind Edward and the martial skill he displayed in defeating Simon de Montfort and the rebels provided a unifying force that was lacking in Henry's reign.

Edward did not want to usurp his father's throne, and since the fighting was done by 1269 he decided to join King Louis IX on crusade in the Levant. This was a decision that Henry did not agree with; he wanted his son to stay in England. But Edward was drawn to the action and independence of his own command that the Crusades offered and felt it was his religious duty. There is no record of Eleanor's reaction but she was surely worried about losing her son in the Crusades to disease or mortal combat. (The Crusades would indeed take the life of Louis IX.) She was also aware of the dangers at home that could easily flare up in his absence, especially if Henry died, an event that could spark internecine war in England. Eleanor was nevertheless a product of the thirteenth century and would have accepted the sacrifice she would have to make in the name of God. Edward made the arrangements for his family and the realm to be placed in the hands of his agents while he was away. In effect, he created a pseudo-regency so that in the event of his death security and peace would hopefully be guaranteed. Edward created a new court, where his mother was not integral, since many of the barons were xenophobic. He was not, but he knew that to keep the peace he needed to create an English royal court dominated by English barons. Edward spoke English and had what can be identified as 'nationalistic' goals to bring together the country. He left the government in capable hands. Eleanor was on good terms with Edward before he left for the Levant, and they had a mutual respect for each other beyond the usual devotion of a mother to her children.

When Henry heard of Louis IX's death at Tunis in 1270 he wanted his son to return. Henry became ill in the early 1271 and sent word to his son urging him to come home. The landscape of Henry's court had changed dramatically by this time, since many of the earlier barons were either dead or away on the Continent. Eleanor felt some isolation because of this but was very adaptable and pressed forward with her interests and the running of her court. Henry's health had been failing since the spring of 1271 and Eleanor was concerned for the security of the realm, since the ghost of rebellion was ever present. She took care over her personal position in the court and how she presented herself, since mistrust for her and what she represented still lingered from earlier events. She made provision for her household. Her children were taken care of through marriage and various titles that she had made sure were endowed upon them.

Her concerns were to shift dramatically as her husband approached death in late 1272. Even on his deathbed the citizens of London were restless in their demands. Eleanor stayed by her husband's side through his final days to comfort him. Gilbert de Clare was summoned to Henry before his last day and had him promise to be loyal to Edward and to quell any disorder that would ensue after his death.

Henry III died on 20 November 1272. He was buried in the tomb of Edward the Confessor, his personal hero, in the Chapel of Kings. It seemed that in death he was honoured more than in life, but he had been a king who from the beginning was dependent on the barons, which made for a tumultuous reign fraught with conflicting loyalties; he was not able to lead, but was led. Henry's reign introduced some very important elements of conditional, constitutional monarchy. The most recent biography of Henry by Darren Baker sums up his legacy:

> Lacking a strong knightly resumé, Henry's best chance to be judged a great king was through sainthood. His piety, charity and pacifism clearly qualified ... His disastrous crusades, abysmal family life and other ills were quickly forgotten as an almost cartoonish figure of goodness and godliness set into the historical record...
>
> Since he seemed like a buffer between the evil John and the dynamic Edward, he was deemed to be neither wicked nor noteworthy, a decent man but woefully not up to the rigours of kingship. At least he fared better than either of them in the monikers that were given. 'Henry the Builder' may not excite the imagination, but it's certainly more flattering than 'John Lackland' or 'Edward Longshanks'.[12]

---

12 Darren Baker, *Henry III: The Great King England never knew it had* (Gloucestershire: The History Press, 2017), p. 355.

Eleanor was now in a different world. Her husband of thirty-six years was dead, her son still in the Holy Land on crusade, and none of her children were with her to console her in her grief. Her mother had died in 1268 and in 1270 she lost her uncle Peter of Savoy, a close family member and advisor, so she was isolated and alone. Eleanor assumed her new role as dowager queen. The succession went smoothly enough for Edward once he received word that his father had passed on, but he did not return to England until 1274. Gilbert de Clare was an able administrator and regent and quelled riots in London. The old seal was broken and a new Edwardian seal was made to represent the new authority of King Edward I. Eleanor was the only royal present in these ceremonies.

Eleanor established her household in Windsor Castle and spent much time with her family. She was still active in Edward's reign advising on marriages, especially that of Edward's daughter. She suffered another bereavement in 1274 when her son Edmund's wife died in childbirth along with the baby, and she comforted her son in his grief. She also lost her two daughters in quick succession in February and March 1276, first her daughter Margaret, Queen of Scotland, and then Beatrice. Eleanor acted as executor for Beatrice, another example of her devotion to her family. She found her grandchildren a source of comfort. She actually raised Edward's son Henry and daughter Eleanor, and Beatrice's son John.

On a different front, Eleanor had to change her household after she was left to her dowager estates and stopped receiving queen's gold once her husband died. She managed her dowager lands with a level of acumen that was impressive, making her a wealthy widow. Her dowager lands, as previously mentioned, were to revert to the crown upon her death. She commanded some authority over her son Edward as king and made requests that were in most cases honoured by him. Edward rarely awarded his mother any more lands or money, knowing that she was comfortable; this proved to be politically prudent during this period. Mother and son had had their differences in the past but they were now bound by mutual familial loyalty that was not going to be broken. We can infer that the power of personality Edward displayed in his reign was equal to his mother's and that this could be where his strength as an intrepid leader came from.

Eleanor exhibited the same anti-Semitism as her son, which does mark a stain on her compassionate nature, though not to the same savage degree. Edward expelled the Jews from Gascony in 1287 and then England in 1290 for economic and political reasons. He needed money to fund his wars of conquest. These medieval pogroms brought immediate wealth to Edward and they found parliamentary favour, since debts owed to the Jewish bankers were cleared and their lands seized.

Eleanor finally entered a convent. This was a familiar path for previous dowager queens, but she did not humbly submit to a convent style of life. She had joined the order of Fontevrault, which had links to the royal family and Eleanor of Aquitaine. It is where Eleanor of Aquitaine, Henry II and Richard I are all buried. Eleanor's final days were at Amesbury in England and not Fontevrault – even as death approached she understood and honoured her title as Queen of England. Eleanor of Provence died on 24 June 1291 and she was laid to rest at Amesbury during a funeral attended by her family and many attendants.

Eleanor was not a popular queen, but she was a strong-willed woman who imposed her will upon her husband's reign in many beneficial ways, especially during the de Montfort rising. She was given more liberty than Eleanor of Aquitaine over her dower lands and in her involvement in government, marriages and appointments to important offices of state. She was a loving, loyal partner to her husband. Eleanor's life represented an evolutionary step forward in queenship in the thirteenth century and her actions would be reflected in those of future medieval queens of England. Eleanor was a true and active participant, for good or bad, in Henry's reign and she redefined the role of queen consort in England.

2

ISABELLA OF FRANCE

Isabella of France generates much debate over whether her gender defines her actions or her actions define her gender.

> Gender can explain why some men are less powerful than others, why some women are more powerful than some men, and other imbalances that the physical equipment of sex does not account for. Discussion of such imbalances, which complicate the social logic of sex as biology seems to decree it, is not always welcome even among feminists, for the imbalances expose the inadequacy of assessment in which women are always oppressed and men always the oppressive: women can be oppressive, men can be oppressed.[13]

One can argue that Isabella overthrew Edward II and ultimately committed regicide. But what Isabella did was part and parcel of what was accepted as political process during the Middle Ages in England. There were examples in both the Anglo-Saxon and

---

13   Allen J. Frantzen (1993), p. 144.

Norman periods where a stronger personality ascended the throne at the expense of a weaker one. Isabella was able to repeat this as a result of the dysfunction of Edward II's reign. She was a woman, but this was not an obstacle to the process.

In Isabella's time, the lands in France had all been lost during the reign of Henry III and the only area still in English possession was the lucrative wine-producing province of Gascony. Much feuding between the monarchs of France and England continued over the province. Gascony was the last remnant of the Aquitaine province of her ancestor Eleanor of Aquitaine. Isabella's father-in-law, the powerful and impressive Edward I, secured Gascony through treaty and war and held the province through Isabella's marriage to his son Edward, Prince of Wales, which was settled in the Treaty of Montreuil.

A treaty had been agreed with Philip IV [of France] that would lead to a permanent peace and the restoration of Gascony, and it was to be cemented in the conventional manner. Edward's son, the fifteen-year old Edward of Caernarfon, was to be married to Philip's daughter, Isabella. Since, however, the princess was only three years old, their wedding would have to wait for some years. In the meantime, there was to be a more immediate match. Edward himself would marry Philip's sister Margaret – sufficiently mature at seventeen, though perhaps not thrilled at the thought of being led to the altar to a man more than three times her age.[14]

---

14   L. F. Salzman, *Edward I*, London, 1968. 147;   *Foedera, Conventiones, Litterae et Acta Publica*, ed. T. Rymer, amended edn by A. Clarke and F. Holbrooke (4 vols). In 7, Record Commission 1816-69. Cited from Marc Morris, *A Great and Terrible King: Edward I and the Forging of Britain* (London: Random House, 2009), p. 318.

One of the themes that comes to the fore with Isabella – and we will see it in other queens – is that when a weak king ascends the throne, a strong queen can counter some of that weakness and assert her own authority. Again, this is a process in the shadow of Eleanor of Aquitaine.

Isabella arrived in England in 1308 as the queen consort, aged twelve. We must separate myth from fact in some of the details and circumstances of this wedding. Prince Edward's favourite, Piers Gaveston, was the one who escorted Isabella and her entourage to him, and it is rumoured that Prince Edward gave Piers gifts from Isabella's family. The historical record does not support the idea. A plausible explanation maybe that Gaveston was entrusted with these items for safekeeping. It was true that Prince Edward seemed to heap affection and attention upon Gaveston, but he was a childhood friend and the person Edward trusted the most. He had never met Isabella before this marriage and she was not his wife of choice, nor was the prince her husband of choice; that kind of love match would have been alien to the royal houses of this period. Marriages were political contracts and this was a fact understood by both parties.

However, dehumanising the individuals to this point does not take into consideration the raw emotional responses which were surely in play. These emotions may or may not have included jealousy and may or may not have been romantic in nature. There was protocol and tradition to be followed, and if this was ignored, then emotions might rise to the surface. Edward and Isabella were to marry to secure a treaty, and she was to provide Edward with sons to ensure a secure succession.

After the marriage in 1308, Edward I ordered the young Edward not to bestow any more lands or riches on Gaveston, and made them both swear fealty on the blessed sacraments. This was to hold through Edward I's lifetime. He even banished Gaveston owing to his undue influence over his son. The reality of the situation is outlined nicely in Michael Prestwich's biography of Edward I:

> It was while the Carlisle parliament [1305] was in session that Edward quarrelled once again with his son, the Prince of Wales. The king took exception to the young prince's relationship with his Gascon favourite, Piers Gaveston. Although this was almost certainly of a homosexual character, the sources do not suggest that this was at issue: what Edward took exception to, was his son's demand that his friend be granted either the county of Ponthieu or the Earldom of Cornwall. The king, still a powerful man despite his years, tore out handfuls of his son's hair, and ordered Gaveston into exile.[15]

These orders would be forgotten after the death of Edward I, and young Edward II would do as he wished, no matter the consequences.

The question of Edward II's homosexuality must be addressed to put Isabella's actions in the proper context. Homosexuality was deemed an immoral and 'unnatural' act against the will of God during the Middle Ages and was illegal behaviour that, if proven, could bring severe punishments. The medievalist John Boswell outlined how homosexuality was viewed from 1250–1350:

> During this time there are many popular diatribes against gay people ... suggesting that they molest children, violate natural law,

---

15   Michael Prestwich, *Edward I* (New Haven: Yale University Press, 1988 [1997]), p. 552.

are bestial and bring harm to nations which tolerate them. Within a single century, between the period of 1250 and 1350, almost every European state passed civil laws demanding death for a single homosexual act. This popular reaction affected Christian theology a great deal. Throughout the twelfth century homosexual relations, had, at worst, been comparable to heterosexual fornication for married people, and, at best, not sinful at all. During the thirteenth century, because of this popular reaction, writers like Thomas Aquinas tried to portray homosexuality as one of the very worst sins, second only to murder.[16]

Nevertheless, as Prince of Wales and later king, Edward would have felt he was entitled to behave in any manner that he desired. His relationship with Piers Gaveston was a kind of royal prerogative. Was the king above the law? Obviously Edward II felt he was, and so his actions would have had juridical repercussions for the monarchy. Balance is the key here; if he addressed the concerns of the barons and ruled justly, then his homosexual behaviour might have been ignored or at least not been a major factor in the resentment that was sown during his reign and ultimately led to his downfall.

There was no doubt that Isabella was aware of her husband's sexual proclivities, but she was young and had little power to do anything about it at this time. As the coronation and wedding proceeded, Isabella's resentment towards Gaveston grew and she

---

16 John Boswell, 'The Church and the Homosexual: An Historical Perspective', 1979. *Excerpts from the keynote address made by Prof. Boswell to the Fourth Biennial Dignity International Convention in 1979.* Cited from Fordham University Sourcebooks website: https://sourcebooks.fordham.edu/pwh/1979boswell.asp

voiced this to her father, Philip IV, King of France. The real bone of contention was her paltry dowry and the fact that Edward II denied her a dower from the treasury and refused her an allowance for her daily expenses from the Exchequer or royal wardrobe. This was a flagrant dereliction of the courtly behaviour expected of all monarchs during this period. As Gaveston's usurpation of patronage and power sowed the seeds of resentment amongst the baronage, then, it also fuelled the jealousy of the young queen. A steady growth of opposition to Gaveston blossomed in Edward II's court, and with Isabella and her French entourage's confirmation of the inordinate favouritism heaped upon Gaveston, a coalition formed with Philip IV's endorsement. The situation came to a head in the spring of 1308 when Philip realised the money he had raised for Isabella's dowry was being lavished upon Edward's favourite at court. This was the last straw, and Philip backed the opposition to Gaveston amongst the baronage of England with money. Parliament forced Edward II to strip Gaveston of his titles and banish him from court.

This was only a temporary respite, since Gaveston came back after fourteen months in exile in Ireland, where he seemed to rule in the king's name in a successful manner. Edward did lavish moneys and manors in England and Wales upon Isabella, but this was to placate the detractors of Gaveston and to pave the way for his return. It seems that Edward played his part as king in this display of political acumen, albeit for his own selfish desires. Gaveston's return disgusted the barons, and he did much to provoke their hatred. Isabella again resorted to writing to her father about Gaveston and the problems at court. In 1310 Edward was forced to accept overseers of his authority, called 'Lords Ordainers', who would 'ordain and establish the estate of our household and our realm'. This was an agreement forced by the barons, who claimed their fealty was rendered null and void by the king's failure to uphold his sworn oath in his coronation. Edward II was forced to agree to all the terms.

Edward decided to start a campaign of conquest in Scotland. He had Gaveston lead alongside him, but this plan backfired since many of the leading barons with military skill did not participate. When Edward came back to his court he found the Lords Ordainers had put restrictions on how he raised money and, more importantly, how he spent it. The Ordainers also demanded that Gaveston be exiled for life. Edward capitulated and Gaveston once again went into exile. Edward reacted against these restraints, however, and in 1312 went to York and summoned Gaveston back to his side. This was in complete defiance of the barons and would lead to war. The leading baron in this fight was Thomas, Earl of Lancaster, who was the most powerful and wealthy baron in the realm. He was also a direct blood relation to both the king and queen, a first cousin to the king and the maternal uncle of Isabella.

Edward was later joined in York by his wife Isabella, who, it later became clear, was pregnant. This was in spite of the neglect that Edward displayed towards his wife and queen, and the consequences would be profound. The barons moved to intercept Edward and Gaveston. Edward left Gaveston behind at the formidable castle of Scarborough. This did not provide the protection Edward had hoped for, and the barons surrounded the castle and forced a surrender, taking Gaveston prisoner.

The Earl of Pembroke took Gaveston into custody, and he promised safe conduct to his prisoner. Pembroke was an older and more temperate baron, who hoped for a peaceful solution to the Gaveston problem. However, Pembroke did not represent the prevailing attitude towards Gaveston, and the Earl of Warwick took custody of the prisoner in June 1312, bringing him to his stronghold at Warwick Castle. The Earl of Lancaster rushed there to adjudicate over Gaveston's fate. Lancaster then took Gaveston from his prison and moved him to Kenilworth Castle before having his men murder Gaveston at Blacklow Hill after a mock trial. Gaveston's head was severed from his body as barbaric proof of his demise. This was a bold move, and the barons were aware there would be repercussions, but they felt it was the only solution in light of Edward II's behaviour over the last four years. Edward's power as king was severely truncated and the barons were confident that his vengeance, which they would assuredly witness, could be contained. However, the murder of Gaveston did lead to a split in the barons' united front.

In autumn 1312 Isabella gave birth to a son and heir to the realm. At sixteen, she had accomplished one of the most vital roles of a queen consort. This was the vital turning point in Isabella's queenship, just as it had been for Eleanor of Aquitaine a century earlier.

Defeat to the Scottish at the battle of Bannockburn had a profound impact on Edward II's reign. When Edward raised an army to go north and fight the Scottish, who were led by the able Robert the Bruce, the English army did not have the most powerful barons in tow. There were two reasons for this reluctance on the barons' part to support the Scottish war. The first revolved around an interesting dichotomy: it was true that a war and victory against Scotland would bring gains to the aristocracy, but it would have also enabled Edward II to gain popularity and exact revenge on those who murdered Gaveston. Secondly, the battlefield would be a dangerous place for any noble whom Edward wanted to see come to an untimely end, as he was the leader on the field. The battle at

Bannockburn was a disaster since there was no unit cohesion and infighting prevailed among Edward's barons. His army was routed and Robert the Bruce was able to secure Scotland from English rule. This battle further entrenched Edward's reputation for failure at court and abroad.

Isabella became Edward's representative while he was away, and this commenced her entrenchment in the power politics of Edward's court. The only hope for the north of England was the Earl of Lancaster, and his relationship with the king was strained. He was content to leave Edward in a weak position. This put Isabella in the unenviable position of mediator between Edward and his barons. This was a period of famine, flood, and war with Scotland, which to Edward's subjects must have felt like biblical chastisement. The barons were at war with each other, especially Surrey and Lancaster, and this further put Edward's kingdom into disarray. Another battle in Scotland in 1319 was another defeat. The king was supported by all his barons including Lancaster, but the support was half-hearted. Edward was forced to agree a two- year truce at Berwick.

Edward and Isabella made a visit to France in 1320 to pay homage to Isabella's brother Philip V, King of France, for the lands Edward ruled in France. This event renewed Isabella's bonds to her French royal family. Meanwhile, back in England, Lancaster cloistered himself in his castle at Pontefract and the Earl of Pembroke ran the country in Edward's name. This unsteady peace was to come to war and rebellion.

Edward II was to fall back into his bad habit of having favourites at court. He appointed Hugh Despenser, a political raptor with an insatiable hunger for power, as chamberlain of the king's household. Despenser moved rapidly to devour the earldom of Gloucester through political machinations and manipulation of Edward. The next prize was land in Wales, also granted. This was a dangerous precedent: not even Edward I would challenge traditional Welsh laws in land acquisition, but Despenser as the new favourite was able to convince the king to take the lands. This led to outright defiance from the barons as it set a precedent that could be used to take land from many of them, so a coalition of forces formed against Edward and Despenser. The new coalition forced Edward to send Despenser into exile in 1320, which gained a brief respite for Edward.

In October 1320 Isabella went on pilgrimage to Canterbury and decided to stop at Leeds Castle to take refuge from the poor weather. This action would set in motion a series of events that would lead to a more tyrannical Edward and an opportunity for him to take revenge for Gaveston's murder a decade earlier, showing that Edward was obsessed and preoccupied with his own personal feelings rather than with creating an environment for a stable realm. The owner of Leeds Castle, Baron Badlesmere, was a recent convert to the Earl of Lancaster's growing rebel party. Isabella's visit may not have been entirely a coincidence but rather perhaps an opportunity to take a look at what borderline loyal barons would do in her presence, a sort of litmus test for loyalty to the crown.

The castle at Leeds denied her access, and when she ordered an entry by force of arms her party was assailed by archers and six of her men-at-arms were killed. This infuriated the queen for another reason beyond the mere rejection of royal privilege: this castle had been held until 1318 by Isabella's aunt and former queen Marguerite (Edward I's second wife) and should have passed to Isabella through inheritance. Edward II, however, chose to pass it to Baron Badlesmere instead, probably to ensure his loyalty, which it did not. These events in Leeds provoked a bellicose response from Edward, who proclaimed that the violence was tantamount to treason. Edward proceeded to deploy knights and siege equipment to breach the castle. It fell rather quickly without support, and Edward's response was brutal to the besieged. He summarily hanged the defenders, and the Lady Badlesmere and her children were imprisoned in the Tower. This heralded martial law and punishment without trial and sent a clear message that Edward was serious about hounding and destroying traitors.

The action in Leeds polarised those involved: all were either for or against the king, no neutrality was permitted. The momentum was with Edward, and by 1322 the Mortimers had surrendered at Shrewsbury and the defenders were again imprisoned in the Tower. Men at arms were killed as traitors. The bloodlust would not be sated until Edward had exacted revenge on his most hated baron, the Earl of Lancaster. He was eventually able to defeat Lancaster and his supporters and imprisoned the earl in his own castle at Pontefract. The great and powerful Earl of Lancaster was condemned to death as a traitor for having conspired with the Scots and seized royal property at Newcastle in 1312. The *Vita Edwardi Seceundi* commented on his fate: 'The Earl of Lancaster once cut off Piers Gaveston's head, and now by the king's command the earl himself has lost his head. Thus, perhaps not unjustly, the earl received measure for measure.'

No lord as prominent as Lancaster had been executed as a traitor since the days of William the Conqueror and the Anglo-Norman baronial conflicts. Lancaster's execution displayed the ruthless and vengeful nature of Edward II, which was released by Hugh Despenser. This was not simple justice but a reign of terror that would turn Edward's people against him.

Isabella was at first relieved that Edward was able to restore his authority in the realm but this changed rapidly as she witnessed the power Despenser had over Edward and that this 'justice' was fuelled by avarice. Isabella was politically isolated from Edward and her own royal properties and income were confiscated by Despenser himself. Isabella up to this point had displayed all the virtues of a good queen. She provided heirs for Edward II, she gave wise counsel through reconciliation with his barons, and she ensured diplomatic amity with France. Isabella now must have felt betrayed by her husband in his willingness to allow such latitude to his new favourite. This takes us back to our original thesis of queenly power and influence in court based upon the model of Eleanor of Aquitaine: consort to the king and close advisor; provider of heirs to ensure a successful succession; and a dowry that strengthens the realm with the queen's authority. Now Edward II was to violate all of these elements and push aside a faithful ally.

Unlike Eleanor of Aquitaine, Isabella had not thus far led a rebellion against Edward, but that would change. By 1322 Isabella was under threat of capture by rebel baron forces and Despenser did little to help her escape, though Edward did send his own troops to ensure her safety, but this too was a late gesture, and Isabella was only able to escape through her own determination and guile. When Isabella was at the Christmas court in York in 1322 she experienced the full reality of the political isolation. Despenser sought to trample underfoot anyone that got in his way, and this all was done with Edward's blessing. Any possibility of a rapprochement died in 1323 with Lord Pembroke. He was on a mission to France to broker some sort of treaty with Scotland, but this was to be his last act and he died of exhaustion.

France had a new king in 1322, Charles IV, Isabella's younger brother. This was to change the political dynamics between France and England and would expose Isabella to Despenser's – and

Edward's – paranoid wrath. Charles IV wanted Edward to pay homage to him in person for his rule over the Gascon province, something Edward II had done for Philip V, Charles's predecessor. Edward refused since he felt, unsurprisingly, that his presence was needed in England to ensure order, and Despenser needed Edward's presence to validate his actions. Charles IV was able to wrest large tracts of land in Gascony from the English defenders and this deepened the gulf between England and France to the worst it had been in a generation. This enabled Despenser to appropriate more land from French aristocracy in England and this would include Isabella herself; she was stripped of her revenue-generating lands and her household was purged on the grounds of that the French were enemies of the state. This severely isolated Isabella on a political and personal front. Despenser's power play through Edward II provoked a more resentful baronage and would create murmurings about tyranny amongst the common people.

The obsession with internal insurgency created a window of opportunity for Isabella to exert her influence on a foreign front. The Gascon war was not going well for Edward and Despenser and they did not have a solution, since financing the war further would not work, with military leaders of dubious loyalty and Edward's refusal to leave the country to pay homage to the king of France, not to mention that Despenser was *persona non grata* in the French court. Furthermore, a war with France would inevitably bring in the Scots on the northern borders, something Edward feared as it was a prelude to a two-front war that Edward wanted to avoid at all costs. Following papal advice Charles IV accepted his sister, Isabella, as emissary to pay homage to end the war in Gascony. This is where the historical myth of Isabella's reputation as a 'she wolf" can be questioned: she operated as a monarch under threat. Her power base and very person were imperilled and she acted as any power player would. She looked for an avenue where she could gain the advantage, maybe at first to rid England of Despenser's influence; but her history with Edward was chequered at best and she saw that she must do whatever she could to gain the advantage. As outlined in the *Vita Edwardi Secundi*:

> The queen departed very joyfully, happy with a twofold joy; pleased in fact to visit her native land and her relatives, pleased to leave the company of some of those whom she did not like. Certainly she does not like Hugh Despenser ... consequently many think she will not return until Hugh Despenser is wholly removed from the king's side.[17]

Edward was reluctant to go to France personally to pay homage to the king of France because of threats in his own kingdom and the humiliating way that this homage would be perceived in Edward's own court. A solution was presented to Edward by his barons: that his son the young Edward be vested with the Duchy of Aquitaine and in the king's stead pay homage to the King of France. Charles IV accepted this proposal and the young Edward was sent to France as envoy to pay homage. In 1325 this would present Isabella with the perfect opportunity to gain the upper hand. Isabella was now not just an accessory to Edward II but an anointed queen and mother to the heir of the throne of England. She became the mouthpiece for protest and rebellion against the tyranny that Edward and Despenser had wrought in England. This

---

17 *Vita Edwardi Seucundi*, pp. 228-9, cited from Seymour Phillips, *Edward II* (London: Yale University Press, 2011), p. 483.

was the enabling event that allowed Isabella to garner support for her opposition to Edward and Despenser.

Isabella's relationship with Roger Mortimer is obscure. Whether she and Mortimer were more than political allies seems probable, but the record does not reflect this directly. Isabella did seek his counsel and aid in raising an army to cross the Channel and rid England of Despenser, but when her husband became a target for revenge is unclear. It is possible that Isabella may have had a romantic relationship with Mortimer, but political exigency was what fuelled their relationship and the shared goal of removing Despenser was their true bond. Isabella, with Mortimer, went to William, Duke of Hainault to get ships, supplies and soldiers, in exchange for a betrothal to her son Edward, the Duke of Aquitaine. This was a hard-earned bargain and massive gamble.

Isabella landed in England in September 1326 with an army of no more than 1,500 men-at-arms. Once she landed, she began to gain support in the countryside and many flocked to her banner. The fact that she had the heir apparent with her, the young Edward, was no doubt a major reason for this defection of Edward's barons. Isabella now provided a viable alternative to the unjust rule of Edward and Despenser. Her mistrust of her husband had grown over the past eighteen years into something like contempt and it had become apparent to her that his removal from power was necessary to secure the throne for her son and a regency for her. Isabella now embraced a kind of premature widowhood according to the *Vita Edwardi Secundi*:

I feel that marriage is a union of a man and a woman, holding fast to the practice of a life together, and that someone has come between my husband and myself and is trying to break that bond;

I declare that I will not return until that intruder is removed, but, discarding my marriage garment, shall put on the robes of widowhood and mourning until I am avenged of this Pharisee.[18]

Even though she was a disloyal wife and possibly an adulteress, this mattered little in the political landscape that ensued. Edward had allowed Despenser to corrupt his royal authority and this was what caused the widescale defection to Isabella's cause. The Barons rallied to Isabella and as she progressed toward London, the situation became more desperate for Edward and Despenser. Isabella was cautious; all provisions were to be paid for since she wanted to be seen as a hero and liberator, not an oppressor. Mortimer was carefully consolidating his military position with soldiers and arms coming with the barons to their cause. Edward and Despenser tried to flee to Wales but their support quickly evaporated and even in Despenser's stronghold of Caerphilly they could not resist the onslaught that was to come. Welsh barons resented Despenser's rule in Wales and turned them over to Isabella and Mortimer in November 1326. The end for Despenser was brutal: he was executed for treason – hanged, drawn and quartered and also castrated, before his head was cut from his body. This type of execution was standard practice (by 1320) for anyone convicted of treason but the castration may have been an added torture designed to allude to his intimacy with Edward II. At his trial, like Lancaster before him, Despenser was not allowed to speak in his own defence. When executed he wore a 'chapelette of sharpe nettles', which

---

18   *Vita Edwardi Secundi*, pp. 240-3, cited from Seymour Phillips, *Edward II* (London: Yale University Press, 2011) pp. 485-6.

represented 'accroaching royal authority'. This would sit well with the bloodthirsty barons, whom Despenser had wronged for many years.[19]

The question of what to do with Edward II as an anointed king was more complex. Isabella trod warily in the deposal of Edward II. It had to be done through law and Parliament. Isabella, Mortimer and the leading barons realised that Edward could still manipulate and disrupt the unity of the realm. There was no precedent for the lawful removal of a ruling king. It was decided to let Edward live in reasonable comfort, albeit a prisoner, so that he would be able to contemplate his sins. The first political hurdle was to remove any allegiance that Edward may garner and to engineer a deposition. This was done through sermon and careful adjudication of his crimes, sodomy was one charge that could be used against him. Edward II's corrupt rule, abuse of power, neglect and abandonment of his realm were all mixed like a toxic cocktail that he would unwillingly swallow.

The obvious solution was to depose Edward in favour of his son Edward, Duke of Aquitaine. The mayor and leading citizens of London were in favour. As recorded in the *Calendar of the Plea and Memorandum Rolls of the City of London*, they wished 'to crown the latter [his son] and to depose his father [Edward II] for frequent offences against his oath and his Crown'.[20] This showed a shrewd understanding of the general atmosphere in England and it proved Edward II's undoing. Isabella was able to present herself as a viable alternative to this despotic and unlawful rule, with her son as the new king and she as the regent. The arguments against Edward II

---

19 Seymour Phillips, *Edward II*, p. 518.

20 Seymour Phillips, *Edward II*, p. 526.

were based on evidence: his stubborn willingness to follow bad and damaging counsel; destruction and unlawful redistribution of lands; and finally, his careless loss of Edward I's acquisitions.

Edward abdicated in favour of his son, Edward, Duke of Aquitaine. There was some opposition but the overwhelming majority agreed with this ruling. The transfer of power went through. Never in English history had a king ruled with the previous one alive and well. This in itself would provide hope to the opposition to Isabella and Mortimer, small as it may be, to foment plots to free Edward II. This was what happened through the spring of 1327 and it seemed self-evident that Isabella and Mortimer had to rid the kingdom of him once and for all. Echoing the famous quote in the 1968 film *The Lion in Winter*, 'What do we do with extra princes?'

The comfort that Edward II enjoyed in captivity changed rapidly after no fewer than three plots to free him were uncovered. It was clear to Isabella that Edward could not be allowed to live, but she or Mortimer could not be implicated in his murder. Edward died at Berkeley castle on 21 September 1327. It was at the time believed to be of natural causes. It seems to be reasonable to assume that either Mortimer, and less likely, Isabella, ordered his death, since they had the most to gain from it. However, the historical record yields nothing, not even the manner of his death. It could be postulated that he was suffocated, if it was indeed murder. The logical argument for that is it leaves no marks on the body and without modern forensic science it is easy to assume natural causes with such a murder. The story of the red-hot iron and burning of his intestines seems an elaborate and messy manner of murder that would also attract attention to the deed. It is likely just that, a story, based on his perceived homosexual behaviour. From 1327 to 1330 there was no accusation of foul play or murder; not until

Mortimer's death in 1330 does the idea of a plot to murder Edward II appear; then the legend grew over the centuries.

Isabella and Mortimer now reigned from 1327 and they were perceived as saviours after Edward II's exceptionally corrupt and ineffectual reign. King Edward III was fifteen years old so this regency would only last a few years, and perhaps this triggered Isabella to make some unwise decisions concerning her enrichment and Mortimer's. Isabella possessed a keen sense of political reality, was intelligent and a wily tactician, pursuing a policy of maintaining her popularity and healing the wounds caused by the previous reign. Mortimer, on the other hand, was preoccupied with the accrual of wealth at any cost. Isabella became the victim of the circumstances of her rule as she slowly tightened her grip with Mortimer's encouragement. The very element that drove Isabella to this point would also be her downfall, since she did not understand the limitations of the monarchy and how to placate the barons to her advantage. So long as Isabella and Mortimer were accepted as the regents that were to rule in young Edward's name, her actions in removing her husband from the throne could be forgiven. But Isabella quickly depleted the treasury to pay debts and to enrich herself and Mortimer. If she had not made that mistake, or had this flaw in her character, she would have been perceived as facilitator of Edward III's succession and a great regent acting for the benefit of the realm, a female William Marshal.

Rumours circulated that Edward was alive and in hiding. The Earl of Kent, who was purported to know of Edward II's whereabouts, was executed. The rumour persisted for centuries and even found its way into modern literature, in the novel *World Without End*. There is scant evidence, although Stephen Spinks in his biography *Edward II, The Man* makes an interesting case for his survival.

Apart from her lavish spending, the seeds of Isabella's fall from power were sown on the Scottish border. Henry, Earl of Lancaster, was opposed to the 1328 peace treaty with Scotland, since his lands bordered the Scottish frontier and he had claims on land holdings in Scotland itself. Scotland had been made an independent kingdom for the first time post-1066 and Robert the Bruce was the monarch. Isabella had married her daughter into the Scottish royal family without Edward III's consent. There were other barons who felt the same way, so the peace treaty was unpopular. Then Mortimer was made an earl. This was the beginning of the end, for Edward III began to mistrust his mother. When Mortimer discovered Edmund of Woodstock (Edward II's brother) was plotting a return of the alive and well Edward II he had him beheaded for treason. It was a fantastical and feeble plot by a weak man, and the reaction from Mortimer and Isabella displayed shades of the Despensers' reign.

Many were disenchanted by Mortimer's stranglehold over government. In the years 1328–30 we see a treaty with Scotland to which Edward III did not give his consent, the marrying off of one of Edward III's sisters without his consent and, finally, the execution of his uncle Edmund without his consent. All of this led the eighteen-year-old king to oust Mortimer and his mother and take control of his realm.

The accusation that Mortimer and Isabella were either complicit in or directly guilty of the murder of Edward II was a charge Isabella could not escape. Ultimately, Isabella and especially Mortimer were guilty of the usurpation of royal power Now that Edward III was old enough to reign in his own name, it became apparent that Mortimer and Isabella were not going to relinquish this authority willingly. The only way to pry the power from Mortimer was from his cold dead fingers. Edward III arranged for his knights to enter Nottingham Castle. They quickly overpowered Mortimer and Isabella. Mortimer was taken into custody and Isabella was forced into her bedchamber. The coup was a success. Isabella and Mortimer's reign was over. Mortimer's fate was never in doubt since he was viewed as a traitor, complicit in the murder of the former king Edward II and a usurper of the power and authority of Edward III. Mortimer's indictment went before Parliament and proceeded with due process. He was pronounced guilty and hanged, drawn and quartered at Tyburn in November 1330. Edward III had the full backing of the barons in this. There was no ambiguity as to the status of the young Edward III as the rightful monarch of England and this was what propelled his early success. Mortimer's supporters were dealt with rapidly.

Isabella's fate was a different matter altogether. She was, after all, the king's mother and she had endeavoured to act to his benefit. Those actions may have been entangled with self-enrichment and revenge, but in the end it was for Edward III that she overthrew her husband's reign. The official line was that she was corrupted and swerved from her royal duty by the traitorous influence of Mortimer. She surrendered the vast estates she had accrued during her three years as regent and was kept under house arrest for a short period before she 'retired' to Castle Rising to live a very comfortable life with a generous allowance from her son.

Isabella's personal quest for power proved to be her undoing. However, she did provide a secure succession, thus fulfilling one of the main duties of a queen consort, albeit through a circuitous route.

Isabella lived her life throughout the first thirty years of Edward III's reign in luxury, but she became more penitent in her old age, going on pilgrimages to Canterbury and collecting religious relics. However, she never lost her love of jewelry, wine and music. As a final sign of contrition perhaps – or, alternatively, a proclamation of innocence – Isabella requested she be buried in her wedding cloak next to a silver casket that contained Edward II's heart.

Queen Isabella has become the 'she-wolf' through the centuries. It was the eighteenth-century poet Thomas Gray who coined the phrase in his anti-French poem *The Bard*. Many chose to vilify her for adultery, cruelty, corrupt governance and complicity in the murder of her own husband. But was it the fact of her gender that attracted such vehement and acidic appraisal? Would a medieval king who brought down a corrupt regime and put his own son on the throne be so vilified? Isabella executed a similar plan of action as Matilda did for her son Henry II, as discussed in the introduction, but she succeeded in overthrowing her husband the king where Matilda had to wait for Stephen's death to put her son on the throne. Both queens produced successful kings of England.

3

PHILIPPA OF HAINAULT

Philippa had the most children of all the queens in this study – one might even say she was too prolific, something that would lead to later turmoil and ultimately the War of the Roses. She was also the model of what a queen should be during the high age of chivalry: loyal to her king and country, and the sympathetic branch of royal authority.

Philippa of Hainault's marriage started at the most inauspicious moment, in the middle of the rebellion that overthrew Edward II and Hugh Despenser. Her dowry was essentially the military support Isabella of France needed to overthrow her husband. The pathos that surrounded the reign and demise of Edward II infected the rise of Edward III, and Philippa was a soothing presence. She came to England in 1327 just as her father-in-law was laid to rest, and there was suspicion surrounding his death. Philippa was married on 30 January 1328 at York Minster. She no doubt understood that her new home was a land embroiled in seething discontent among the populace and barons. The general atmosphere of discontent was characterised by Mortimer's ignominious treaty with the Scots, as outlined by B. C. Hardy:

Additional brilliance was lent to the ceremony by the presence of hundred Scotch lords who had just arrived to negotiate the promised peace. This, afterwards known as the 'Shameful Peace', was concluded entirely against the will of the English people on March 17. By its conditions, David Bruce was to marry the King's sister Joan, the Scots were to pay 20,000 pounds Sterling in three yearly instalments, and England to restore the crown jewels of Scotland, 'Ragmans Roll', and the Scone coronation stone, all of which have been carried away to London in triumph in the reign of Edward I.[21]

This was the realm Philippa entered, a regency run by Edward's mother and her lover/partner Mortimer, an unsettled kingdom. There is no clear record of the relationship Philippa had with her mother-in-law, dowager Queen Isabella. We can assume that the new queen was subordinate to Isabella and the lands and estates were run by the regency, which meant limited power to exert influence and authority in her new position as queen. She did, however, play the part of the graceful queen well, which would charm her subjects – something Isabella was never capable of doing.

The period 1328–1330 saw the young queen and king more firmly established in their rightful position by the birth of their first child. Concurrently, the regency was becoming untenable. It is important to understand the pregnancy as a triggering event that spurred Edward III to action against the regency: 'The queen's pregnancy proved in the most potent manner the maturity and vigour of her husband. It also

21 B. C. Hardy, *Philippa of Hainault and Her Times* (London: John Long Ltd. 1910), p. 48.

impacted directly on her own status.'[22] Mortimer and Isabella were serving themselves and not the kingdom, and had brokered that most unpopular treaty with the Scots. This created an atmosphere for change. Edward III witnessed the arrest and execution of his beloved uncle Edmund, Earl of Kent, another spur to action. Philippa displayed compassion for Edward during this period of the regency. Once their son, Edward, was born in June 1330, events moved quickly from then to autumn. B. C. Hardy sums up the mindset of Edward: 'While Philippa dreamed happy dreams over her baby at Woodstock, Edward, himself the father and waking fully to his responsibility as king of the realm, saw grim work before him.'[23]

Edward took control on 19 October 1330 when he seized control of the government, imprisoned his mother and executed Mortimer. Edward was fully backed by the baronage in taking control of the throne. The accusations against Mortimer were concise and conclusive. He was guilty of undue influence over the royal family, guilty in the murder of Edward II and he sowed discontent and sedition between the Queen Isabella and the then king, Edward II. Furthermore, his acts against Lancaster and Kent were acts of treason and he was to blame for all the problems with the minority regency. The charges were carefully crafted to shift all blame away from Isabella.

What to do with dear Mama? Edward acted to protect his mother, whom he still held in high affection, but he was not under any illusion that she was completely innocent, since her removal from the political scene was complete. She was allowed to live in comfort at Castle Rising, where she spent her days as dowager

22 Mark W. Ormand, *Edward III* (New Haven: Yale University Press, 2011), p. 84.

23 Hardy, 67.

queen and of course was present for ceremonial occasions at court, but her power was gone and she was under the careful watch of Edwards III's men.

Philippa now enjoyed the full benefits of her dower, which had been denied by Isabella and Mortimer during her first two years as queen. (Philippa's coronation had been delayed by two years as Isabella did not wish to relinquish her own status.) Philippa was to be centre stage in the pageantry of Edward III's court. She was as visible as Eleanor of Aquitaine, but without the rebellious nature. She was the model of a medieval queen, and lauded in the literature of the day:

> Faire Philippe, William Hannault's child, and young daughter deare, Of roseate hue and beauty bright, in tomb lies hilled here, Edward the Third, thro' mother's will and nobles good consent, took her to wife, and joyfully wither times he spent. Her uncle John, a martial man, and eke avaliant knight, Did link this woman to this king in bonds of marriage right. This match and marriage thus in blood did bind the Flemings sure To Englishmen, by which they did the Frenchmen's wrack procure.
>
> This Philippe, flowered in gifts full rare and treasure of the mind, In beauty bright, religion, faith, to all and each most kind. A fruitful mother Philippe was, full many a son she bred, And brought forth many a worthy knight, hardy and full of dread. A careful nurse to students all, at Oxford she did found Queens College, and Dame Pallas school, that did her fame resound.[24]

This passage sums up clearly the essence of Philippa's reign as queen and surely indicates the beloved status she enjoyed in the kingdom.

---

24 Froissart cited from Hardy, p. 302.

The early reign of Edward and Philippa saw a succession of children and the Scottish wars that Edward led. The stabilisation of the reign was paramount, and Philippa was the poster child for the stalwart and loyal queen, which contrasted sharply with the previous queen. Philippa was to become the cultural ambassador of the court and a tempering influence upon Edward III. She was shocked at the perceived poverty of England in comparison to the prosperous county of Hainault in the Low Countries; her homeland had a much smaller population than England, of course, but poverty had worsened during Edward II's reign and Isabella's regency. Hainault was comparatively akin to Qatar today.

Philippa in many ways was the maker of manners and the core of the court's mode of behaviour, where chivalry was the keynote. The social conduct of the court was sustained by the presence of the queen and she became a behavioural touchstone for all to follow. Her impeccable presentation and her full support of Edward III's policies no doubt contributed to the success of this period. She provided a counterpoint to the boorish Plantagenet mentality of the knights and leading barons of court. This was a period of relative tranquility for Philippa, and her persona was greatly enhanced in the establishment of Edward III's court.

Edward was greatly distressed by the Treaty of Northampton, which was brokered by his mother and Mortimer. This 'shameful peace' had to be rectified in King Edward's eyes. Between 1332 and 1333 Edward won two victories over the Scots and put Edward Balliol on the Scottish throne. However, during these battles with Scotland, Berwick, a northern stronghold, remained in Scottish hands and Queen Philippa, who accompanied her husband on campaign, was threatened by a Scottish lord. Edward secured Berwick before rescuing his wife. This was a cool and calculated response by Edward III, which displayed his equal love for queen and country.

The queen encouraged and helped set up a thriving wool-manufacturing industry in England, bringing a small colony of Flemish weavers to Norwich. The encouragement of the king and queen helped grow this industry, despite the inherent xenophobia of the indigenous population. Philippa's enthusiasm for the new industry helped spread it throughout Norfolk and eventually the whole of England.

Philippa's large brood began with the birth of the Crown Prince Edward in 1330, followed in 1332 by Princess Isabella, named after Edward's mother or Philippa's sister, depending on how one interprets Edward's relationship with his mother. A third child was born in 1334, the most fair Princess Joan. The royal family was growing ever so fast, and Edward and Philippa were busy arranging politically advantageous marriages for the girls.

An interesting dilemma that Philippa and Edward faced was how to secure their children's future (and good political alliances) without disturbing the succession. Either Philippa's children had to gain titles and baronages in foreign lands or the king and queen had to reward their sons with English earldoms. This royal system did not help secure the future monarchy. The recent history of Edward II and his siblings proved that junior royal family members could produce strife, and his brothers ultimately paid the price with their lives. However, Edward III and Philippa were to maintain a secure and prosperous monarchy for thirty years.

It is too easy with hindsight to foist blame upon Philippa and Edward for the future problems in dynastic succession towards the end of the fourteenth century. The royal family under Philippa and Edward was to create a solid and successful monarchy that was envied by the Plantagenets of the fifteenth century. It would last through both their lifetimes. Philippa and Edward arranged marriages for their children that would benefit the monarchy. The 1340s proved to be a period of success, and a true symbiotic political system arose between the king and his aristocracy.

War was the binding agent that secured the success of Edward III's reign. W. M. Ormand sums up the policy of Edward and Philippa and its resemblance to that of Eleanor of Aquitaine and Henry II:

> Henry II and Edward III had both succeeded to a battered inheritance and had both chosen an expansionist policy in order to quell unrest in England and provide lands for their numerous offspring. If Edward could avoid the feuds that had broken out in the Plantagenet family during the last century, he could indeed profit much from Henry's example.[25]

This is a prime example of the influence of the Angevin legacy upon Edward's reign. The Continental empire would embroil France and England in a lengthy war for control of Aquitaine and Gascony. The Hundred Years War was essentially a family endeavour that would encompass all of Philippa's life.

In 1340 Philippa gave birth to her third surviving son, John of Gaunt. Another son was born in June 1341 – Edmund of Langley, who would be the founder of the House of York and thus the

---

25 Mark W. Ormand, 'Edward III and his Family' in *Journal of British Studies*, vol. 26, no. 4 (Oct. 1987), pp. 407-408.

'father' of the internecine wars of 1455–85. Philippa had produced a good string of heirs and spares, but this was also a liability. The young royal couple enjoyed their large family but Philippa's royal household was in financial deficit, partly due to the cost of wars in France and partly because the inheritance Philippa and her sister were due from Hainault had not materialised. The queen did maintain ties to her homeland but in a restrained manner, unlike Eleanor of Provence, which served to guard against the fear and resentment of foreigners that the baronage of England constantly displayed throughout this period.

After 1344, Philippa's life was dominated by war, particularly in preparations for a large invasion of France. Her son Prince Edward, recently created Prince of Wales, was to embark on this adventure. One can surmise that Philippa was doubly anxious as her eldest son and husband went to war. The Battle of Crécy in 1346 has been written about many times, but its impact on Philippa is our concern here. Edward III won a crushing victory over the French with the use of the longbow and a well-oiled war machine. Edward, Prince of Wales, was blooded at Crécy, positioned as commander of the vanguard cavalry units, winning him fame and beginning the remarkable career of the man who would be known as the 'Black Prince'.

The victory at Crécy secured the monarchy at home, and Philippa saw the cohesion it provided for the baronage and the tightly knit feudal system that Edward III was building. The Order of the Garter was formed, binding the aristocracy to the monarchy, and proved to be good public relations for the realm in general. The order was formed in 1349, and Philippa was the central female character and the symbolic ideal of queenship which it served. This new order of knights was to draw upon the rich heritage of martial and chivalric history to create something akin to a warrior state. It drew its inspiration from Julio-Claudian Roman emperors, Carolingian heroes (such as Charlemagne) and Arthurian legend, which appealed to the romantic notion of knighthood.

This period was the apex of Edward III's reign. Philippa travelled on campaign with her husband, when childbirth did not prevent it. The imagery and coherent political atmosphere was ever-present in this war-making state and the aristocracy was bound to its success; although the propensity for bellicosity was in fact fuelled not by chivalry but the ever-present avarice of the royal institution, aristocracy and gentry alike. Nowhere in the Middle Ages do we see such success in creating a monolithic feudal order since Henry II's Angevin empire, but Philippa provided the one element that Henry II and Eleanor of Aquitaine lacked: royal marital unity. This was one of the major pillars of success that underpinned England's successful campaigns in France. When Edward was away during the Crécy campaign, Philippa was instrumental in mustering troops to defend the besieged town of York from a Scottish incursion by King David. At the Battle of Neville's Cross the Scottish army was defeated and King David was captured. It seems that Philippa was the rallying point, but the story that she rode into battle on a white steed to inspire the men is dubious. She oversaw King David's subsequent imprisonment in the Tower. This displayed the solid base Philippa contributed to the crown and helped define an ideal of loyalty and fealty to the realm that would serve as an enduring example of the power of the English queen.

In the domestic sphere, Philippa attracted criticism from the gentry when she tried and failed to extract greater profit from her lands, as Eleanor of Provence had done in the past. Philippa was to show sound management skills and enterprise in the execution of other affairs of the royal estate, and the war-machine did generate funds, but this economic success was to prove to be ephemeral and would disappear when martial profits dwindled. Philippa was far more practical and far-sighted than Edward III in the management of estates. She was not engulfed in the lifestyle of opulence and the tournament, which her husband relished.

Philippa's prime concern was the royal family. There was Joan, her favourite daughter; Prince Edward, a gallant knight and heir apparent; Isabella, the favourite daughter of the king; the sturdy John of Gaunt; Edmund of Langley with his ever-present companion the Earl of Pembroke; and another older boy, Lionel, and his wife; and the young Mary and infant Margaret. Philippa was seeing the nest empty of the older children, as the young adults started to find their own way in the royal court. The younger children, however, were still under the watchful eye of the queen. She busied herself providing estates to secure her children's futures. Edward III did try to bestow many estates upon his children, but they were always managed by Queen Philippa. Unfortunately, some of these grand estates and castles were more of a financial liability than an asset. The management of these royal estates was particularly challenging in the prevalent warlike atmosphere.

The habits of plunder and lawlessness that Edward III's soldiers displayed on campaign came home with them. Philippa had on many occasions to deal with the recklessness and destructive behaviour of the common soldiers. The queen had to balance her reprisals with careful consideration of the popular opinion of the monarchy. However, Philippa would not turn a blind eye when these violent incursions fell upon her children's interests; this would spark her maternal instinct and awaken the dragon in her in defence of her brood.

Philippa's thriftiness with the royal allowance was exceptional, no doubt a product of her sensible, commercially minded Hainault upbringing. Edward habitually borrowed from the royal household budget to fund his tournaments and his campaigns abroad, which made her task even harder. Her financial common sense was no doubt an unheralded asset that helped maintain the grandeur of Edward III's reign.

Beside her domestic toils, Philippa famously displayed the quality of mercy in the face of her husband's wrath in the heat of battle. The story of the six captives at Calais has been told on many occasions and was chronicled by Froissart. Edward intended to summarily execute six chief burghers of Calais until Queen Philippa intervened:

> Then did the noble Queen of England a deed of noble lowliness, seeing she was great with child, and wept so tenderly for the pity that she could no longer stand upright; therefore she cast herself on her knees before her lord the King and spake on this wise: Ah, gentle sir, since the day I crossed the sea with great peril to see you, I have never asked for one favour; now pray I and beseech you with folded hands for the love of Our Lady's Son, and as proof of your love to me, that you will have mercy upon these six men.[26]

Whether or not this story is completely accurate, it does show the moderating effect Philippa had upon Edward in his martial pursuits and would fall into line with the concept of chivalry that had captured the imagination of so many.

---

26 Froissart cited from Hardy, pp. 176-77.

Putting aside war and the royal domestic duties of the queen, the spread of bubonic plague would also have an impact on Philippa's reign. The Black Death that gripped Europe came to England in June 1348. It wreaked havoc and destruction on an unparalleled level and transformed England.

> In all 25 million died of it in this continent. Boccaccio has told the tale of it at Florence; and in Avignon Petrarch's Laura was one of the first victims. The horrible circumstances of the disease, the rapidity of its progress, and the practical inevitability of death once the person was attacked, all added to the almost supernatural terror it inspired. The first sign was usually a discoloured swelling under the armpits, after which other swellings might appear, or blood be coughed up, the symptoms appearing slightly, but a violent thirst and then a sudden coma followed always, and in a few hours, all would be over. Breath no sooner ceased and black patches appeared upon the skin, spreading over the entire body, decomposition set in in a few minutes, and a loathsome and sickening smell issued from the corpse. Infection was so strong that it was said to be sufficient to look upon a person afflicted to receive the attack oneself … A very few people, it is true, recovered from the illness, but the recovery was looked upon as miraculous. No doubt the [un]sanitary habits and dwellings of the age fostered its progress, the almost impossibility of immediate burial for the victims accelerated its spread. Some few laws were hastily passed to check its advance, but with a futility to be expected.[27]

This vivid description can conjure up the despair that the queen felt when this blanket of death descended upon her own family.

---

27   Hardy, pp. 197-98.

The Black Death reached Bordeaux in July 1348 and it struck the area with a swift, merciless blow that assailed the weak and strong alike. Philippa's favourite daughter, Joan, was infected in September and the illness rapidly claimed her. No doubt the news came as a devastating blow to Philippa and Edward, and the loss of their child cast a dark shadow upon their lives. This was in the midst of the euphoria over Edward's successful campaigns in France. The Bishop of Carlisle immediately returned to court to give the last reports of poor Princess Joan's life. Edward and Philippa never forgot those who comforted Joan in her final hours and these people were rewarded and recognised by the king and queen. The popular culture reflected the impact of the plague in songs such as 'Ring a ring o' Rosie' and Holinshed recorded a dubious result of the sickness and its impact on the physical characteristics of the population: all the children born in the year of the Black Death allegedly had 'four cheek-teeth less than usual, namely twenty-eight instead of thirty-two, which people before that time commonlie used to have'.[28]

The 1350s were full of campaigns and victories. The burgeoning navy was able to defeat a combined French and Spanish fleet, to much celebration at court.

Philippa concerned herself with the plight of her second cousin Joan of Kent; Philippa's son Prince Edward was interested in her, but she was already married to Sir Thomas Holland (*see* following chapter). Philippa seemed to have sympathy for Joan of Kent amid a political process that treated her as a prize to be won. However, Joan remained married to Sir Thomas Holland throughout the 1350s. Philippa may have been aware of the attraction her

---

28 Holinshed cited from Hardy, p. 202.

eldest son held for Joan of Kent, but discretion was truly the better part of valour in the dubious circumstances of the marriages of young Joan of Kent.

Philippa gave birth to her last child, Thomas of Woodstock, in January 1355. There was festive jousting in the royal court with the older children on display. Philippa's son Lionel was knighted, and John of Gaunt was made admiral of the English navy.

Her eldest, Prince Edward, led an army to Bordeaux from Plymouth, with Edward III along for the ride. Also present were Philippa's sons Lionel and John. Philippa and her young son Edmund of Langley were left in charge of England. However, when the king heard that Berwick had been attacked by the Scots, he immediately left France for the north of England. He left the whole French campaign in the hands of the able Prince Edward.

Edward III was able to relieve the attack on Berwick and subdue the Scottish threat. He announced his intentions of governing Scotland himself and marched farther north into the country. The Scots responded with scorched-earth tactics, but despite this devastation Edward was able to push forward to Edinburgh. However, the occupational force Edward III left in Scotland held only a precarious grasp on the region and eventually the English army retreated south. Scotland was left in disarray.

Meanwhile, Edward the Prince of Wales returned to Bordeaux, which was always his headquarters. This was a campaign offering booty and thus was very popular with the baronage. It showed that France was vulnerable could enrich the English aristocracy.

The fortunes of war shifted dramatically in the autumn of 1356 when Philippa's eldest son learned that King John of France lay close by with an army at least five times as large as his own. Philippa's son prepared his men for battle at Poitiers. The odds were against the

Black Prince but on Monday 19 September the English destroyed the French cavalry and great numbers of the French aristocracy under a hail of arrows. Skilful use of archers and foot soldiers won the day.

The prince had fought all that morning 'like a fell and cruel lion' but, like his father, he could be generous to a fallen foe; he received King John with the most chivalrous courtesy. The same evening he entertained him at a great banquet, where he waited upon the king himself, refusing to sit beside him. He tried to lift King John's despondency with the words, 'Although, noble sir, it was not God's will that you should win the day, you singly have won the prize of valour, since it was apparent to every Englishman that none bore himself so bravely as you.'[29]

Philippa could not have been more proud of her son Edward and his victory at Poitiers, and she was praised for the warmth of her reception of the captive King John at the palace of Savoy. This victory was the zenith of Edward III's reign and Queen Philippa basked in the accomplishments of her eldest son. Public approval was at its height during the late 1350s and Philippa was greatly adored by the English people. Philippa as the matriarchal head of this fairy-tale chivalric kingdom was celebrated in art and song. All of Europe looked upon England with envy and saw the majesty of Philippa and Edward III's court, something that would inspire emulation and envy for the next century. The dark years that were to come would not tarnish this optimistic time; in fact, they would make it shine all the more as a golden age.

In retrospect we can see that the size of Philippa's impressive brood would serve to undermine the stability of the English throne in the next century. Nevertheless, England now had a worthy

---

29   Hardy, p. 242.

successor to Henry II and Eleanor of Aquitaine's great Angevin empire, and without the internal strife and conflict that dominated that late twelfth-century reign. It seemed that Edward and Philippa had created a successful dynasty that was the very model of medieval English ideals.

Philippa's major focus during the latter part of her life was her children, and especially her younger brood. She oversaw their estates and future manorial incomes, and their marriages. The dowager queen, Philippa's mother-in-law, died in late summer of 1358. The last twenty-eight years saw Isabella in quiet retirement with no involvement in public or political affairs. Her son Edward III mourned her loss and demanded a royal interment. Philippa was in full support of her husband's wishes.

The wedding of John of Gaunt to Blanche of Lancaster at Reading in 1359 was a much-celebrated and festive occasion. It was honoured with tournaments and people attended in great numbers. Philippa was looking to the future with satisfaction since the successful marriages were producing a strong Plantagenet dynasty. Her only worry was for eldest son, Edward, who was still not married. Given that he was the heir apparent, this was of paramount concern for Philippa. Queen Philippa was of course present at her son John of Gaunt's wedding and the surprise appearance of King Edward III and Prince Edward was well received – it was thought that they were not going attend due to the planning of the upcoming campaign in France. This was a well-staged piece of royal theatre.

The queen's travelling days were over and she was left in charge of the realm in Edward's absence. She mounted a successful defence of the kingdom at home in the face of some French incursions upon English shores. Lord Thomas staged a well-planned defence and the French were repelled. Meanwhile, Edward III mounted a successful campaign in France and was able to secure Aquitaine, which included Guienne, Ponthieu and Calais. In exchange, he renounced his claim upon the kingship of France. He was also paid a hefty ransom for the return of King John. Edward III headed home, exhausted. He left Prince Edward in charge of Aquitaine. Edward held a parliament to ratify the peace he had brokered with France and the Archbishop of Canterbury celebrated the victory with a Mass. Philippa was relieved to have her husband back in England.

In 1361, Prince Edward secretly married Joan of Kent, who was by now a widow. The queen had been aware of the hold Joan had over her son Edward. The countess 'was fat and almost forty, but the Prince of Wales followed her still like a shadow'.[30] The two main areas that concerned Philippa and Edward III were Joan's dubious marital history and lack of any diplomatic connections that would increase the wealth or power of the kingdom. Another point of contention was that the union was deemed invalid in the eyes of the Church, owing to consanguinity. Prince Edward and Joan were unmovable, though, and the king, against his wishes, arranged for a swift papal dispensation to allow the union. There was a public remarriage at Windsor, which Edward III refused to attend; the royal protest shows he respected his son's right to make a decision on whom to marry but did not approve of his choice of bride. Philippa attended with her younger sons, her daughter Isabella, Queen Joan of Scotland and the Countess Maud of Hainault, apparently content that her son was happy with the

---

30 Hardy, p. 266.

choice of his bride. This accords with how Philippa had always wanted what was best for her children.

Philippa's last decade of life is dominated by her sons. Edward's marriage to Joan produced a son and heir, Edward, in 1370. Unfortunately, he was to die at seven years old. Philippa remained active into her middle age, but she dislocated her shoulder in an outdoor hunting accident at Cosham. This accident seemed to limit her travel, though she still did so throughout the 1360s. Her younger son John of Gaunt had inherited Lancaster through his wife Blanche. Maud of Hainault had died in 1362, and this left the entire Lancaster fortune in Blanche's hands, making John of Gaunt one of the most powerful and wealthy of the cadet branch of the House of Plantagenet. This would have an impact on the later years of Edward III's reign and also the reigns to come.

Philippa had the satisfaction of hearing that Edward and Joan of Kent's second child was born in 1367. The news came from Bordeaux that a son named Richard had been safely delivered. This news no doubt delighted Philippa. However, this was the only good news for her in 1367. First, she suffered an attack of dropsy and then to further her suffering news arrived of her favourite son's death. Lionel of Antwerp had died in the heat of the Italian summer; he had been overindulging in drinking and other pleasures for months. Philippa never really recovered from the illness, or the sad news.

Philippa's husband in his twilight years left the conduct of the kingdom to his sons and ministers. Edward III had been infatuated by an attractive court lady, Alice Perrers. Alice was one of the queen's ladies and remained one until Philippa died in 1369. Edward took Alice as a mistress much earlier and granted her estates and money. Her husband's infatuation with Alice and his indiscretion no doubt contributed to Philippa's anxieties in her final year of life. The further renewal of the war with France in 1368 was also distressing to her and she was worried as Prince Edward had been stricken with an illness, which limited his ability to administer the Duchy of Aquitaine. Philippa's health finally failed in late summer 1369. 'Dead is she and buried, that kind lady who in all honour without blame past her life. Alas what news for all her friends!'[31]

The throne after Philippa's death was a shadow of its former glory. Edward III's great schemes and victories had faded and France was reasserting itself after the weakness that Edward III exhibited in the last few years of his reign. She had given him twelve children, none of whom ever wore the crown and only five of whom survived her. Prince Edward, the gleaming hope for the future, was stricken with disease in the last years of his life. He died in 1376, leaving his young son Richard as heir to the throne. King Edward III was never the same man after Philippa's death.

The only child of Philippa and Edward who exerted any power or influence was John of Gaunt. It may have seemed that Gaunt had overreached himself towards the end, but he was to be the uncle of the new king, Richard II. The rumour that persisted was that Gaunt would usurp the throne from his nephew Richard, but the Duke of Lancaster made no attempt in 1377 to wrest the crown from young Richard and served as regent and advisor to the young king.

Edward III made no provisions for a regency upon his death, a rather short-sighted decision in the light of English royal history. However, it was the failures and complete misunderstanding of English government of Richards II's reign and not the dynastic policies of Edward III that effectively split the Plantagenet family

---

31 Froissart cited from Hardy, p. 301.

in 1399. Circumstances forced these issues, not any failure of Edward III as king. Perhaps if Philippa had lived longer there may have been more stability within the Plantagenet family. She had proved to be the very model of a queen consort and she worked faithfully and tirelessly for the crown. She can be considered a true mother of the English people during her reign, and she maintained a balance between royal and familial duties that can only be admired in such a tumultuous and warlike time.

4

JOAN OF KENT

During her childhood Joan, the fair maid of Kent, was a refugee from the revolt led by Isabella of France and Roger Mortimer. Her father, Edmund Plantagenet, the younger half-brother of Edward II, was the victim of the short period of Isabella and Mortimer's regency, 1327–30, and was executed for treason under suspicious circumstances during this time. Joan was the wife of the Black Prince, Princess of Wales and also the mother of Richard II. She exercised power and influence during the late 1370s and early 1380s until her death in 1385. She represents the consortia power of a queen mother but was never a queen in her own right. She and Katherine Swynford are the two influential women who were close to the throne but were never queen of England. They both represent an important link in the chain of queens in this study. Like Eleanor of Aquitaine, they exerted their influence through their maternal relations to kings of England. While Joan was the mother of a king, Katherine Swynford was the matriarch of the Beaufort line, which led to the Tudor dynasty. Joan was described by many contemporaries as a rare beauty of the age. The romantic notions that surround her will be dispelled and this essay will elucidate the true woman she was. Joan of Kent, Princess of Wales, never became queen due to the premature death of her husband, Edward the Black Prince, in 1376, a year before his father, Edward III. Joan of Kent exerted influence over her husband and her son, and had ties to the Lollard movement. Froissart described her as '*la plus belle de tout le royaume d'Engleterre et la plus amoureuse*' – 'the most beautiful woman in all the realm of England, and the most loving'. She was a medieval beauty but possessed abilities beyond the superficial appeal of her looks.

Joan of Kent's early life was surrounded with uncertainty, beginning with the tumultuous events of the overthrowing of Edward II by his queen Isabella of France and Roger Mortimer. In 1330 Joan's father, Edmund, Earl of Kent, was found guilty of treason for plotting to restore his half-brother Edward II, whom he believed was still alive, to the throne. Mortimer may well have been responsible for leading Edmund to the belief that his half-brother still lived, in a form of entrapment, and it can be inferred that Isabella and Mortimer wanted to dispose of him for two reasons: the influence he may have had over the young Edward III, who was known to be fond of his uncle, and the lucrative estates he held. Edward III may not have approved of this execution but Isabella and Mortimer were the ones holding the power in 1330. It seems that the execution of Edmund shocked contemporaries and the severity of his sentence shook the very foundation of Isabella and Mortimer's regency. The execution was a vindictive act used to control the baronage with terror, but it had the opposite effect. The avarice and greed shown by Isabella and Mortimer in respect to the wholesale confiscation of Edmund's lands and estates by the treasury was seen as a selfish act no different than Edward II's and the Despensers' later reign. Justice was to be swift, for only seven months after Edmund's execution, Edward III engineered to be rescued with the help of some faithful knights, overthrew the regency and rightfully claimed the kingdom for himself. Roger Mortimer was executed for his crimes and at the top of that list was the execution of Edmund, Earl of Kent. Most of the lands and estates taken from the Earl of Kent were restored to Edmund's sons, thanks to their mother Margaret's persistence in applying for compensation. Overall, Edward III was quick to follow a path of reconciliation and to restore order to the realm. He was even-handed and did restore most of the earldom of Kent but some lands had to be distributed among other loyal barons as a reward for their support in overthrowing the regency.

After the dust had cleared, Margaret was fully occupied by running the vast estates of the earldom of Kent (Edmund's sons were too young to inherit the estates) and her daughter Joan and son John were put into the care of the royal household. The king and queen were undoubtedly the major proprietors of Joan and John's childhood. The royal children of Edward III and their companions, which would have been Joan and John, were under the careful supervision of Queen Philippa. Joan would have been literate in French reading and writing for a young woman of her status. She would also have had a knowledge of some Latin due to religious training. Joan would have been raised as the other young woman of the royal household with skills in dancing, singing, playing musical instruments and a form of embroidery. On the physical side she would have been taught to ride and engage in royal sport of the era. Her brother John would have been trained at the appropriate age in the martial skills of a knight. Religion would have been a cornerstone of their education and canonical teachings would have been inculcated at an early age upon Joan and her brother. Joan would have travelled with Philippa, who followed her king in his political dealings in the realm. This would have been a stable and safe environment for Joan and would subsequently create a strong-willed independent woman.

As discussed before, children of noble birth would have had their marriages pre-planned by their respective guardians to ensure political alliances and stability for their families and for the realm. In 1338 Joan accompanied the Princess Isabella to Europe with the king and queen to secure alliances for Edward III's future plans of the conquest of France. The reason for Edward's war was his claim upon the French throne, which was through his mother Isabella, Charles IV's only sister, making Edward the closest male relative. The French preferred the claim of Philip of Valois, who became Philip VI. He took advantage of England's war with Scotland (the Auld Alliance[32]) to confiscate Aquitaine for the French crown in 1337. (The Angevin inheritance goes back to Eleanor of Aquitaine and this duchy was part of the English realm lost in the previous century. Again, the shadow of Eleanor of Aquitaine was a powerful and symbolic element of the English monarchy and stems from the dower of a queen.) Edward reacted by asserting his claim to the French throne. Edward wanted to secure the textile trade in Flanders and needed allies to support his war with France, hence the journey to Antwerp.

---

32   The Auld Alliance was between Scotland and France and originated in 1295 to control English expansion during Edward I's reign. It extended until the Treaty of Edinburgh of 1560.

By early spring 1340 Joan had been away from her mother and family for two years and was under the supervision of Lady Saint Omer, who was entrusted by Queen Philippa to be the guardian of the royal princess and Joan. The preparations for war and Edward's political alliances no doubt created an atmosphere of uncertainty for everyone. At the age of twelve, Joan would have been displaying her impeccable visage of beauty and she was also of the age of consent, according to the canon law of the time.

This brief period in early spring 1340 produced an environment that made Joan susceptible to the advances of one of the king's household knights, Sir Thomas Holland. He was a lowly knight in the service of the Earl of Salisbury, and the second son of a Lancastrian knight who did not support his lord, Thomas, Earl of Lancaster, against Despenser and Edward II in 1322. These past events led to the Earl of Lancaster's execution and the betrayal of Sir Robert Holland (Sir Thomas Holland's father) had been a shock to the English baronage. This act of betrayal was not forgotten amongst the nobility. Given this shadowy past, it would not be looked upon as a favourable match for Joan, and Sir Thomas was well aware of this. Sir Thomas was more than ten years her senior and his reputation as a knight may have been attractive to a young girl like Joan. He proposed and they engaged in a clandestine marriage without royal consent. This was a completely unorthodox move by Sir Thomas and would have risked the disapproval of the king and possibly led to his removal from royal service. Although marriage to social inferiors did occur on occasion, to do so in secret was quite rare. Canon law considered the age of consent for a woman to be twelve and as long both parties had the capacity and expressed consent – '*de praesenti*' – then the marriage would be valid.

However, this marriage was of an irregular nature and could be easily contested by either party, or the parents could intervene on the part of either party. Joan was swept away by emotional 'love' for an older knight with notions of chivalric romanticism. Sir Thomas did distinguish himself as an able military man under Edward III, received his knighthood from the king and served in the campaigns in Scotland with valour, but these accomplishments would not be sufficient to allow the match in the eyes of her parents or guardians.

The historical record is unclear as to when Thomas first drew the attention of young Joan, but he would have had limited financial means as a knight and this can only be seen as an opportunistic social move to better his lot in life. There may have been an emotional attraction between the two, of course, but her status and wealth no doubt had a huge influence on the twenty-four-year-old Sir Thomas. The validity of the marriage would only be restricted by law by consanguinity, compaternity or previous spousal marriages, none of which were present here. This would still not make it any easier for the young couple once it came to light. This marriage seems to have been fuelled by youthful vigour, but it would not help the social status of Sir Thomas Holland if it was not given formal approval and support. Sir Thomas calculated that it would take time for him to secure the proper approval of the court and family and he was gambling that time was on his side. He had military obligations to fulfil and so he left his new bride and asked that their marriage remain a secret until his return from France. The court was preoccupied with the pending war with France and he was involved in the naval battle of Sluys in 1340 and was active at the siege of Tournai.

Thomas was released from military service after Tournai, and in 1341 he was looking for a way to further distinguish his career. Since he was not in official military service, he saw the crusade with the Teutonic knights against the Tartars as a good opportunity to do exactly that. He obtained the king's permission to go on crusade and may have seen Joan briefly to explain his predicament and assure her he would return and claim her as his wife.

It may be assumed that he distinguished himself notably during the bitter fighting that took place in the frontiers of Prussia in 1341. The portrait of Chaucer's 'verray, parfait, gentle knight' is obviously a tribute to the prowess of men like Holland, who had not only 'reysed [in Lettow] and in Ruce', but who also 'hadde the bord bigonne/Aboven alle nacions in Pruce'.[33]

The marriage to Sir Thomas Holland created much distress in Joan's life. In early 1341 she was reunited with her family and her mother announced she was to be married to William Montague, son of the Earl of Salisbury and childhood friend of the court. Joan could not contact Sir Thomas since he was away on crusade and she was forced by circumstances to tell her mother about her marriage to him. Her mother Margaret was displeased and showed no sympathy for Joan's plight. Her mother's reaction was probably of disbelief and she effectively bullied her into the marriage with the Earl of Salisbury. It can be surmised that her family decided to ignore her original betrothal on the assumption that it could be dissolved in favour of this more acceptable and profitable union. So in early 1341 Joan and William were married

---

33 Karl P. Wenterdorf, 'The Clandestine Marriages of the Fair Maid of Kent', in *Journal of Medieval History* 5 (1979), p. 207.

bigamously. The wedding was a public affair and had the full approval of the king, which was politically acceptable among the royal household and the baronage. It seems that the Earl of Salisbury may have been aware of the clandestine marriage of Sir Thomas and Joan, since it seems unlikely that her mother and uncle would have hidden this information from the earl to avoid future complications. Salisbury had the advantage of serving with Sir Thomas on earlier campaigns and knew the measure of the man, so perhaps he felt that Sir Thomas could be compensated for his earlier transgression and forget the whole matter of his marriage to Joan. This is speculation but it seems to follow the course of events, as we will see.

The other aspect of the affair is what part the king and queen had played. It seems likely that they were aware of the secret marriage of Joan and Sir Thomas. One can surmise that perhaps the king and queen felt a bit responsible since Joan had not been so closely supervised while under the care the royal household. Again this is speculation based on the circumstances, but it seems to be a logical conclusion since the king and queen seemed to keep themselves distant from this dilemma. King Edward may also have felt that it was Salisbury's problem and he had full confidence that he would resolve it. However, since this affair dragged on for over eight years it seems that discretion was to be the better part of valour for the king and queen. Everyone involved probably assumed this was a young girl's crush and that she was somehow manipulated into this marriage by the young, dashing knight.

However, in 1342 Sir Thomas returned from his crusade in Prussia and made his intentions clear to Joan's mother. Margaret and Joan's uncle hoped that the Earl of Salisbury would be present to deal with this 'misunderstanding' but unfortunately for them he was in France handling matters of state. Since the earl was in France, Joan's mother, uncle and William Montague refused Sir Thomas any rights in his marriage claim. Joan was still unwilling to renounce her marriage to Sir Thomas, so this would become complicated. In this medieval world the wealthy and powerful felt they had certain advantages, and so waiting for the lowly Sir Thomas to make the first move was in their best interests. Sir Thomas was not capable of affording expensive legal proceedings to prove his claim and he had military obligations by mid-1342. Joan's fortitude and steadfast loyalty to Sir Thomas was a commendable trait, but her wishes were completely ignored by all parties involved.

After the military actions in Brittany were over Sir Thomas and the Earl of Salisbury went on crusade in Granada against the Moors. This would further delay any action and further Joan's turmoil with her mother, uncle and William Montague. A fact that seems quite evident is that these men, Sir Thomas and the Earl of Salisbury, were jockeying for political advantage to claim their prize, a callous and cavalier attitude towards this young woman by allowing the crusade to delay proceedings. Sir Thomas was obviously furthering his military reputation and hoping through chivalric service to the king that he may be seen in a better light, but the other side seemed to be employing stalling tactics. The crusade in Spain ended in late 1343 and it was expected that Joan would see a conclusion to her marital strife. Joan was still holding fast to remaining married to Sir Thomas, so a Church decision was not an avenue for her mother and William to pursue.

The Earl of Salisbury unexpectedly died while at a jousting tournament in 1344 and this would only exacerbate the issue. The young heir, William Montague, was too young to claim his father's estates, and therefore did not have the power to fulfil or make any promises to Thomas. Everyone turned to the king to solve this marriage dilemma, but it seemed he was deliberately distancing himself from it. King Edward III's inaction can be seen as a political move since he was preparing for a war with France and did not want any distractions, or perhaps he was sympathetic to the cause of Sir Thomas and Joan but did not want to openly declare a side. There is no record to follow on this matter but speculation may serve to fill in some of the gaps. Joan's family and William Montague would now try again to get Joan to repudiate her marriage, but her steadfast loyalty to Sir Thomas remained and this matter would drag on for another five years. My analysis of the marriage of Joan and Sir Thomas is that perhaps Edward saw the inevitability of it and thought that it might prove to be an incentive for future recruitment of able-bodied men to serve the king. While Edward would not condone this social climbing, it could serve to be an encouragement for men to serve in a long and protracted war.

The war in France began in earnest again in 1345/46 and led to one of the most celebrated victories of the war, the Battle of Crécy, in which Sir Thomas participated bravely. A fortunate event for Sir Thomas was at the Battle of Caen where he captured a noble fighting on the French side, Count Raoul d'Eu. This was a large honour for Sir Thomas and the ransom would bring him wealth. The capture of French nobles produced revenue for many, including the king, during the Hundred Years War, which was was now becoming a profitable enterprise. Sir Thomas fought in the cavalry vanguard of Prince Edward, a very dangerous unit to be in since it took the brunt of the brutal assault. Holland distinguished himself and was able to enhance his reputation at court once again. It seems his star was on the rise.

Sir Thomas could now, with his revenue from the ransom for the count, proceed with a petition for the papacy to intercede in the marriage of Joan and William, hoping the pope would annul the latter's marriage. This of course infuriated William Montague and he subsequently detained Joan at his residence. Since he did not have access to his full estate due to his age this action was all he could muster. The king did not intervene in any way for either Sir Thomas or William but he did grant part of the inheritance he was due to show no favouritism. Now William could respond to Sir Thomas's challenge. One point to note was that no one considered Joan's wishes in the matter and her mother was even aiding William in his pursuit.

During the marriage proceedings the king instituted a new order of knights called the Order of the Garter which the most prestigious knights were invited to join and Sir Thomas and William were both members. Perhaps the king wanted to display impartiality in the marriage debate. The Order of the Garter seems to have been first displayed at the tournament at Windsor in 1348 and in typical chivalric fashion Sir Thomas and William were on opposite sides during the tournament, the debate being played out on the field, which gave it a sense of the cliché 'may the best man win'. The objectification of Joan of Kent was apparent in these actions and there was little if any consideration for her wishes; she was a prize to be won and King Edward perpetuated this idea to his own advantage.

The papal proceeding went on for over a year and finally, in 1349, Cardinal d'Albi declared the marriage between William and Joan as invalid and found the previous marriage between Sir Thomas Holland and Joan of Kent valid. Further, the cardinal ordered a public ceremony for Joan and Thomas. This was all confirmed in late 1349 by the pope and he ordered the judgement to be carried out by the bishops of Norwich and London. One of the reasons for the long delay was the spread of the plague in the summer of 1348, which had a dramatic impact on communications and travel throughout Europe. William conceded in 1349 and Sir Thomas and Joan would now be able to live as husband and wife. A victim of the plague during the proceedings was Joan's mother Margaret, who died in September 1349, a sadness for Joan since it seemed that mother and daughter did not reconcile before her death.

Married life began in 1350 and Joan and Sir Thomas moved into one of his Broughton manor houses in Buckinghamshire that he inherited from his mother, who had also recently died of plague. Sir Thomas had to supplement his income with military service since his properties were not adequate to support the lifestyle Joan had been used to. Holland maintained his reputation and connection to the court and had Prince Edward as the godfather of their first child, Thomas. This was a choice based on the relationship Joan had with her cousin and the fact that Sir Thomas had served with the prince at Crécy, probably allowing Thomas to gain favour with the prince through comradeship in arms.

Joan and Thomas were able to spend some time together before the tragic event of 1352, when her brother suddenly died of an illness. Joan lost her last close family relative, with whom she had grown up. This loss did have the benefit of Joan inheriting the earldom of Kent, which was one of the most lucrative in England. The surviving wife of her brother John, Elizabeth, was to inherit one third of the earldom for her upkeep, but this was to revert to Joan and her offspring upon her death. The inheritance cleared all of Sir Thomas' debts and made him a peer, making Joan and Thomas wealthy. However, the king would not grant the title of earl to Sir Thomas yet, which may be due to the nature of his marriage to Joan. Joan and Thomas moved into the most prominent property of the earldom at Castle Donington. This was to be their residence for the remainder of their marriage and an excellent place to raise their children.

The war did consume Sir Thomas' main interest from 1352 to 1360 and warfare was where he seemed show the most skill. On occasion Joan would accompany Holland on his campaigns in France, a sign of devotion on Joan's part to her husband's career. Sir Thomas was Governor Lieutenant in Brittany for Edward III, a prestigious position that reflected his rank and skill in warfare. Sir Thomas and Joan had three other children between 1350 and 1358, which confirmed a happy personal relationship between the two.

The campaigning in 1356–58 had been long and arduous, but Sir Thomas reached the pinnacle of his career during this time when he was appointed Earl of Kent and Captain-General of all English holdings in France and Normandy. Sir Thomas had gained some of the highest honours for a knight of his class and was the star of the court for his service and close familial connection to the royal family. He was now called back to Normandy in September 1360 and this was to be his last fateful duty to his king, for in late December 1360 Sir Thomas succumbed to illness and died. This was devastating news to Joan, and for Thomas to die at the pinnacle of his career and at an age of vigour was a shock to everyone at court. He was succeeded by his eldest son as the Earl of Kent to carry on his legacy.

At the age of thirty-two Joan of Kent was a widow and one of the most desirable women in the court of Edward III. It seems that Prince Edward had been interested in Joan for years but she was married and therefore unavailable. Since Prince Edward had known Joan throughout his life it seems logical to assume he harboured feelings for her but there were many distractions and her marital background would deter any of his passions. Now that Joan was a widow it seemed that Prince Edward wished to marry Joan and being the heir apparent combined with his chivalric resume was an attractive prospect for Joan. She had also known him his whole life and had close personal ties with the royal family.

The marriage of the most beautiful woman in the kingdom (according to Froissart) and the most famous knight was a star-studded match. Joan's marital history and her familial relationship with Prince Edward would, of course, be a stumbling block, and a papal dispensation would be required for them to marry. Edward and Joan were related within the prohibited degree of consanguinity and they applied for a per *verba da preaesenti* papal agreement with Pope Innocent VI. The Black Prince secretly married Joan in 1361, which Edward III used to strong-arm the pope into giving the dispensation and declaring that all future offspring were legitimate. Their marriage was declared legal by the pope in September 1361 and they were now publicly the greatest chivalric knight and the most fair lady of Kent. In 1362 King Edward granted his son the title Prince of Aquitaine, which was in practice an independent ruler of that region, no doubt in preparation for his eventual inheritance of the English throne.

Edward III and Prince Edward received papal authority for the marriage and the succession would now be totally secure and lawful without any contention. The Black Prince provided generously for Joan's Holland children and this created political and social opportunities that would befit the Princess of Wales and the heir to the English throne. The Holland children were part of the prince's household and would be under the protection and authority of the royal household, which would serve the political wills of the royal prerogative. The spectre of social climbing was probably present in the fact that this marriage to the Prince of Wales was advantageous to Joan's family and would engender jealously among some of the baronage. Joan of Kent was the leading lady of the court after Queen Philippa, since there had not been a precedent for a Princess of Wales. She would also share the title as Princess of Aquitaine as consort to Prince Edward, this being confirmed by the Treaty of Bretigny, which declared Edward III's ascendency over the French king.

Prince Edward and Joan arrived in Aquitaine in 1363, a historical event marked by the precedent of Eleanor of Aquitaine and a nostalgic representation of the great Angevin empire of Henry II. Joan may have been influenced by the mark left by Eleanor of Aquitaine, now that she was the Princess of Aquitaine. However, Aquitaine was not the profitable province it had been 200 years ago; it was war-torn and had been ravaged by famine and plague. This is another example of how long and far Eleanor of Aquitaine would cast her shadow upon our story of the queens of England. It was a daunting task to revive Aquitaine, but Joan and Prince Edward were able to secure the Aquitaine province and kept a splendid court to promote English rule over the area. Administration of Aquitaine did require internal taxation and was not completely supported by the local baronage, but through sheer personality Edward was able to prevail in most areas of finance. Joan was modelling herself after her mother-in-law Queen Philippa, in running a court that completely supported her husband. Joan was a model consort and advised and encouraged Edward's rule in Aquitaine.

They based their court at Bordeaux, the hub of the commercial wine trade, which brought considerable profit to this province. The city also provided sea access, which was vital for commercial and military activities. Joan gave birth to their first son in March 1365, which was much celebrated as it provided an assurance for the succession. He was christened Edward after his father and grandfather, in the expectation that he would accede to the throne in due time. This would have been a happy time for Joan and Prince Edward, since many of their expectations were being fulfilled as the heir apparent couple of England. Prince Edward was active in gaining the political favour of his nobles and the occasion of the birth of his first child made for celebrations. This was to follow with Joan and Edward's second child, Richard, who was born in Bordeaux in 1367. Joan had provided an heir and a spare for her prince, to resort to common vernacular, and this was of course received with great excitement by her husband. However, war was on the horizon. Prince Edward would be beckoned by yet another fight, this time in Castile.

Joan saw her husband and stepson go off to war to aid Pedro of Castile to regain his throne from his rival relative, Henry of Trastámara, who was supported by the king of France, Charles V. This was a perfect opportunity for the new king of France to strike back at Edward III, albeit not directly to avoid open warfare, but in an attritional manner to slowly regain his French kingdom. Prince Edward got tacit approval and support from his father and was sending a force to aid his efforts in Castile. Pedro was not considered completely reliable, but he was a co-belligerent against the king of France. The campaign was a success. After six months of marching and fighting, and with the help of the king of Navarre, Prince Edward was able to defeat Henry at the Battle of Nájera. This was to be Prince Edward's last great victory in the field, since it seems he had contracted a disease while fighting. Although it is unclear what it was, through my research I would lean towards malaria. The other diseases that have been proposed are not consistent with diagnostic medicine, since dysentery would kill its hosts in a much quicker time than the nine years from his contraction of the disease and his eventual death in 1376. However, since diagnosing diseases was not even a science during this time it could have been a combination of factors that led to his prolonged illness and death, but malaria seems to be the most viable culprit due to its intermittent symptoms and its progress through the human body.

Joan was concerned once her husband returned and she saw the state of his health. Furthermore, the economic debts incurred during the war put strain on Aquitaine and the leading barons started to reveal their true colours. The support that Prince Edward had secured seemed to evaporate overnight after he returned from Castile. The taxes he imposed were unpopular and now the Aquitaine French barons started a wholesale defection to the French king. Like sharks, they sensed blood in the water, and with Prince Edward's weakened state, they saw opportunity to defect and throw off the yoke of English rule. Charles V of France declared the annexation of Aquitaine in late 1369 and made many promises to that effect to the local baronage. In 1370 Edward III sent a force to reinforce his claim on Aquitaine, but it was too late. The last campaign in 1370 at Limoges was administered by Prince Edward from a hospital litter. He had won through grit and determination but the city was completely destroyed, and this tarnished his honour in France and he had lost the loyalty of the local barons in both Aquitaine and Gascony.

Joan was grief stricken when her eldest son, Edward, was taken ill and died in Angoulême. This was a heavy loss for the Black Prince and Joan. In his ailing state, the Prince saw fit to return to England with Joan. In 1371 they arrived with their retinue and their surviving son, Richard, in England with hopes of a convalescence for Prince Edward. This was a hard time for Joan. With the death of her eldest son and her infirm husband, she now had to take on the responsibility of running the household. Her loyalty to the royal family and her husband was to be admired; she now had to ensure the succession, since her father-in-law, the king, was also old and ill and neither the king nor his son were getting better. The political responsibilities were being transferred to Prince Edward's younger brother, John of Gaunt.

In England there was less enthusiasm for the war in France, since it was very costly to maintain and the recent losses had made a negative impact on the economic health of England. John of Gaunt led a military force to recover Aquitaine in 1371, but it was a dismal failure and this reflected poorly on Gaunt, even though it is suspected that any expedition would have failed even with a healthy prince and king, since the tide of war was turning against England in France. The military machine Edward III created was coming to a halt due to the plague and labour difficulties at home. The war was self-sustaining due to its profit when it was successful but once the money stopped flowing, the ability to maintain military forces in the field put an extreme strain on the economy and many of the nobility were not willing to support a war that did not turn a profit. France also had a stronger king (Charles V) who was willing to wage a war of attrition rather than annihilation, the latter of which favoured English victories.

The years 1372–76 were tough on Joan as she saw her husband steadily decline in health and vigour, and this was particularly disturbing since he had been the shining star of chivalry and had a brilliant military career marked by the boundless energy he displayed on campaign. Now he was a shell of the man he once was and Joan nursed him the best she could. However, she never got directly involved in the political scene, and this seemed to be a prudent course of action after Joan's marital history. This decision was jointly made by her and Prince Edward to safeguard their young son Richard, who would soon succeed to the throne. The tightly knit royal court that Edward III had in the early glory days declined and fragmented due to a lack of support by the younger nobility and the death of the old-guard nobility who had supported Edward III and his son on the earlier successful campaigns in Crécy and Poitiers.

Joan and Prince Edward were involved in educating young Richard in the best manner possible to prepare him for his new role as heir to the throne, and later monarch. This was a dark time as Prince Edward saw his earlier victories in France lost by the weakness of the royal court and failed military actions, so he and Joan turned to the more immediate problem of the succession. Joan watched as her husband's health slowly deteriorated, and in 1376 the barons showed their full disapproval of the then current state of the realm with charges of corruption brought against many in the royal circle. It was also apparent that they were not happy with John of Gaunt's handling of the military activities and his reputation suffered greatly, something that would come to a head five years later in 1381 with the Peasants' Revolt.

Edward the Black Prince died on 8 June 1376 and this left Joan of Kent a widow again. The loss of such a great knight and prince had a resounding impact on England, creating a sombre mood. The flower of chivalry had been lost forever and Edward III was so distraught that it is suspected that his son's death led to his own death only a year later in 1377. Prince Edward prepared well for his death to alleviate any burden upon Joan or his son Richard. The major concern for Prince Edward on his deathbed was the legitimacy of his son and his marriage and to ensure a peaceful succession. It is known he harboured great affection and love for his wife and son, but his duty would always come first. Joan found herself again a widow and in a position of wealth, in which she managed her own estates and one third of the prince's estates. This was a good position of power and wealth to support her son, who ascended the throne in 1377.

Joan of Kent had fostered a mutually respectful relationship with Prince Edward's brother, John of Gaunt, and this was particularly important in the coronation of her son Richard as king. John of Gaunt was the oldest surviving son of Edward III and he was to be regent for the young King Richard. The year 1377 proved to be a difficult time for the realm and John of Gaunt came under considerable pressure from parliament over the support he had for the Lollards. The leader of this sect, John Wycliffe, was put on trial that year. William Courtenay, Bishop of London, and John of Gaunt, clashed verbally during the hearing and this resulted in the dispersal of the court and a riot. John of Gaunt escaped by water to Joan's Kennington Castle. She accepted and protected him, something he would never forget. Joan was a calming pressence and she was able to appeal to the mob. Their fears were allayed by her fast action and swift persuasion. Her status in the realm had been elevated and she was able to employ this reputation with a modicum of political skill that prevented any further violence. This counsel would be helpful in Richard's regency as Joan would be the voice of reason and conciliatory politics.

Joan and John of Gaunt arranged for a magnificent coronation for young Richard and they were careful to maintain the legal aspects of the succession. The oath of succession sworn to by Richard, with careful wording, became a fait accompli. The celebrations took place throughout London but the young king was overwrought and he fell asleep towards the end of ceremony. The ten-year-old was just beginning his reign. John of Gaunt was directing the royal household and running the day-to-day operation of the realm. Joan was, of course, consulted and she contributed in a protective way because she was keen to shield him from any discord from the anxious barons. She arranged to surround young Richard with many people who would encourage his royal status and remind him of the greatness of his father, a reputation that would perhaps be hard to uphold by anyone. Richard's kingship impacted on his family and it made his half-siblings, the Holland boys, royal kinsmen. They would one day be earls in their own right and close supporters of King Richard. Joan was careful not to draw too much attention to these actions as she did not want to alienate her family or young King Richard from the barons. The next few years went well for the young king and Joan but the growing economic problems that arose from the aftermath of the war in France and the plague started to rear their ugly head in 1380.

The Peasants' Revolt in 1381 was sparked by the poll tax and was an event that shook the very core of the English realm. By 1381 the war in France had been going dismally and its popularity had waned considerably. The revolt was predominantly aimed at the baronage, especially Richard's uncle John of Gaunt. The king and Joan were not part of this contempt for the ruling class. The peasants, led by Wat Tyler and John Ball, were hoping to get their respective demands met by the young king. When Joan encountered the angry mob while in her carriage en route to her son Richard, she was not threatened or harmed in any way, such demonstrates the high regard in which she was held among the people in general. Luckily John of Gaunt was away in Scotland so he was not a ready target for the revolt.

Richard and his council decided that it would be best to meet with the rebels and see what their demands were. The king went via barge to meet the rebels at Mile End. Joan apparently sent off her son but did not accompany him. Richard probably wanted his mother to remain in a safe place. It seems that as soon as the king and his small entourage left the Tower of London, the rebels stormed it and exacted their revenge against many of those who were there. However, Joan and Henry Bolingbroke (John of Gaunt's eldest son) were not harmed. Henry was hidden by a servant and Joan was whisked away after making it to a safe place – the queen's wardrobe.

Joan was worried due to the violence of the rebel but had found some comfort in the fact that their venom was mainly directed at the baronage and not at her or her son, the king. One of the victims of the violence was the Archbishop of Canterbury, who was summarily beheaded, as was the Treasurer Robert Hales and Sir John Legge, the creator of the dreaded poll tax. Richard met the rebels at Mile End, heard their demand for freedom and agreed to their terms (he really had no other choice), and was very conciliatory to the angry mob.

The next day Richard headed out to Smithfield to meet with Wat Tyler, the leader of the rebels, with his contingent. After the success of the raid on the Tower, Wat Tyler felt he could negotiate more extreme terms with the king. The events that followed are a bit cloudy but it seems that one of the king's squires had a physical confrontation, and then William Walworth (Mayor of London) struck Wat Tyler with his sword and killed him. Once the rebels realised what had happened, they started to become unruly but the king stepped in and presented himself as their leader. This was a very spontaneous action on the part of the king, who probably realised he was the only one the rebels would trust to bring their demands to fruition. The plan worked, and the crowd of rebels started to disperse.

Richard was then reunited with his mother and went back to London. This was where the king was able to garner support among the barons and knights and rescinded the promises he made to the rebels. Orders were given to enforce the peace and the ringleaders were gathered up, including Jack Straw and John Ball, the most prominent of the rebels, who were then executed for treason against the crown. The situation over the next few weeks was brought to a resolution, and some of the demands were addressed, but the king and barons were able to maintain power.

This was one of the worst threats to the crown since the French invasion earlier in the century. Joan looked at her son in a different light and started to realise he had the leadership ability of a king. It can't be denied that Richard benefited from being the son of the greatest knight in the land and that his mother was held in high esteem by all of England. This reputation gave Richard the freedom to act and the stalwart confidence to defend his realm.

Joan's careful planning and impeccable behaviour at court had paid dividends for her son and this was the legacy that Richard would inherit. One of the last efforts Joan made for her son was the arrangement for his marriage to Anne of Bohemia. Anne was the daughter of the king of Bohemia and did not come with a dowry, which concerned many of the barons. It was not a particularly popular union but Joan felt it to be a good match, as did John of Gaunt. The marriage avoided any complicated political entanglements with France or Spain, which were more obvious choices. This marriage was free of any military and political alliances that England at this time could ill afford. Joan's close relationship with her husband's brother, John of Gaunt, and her steadfast loyalty to her family was a true testament of Joan's abilities and her great poise while all of England was watching.

Joan's last years were in retirement at Wallingford Castle, which seemed to have been her idea since her son did not wish her to leave court. However, she felt that it was his time and her constant presence might distract from his kingship. Right before her death in 1385, there had been a rift between John of Gaunt and King Richard and Joan would intercede one last time as peacemaker and she managed to smooth the waters between the king and his most powerful magnate. She warned Richard of the sycophants in his court and the need to maintain a proper balance among the barons at court. Subsequently she requested that John of Gaunt go to Westminster to have an accord with the king, and in this she was successful. Again in her last year she was the consummate peacemaker and her loss would be gravely felt in the coming years of Richard's reign. At this juncture, it seems that Joan had become frail and overweight and she had lost the light that she had emitted from her earlier days. She was fifty-eight years old.

Joan's son, John Holland, had been in an army going north to quell the border of Scotland in late July 1385. Earlier, he had had a bitter fight with the Earl of Stafford and, in the melee, he killed him. When this news reached Richard's court, he was greatly disturbed and he had his half-brother arrested and took away all his estates. He did not have him tried for murder but was nevertheless extremely angry with him. Joan tried to intercede again but her health was failing and she could only send messages, which did not have the same impact as a personal visit. Joan was so overwrought that she fainted. She passed away on 8 August 1385. The news of King Richard's mother's death hit him hard, but there is no official record of his grief. Joan was laid to rest at the chapel in Stamford and wanted a less grandiose memorial than her husband's, father's and mother-in-law's, which showed her humble nature, even serving the realm in her death, carefully avoiding bringing too much attention to herself. Joan of Kent was a moderate and temperate influence on her son and her passing would remove some of the conciliatory actions of Richard's reign and would lead to a more tyrannical rule without her.

Joan of Kent displayed some of the major elements of queenship, bringing with her a considerable dowry and particularly in ensuring a peaceful succession. She also followed in the footsteps of Eleanor when she fiercely defended her family against the many trials she encountered in her lifetime. Although she was a more reserved and less meddling princess consort than the women who preceeded her, in the end she portrayed the ideal of the steadfast queen during a tumultuous time of war and plague. Joan of Kent never was a queen in her own right but she was mother to a king and the consort of the greatest prince in English history, albeit with a tragic ending. In the recent biography by Penny Lawne we have a nice summing up of Joan's life:

Joan's most famous legacy was her son, Richard. Once it became clear that the Prince [Edward the Black Prince] would not live to succeed his father, Joan devoted herself to the future of their son, to the extent that she was prepared to suppress the interests of her older sons until Richard was secure on his throne. Much of her influence was beneficial. Her popularity and her good relationship with Gaunt eased Richard's peaceful succession; Gaunt's support for Richard's accession was crucial, and although his loyalty to his brother had never been in doubt there were many who feared he would not support the son and would make a bid for the throne himself. That Gaunt was so stalwart in his support of his nephew was in no small measure due to the affectionate and fond relationship he enjoyed with Joan, and their mutual trust and respect.[34]

Joan of Kent is an important study for this work since she represents the cool, intrepid style of queenship that would mark the era, but her non-political role indicated conservativism. However, when her interests were at stake, she displayed the same vitality and insight that Eleanor of Aquitaine and the other queens in this study used to determine the right course of action. Her unorthodox marital history and her long association with the royal family and ultimate

---

34 Penny Lawne, *Joan of Kent: The First Princess of Wales* (Stroud: Amberley Publishing, 2015), p. 268.

marriage to the Black Prince indicated her importance to the Plantagenet line, albeit her son Richard would be usurped by her nephew, an event she fortunately did not live to see. The romantic mythos that surrounded Joan of Kent still permeates the literature and popular culture of today. Froissart maintained she was the most beautiful woman of her time and was filled with love and affection; what more could the realm want from a queen?

5

KATHERINE SWYNFORD

Katherine Swynford, along with Joan of Kent, is one of the two subjects in this study who never became a queen in her own right, but was extremely influential in the Plantagenet royal line. Swynford, like Joan of Kent, married a son of Edward III, John of Gaunt. Katherine had been involved in an extramarital affair with Gaunt for many years. Her historical legacy has been clouded by the publication of Anya Seton's famous novel *Katherine*, first published in 1954, which muddied the waters of research and still has an impact on how we view Swynford during this period. Conversely, the novel also triggered more recent sound historical research and was the impetus for a more thorough and objective view of Katherine Swynford and her influence on the Plantagenet royal dynasty. An interesting quote from Madeline Caviness outlines the perception of femininity and its duty in royal lineage. Katherine Swynford indeed bucked this trend and became an important dynastic foundation of English royalty.

In the fraught atmosphere of a failing dynasty, betrayed by female lasciviousness and punished by a lack of male heirs, more than lessons of conventional piety had to be directed at the girl-bride who was supposed to become the chaste mother of indubitably legitimate male children.[35]

What will be apparent is that Katherine was able to overcome many obstacles in the form of the notions about medieval consorts and female behaviour. She would be in a position of unprecedented power when her offspring formed the Beaufort line, which later weaved itself inextricably into the lines of decent of English royalty that continues up to this day.

Katherine's heritage connects to the Hainault and English thrones. The Roet family, from which Katherine originates, seems to indicate some noble ancestry. Katherine Swynford was born to Paon de Roet in about 1345 and she was the middle offspring of his three daughters. Her younger sister Philippa was born in 1347. The eldest daughter was born in 1335 and entered a convent and served the church throughout her lifetime. These dates are not completely certain, but recent research seems to place their respective births at these dates. Paon de Roet was in service to Queen Philippa as a trusted part of her retinue. Little is known about Katherine Swynford's mother, but it seems that she was of English birth.

---

35 Madeline H. Caviness, 'Patron or Matron? A Capetian Bride and a Vade Mecum for Her Marriage Bed' in Nancy Partner, ed., *Studying Medieval Women: Sex, Gender and Feminism* (Cambridge, MA: The Medieval Academy of America, 1993), p. 36.

Since the focus of this essay is Katherine Swynford we will focus on her upbringing. Her younger sister will be of interest since she married the famous poet, Geoffrey Chaucer. There is little evidence concerning the life of Katherine's eldest sister, Isabella. Paon de Roet was a knight of some distinction and served with Edward III at Crécy and Calais. He became marshal of the queen's household due to his service in France. The era Katherine was born into was fraught with war and plague. It seems that Katherine might have had an elder brother too. He may have served with the Black Prince, but little is known of his life in service. Paon de Roet served the household honourably and it seems he may have died around 1355. Katherine's mother may have passed away earlier in 1352. This left Katherine and her sister Philippa in the care of Queen Philippa.

Katherine and her sister were brought up among the royal brood. Evidence suggests that Katherine was fluent in Dutch and Norman French (the language of the English court), and she learned English later in life. Katherine was also tutored in the same skills as the royal children, which would have included sewing, learning to play musical instruments, dance and religious instruction. She also learned the prerequisite etiquette and social skills of the English aristocracy of this period. This favourable upbringing would no doubt have undue influence on the sisters' respective lives and equip them to move in the social circles of the English nobility of this period.

The early life of Katherine's sister seems to indicate a placement in the Countess of Ulster's household as a rokestere (cradle rocker).[36]

---

36 Margaret Galway, 'Philippa Pan: Philippa Chaucer', *Modern Language Review*, 55 (1960), pp. 481-2.

Philippa returned to the queen's household after the death of the countess. In 1366 Philippa married the poet Geoffrey Chaucer, whom she had met during her tenure of service for the Countess of Ulster. When John of Gaunt married Constance of Castile, who was his second wife, Philippa entered the household of the new Duchess of Lancaster, Constance. Philippa had a nice life with Chaucer and lived with her sister in Lincolnshire. She died some time around 1386. Insight into Katherine's sister's life is available due to her marriage to Geoffrey Chaucer and his writing and record keeping.

The earliest accounts of Katherine's life are reflected in the public records for the year 1365. She was in service to the Duchess of Lancaster and it seems that she was close to the family since she was permitted to receive mass in a private ceremony. The record for this year also indicates that Katherine had been married to Hugh Swynford, who was a retainer to the Duke of Lancaster. It seems that Katherine and Hugh Swynford were married somewhere between 1363 and 1365.

There is strong evidence that Katherine, who was previously thought to be born in 1350, was probably born in about 1345. The later date of birth would have meant that in 1365 she was been fifteen years old and this was far too young for woman who was a commoner to be married, contrary to modern-day popular belief. Only the highest-ranking individuals of the nobility were married very young in order to secure political and military agendas. Since Katherine and her husband were of lower social rank, she was most likely married in her early twenties. Furthermore, Katherine Swynford was the caretaker of the Duke and Duchess of Lancaster's children around this time. Conventions of the time would indicate that this prestigious position would not be held by a woman under the age of twenty. There is no doubt that Katherine had been awarded this important post because of her early childhood training under the guidance and tutelage of Queen Philippa.

Since the records for John of Gaunt are not complete, it may be inferred that Katherine was placed by Queen Philippa into the service of the Duchess of Lancaster to help with the recent birth of a child in 1360. However, the records do indicate Katherine's presence in the Duke and Duchess of Lancaster's household by 1365. Thus this can be considered informed speculation on whether Katherine had contact with the Duke of Lancaster before 1365 or in the household of Blanche Lancaster.

The marriage of Hugh and Katherine Swynford seems to indicate a union of two consenting people who had developed true feelings for each other. It can be deduced that Katherine met Hugh Swynford while in service to the Duchess of Lancaster. Hugh was a knight in the Duke of Lancaster's retinue. Katherine may also have harboured feelings for John of Gaunt, but the social rules of the time presented barriers that Katherine could not overcome. Furthermore, since John was of royal blood, he had to wed marriage partners who would benefit the the royal family. No doubt Katherine de Roet would not be an acceptable political or economic match for John of Gaunt. A century later Edward IV would oppose the system when he married Elizabeth Woodville, which created a tumultuous era.

Katherine made a logical choice to marry Hugh Swynford, for he was of some means and was a knight of the gentry class. He was also a landowner of modest means and there may have been some romantic interludes between the two before the marriage. This makes chronological sense if we date the relationship as a mistress to Gaunt from around 1370 to 1372. Katherine, in many ways, was thinking like a noble and secured her future in the best manner she could by marrying Hugh Swynford – a marriage of convenience rather than choice.

The question arises, then, did Katherine have a relationship with John of Gaunt before her marriage? Did Katherine plan to be John of Gaunt's mistress, and further was Hugh Swynford aware of this arrangement and was he even compliant to his master's wishes? These are all intriguing questions but there is little evidence to prove or disprove these theories. However, it is clear that Katherine was in the household of John of Gaunt and had developed some kind of a relationship with him from the start, but the very nature of this relationship is still conjecture. Katherine had two children with Hugh Swynford – Blanche and Thomas. The daughter, Blanche, born in 1366, was the older of the two. Further evidence of Katherine's closeness to the Duke of Lancaster was that John of Gaunt was godparent to Blanche. This may have indicated a 'closeness' in his relationship with Katherine, since he would be godfather to a member of the social class below his.

Another point to consider about John of Gaunt and Katherine Swynford's affair was the benefits and favours gained by Katherine while in service to the Lancasters. The positions of Katherine and Hugh Swynford in the Lancaster household were of high honour. We cannot be certain that this was strictly due to their high-quality training. On the contrary, it could be argued with a healthy dose of speculation that perhaps Katherine had an arrangement with the Duke of Lancaster, whereby she would be his mistress if certain favours would be awarded to her and her husband. This quid-pro-quo arrangement would not be out of character for this time period and in many cases would be an acceptable means of upward social mobility. However, this is certainly not an arrangement that would be documented, which would be the reason for the lack of sources to back up this theory.

Katherine took charge of the duke's household upon the death of Blanche, Duchess of Lancaster, in 1369, which, coincidentally, was also the year of John of Gaunt's mother's death (Queen Philippa). This double tragedy would surely have affected John of Gaunt and perhaps Katherine was the person to console the Duke of Lancaster. Again, this presumes there was a personal relationship that had ensued before the death of these two important women in John of Gaunt's life.

Katherine Swynford's husband died two years later in 1371 while on campaign under John of Gaunt's leadership. The general consensus among historians is that the relationship between John of Gaunt and Katherine as his mistress began around 1372, since there was a steady increase in grants and gifts to Katherine from John of Gaunt from this period onwards. The historical records indicate that the affair of Katherine Swynford and John of Gaunt was most likely public knowledge by 1375, but as I have indicated it seems that perhaps the relationship may have started earlier and both parties wanted to avoid a scandal at the time. Historians believe that the Duke of Lancaster may have begun his affair with Katherine Swynford at the same time he married his second wife, Constance of Castile. Alison Weir outlines that the historical record indicates a documentation of the period 1372–83:

Much of what we know of Katherine Swynford's years as John of Gaunt's mistress is recorded in John of Gaunt's register, which survives for the periods 1372–76 and 1379–83. This covers much of the period in question, although three vital years are missing, as are the years following their parting. These missing records would surely have contained more clues to the truth of the relationship between Katherine and John, so their loss is only to be lamented. Nevertheless, as will surely become clear there is much that can be inferred from the information that has come down to us.[37]

John of Gaunt's second marriage was to further his political ambition of acquiring the throne of Castile. This never came to be, but seemed to be the pivotal motivation behind the second marriage. I think that the mistress relationship may have been going on before he married his second wife, though there is no evidence to prove or disprove this. Now, the question arises, did Constance of Castile marry John of Gaunt, fully aware of his liaison with Katherine Swynford and possibly accepting it as a condition of the marriage? There is some evidence that may indicate this, since the Duke of Lancaster and Constance of Castile named their daughter Katherine. This could be an indication of the acceptance of Katherine Swynford within the intimate household or just plain coincidence. There is no record to prove either theory.

It is certainly rather interesting that there could be a connection between wife and mistress. This would surely indicate an open marriage, but mistresses were not uncommon among the nobility

---

37   Alison Weir, *Mistress of the Monarchy: The Life of Katherine Swynford, Duchess of Lancaster* (New York: Ballantine Books, 2009), pp. 129.

during this era. The works of the Benedictine monk Thomas Walsingham described an illicit and inappropriate relationship between Katherine Swynford and the Duke of Lancaster in 1378. Walsingham seemed to be more interested in attacking John of Gaunt's political and moral character than in any vitriolic description of Katherine Swynford. Perhaps this condemnation was directed at the political ambitions of John of Gaunt since Edward III died in 1377 and this may have been part of an agenda to prevent John of Gaunt seizing the throne for himself. Walsingham wrote about another illicit affair and mentioned the inappropriate behaviour Edward III displayed with Alice Perrers. The description of Edward III's affair is a diatribe against the sins of woman and suggests that the king was powerless and too weak to break her spell on him:

> At that same time there was a woman in England called Alice Perrers. She was a shameless, imprudent harlot, and of low birth, for she was the daughter of the thatcher in the town of Henney, elevated by fortune. She was not attractive or beautiful, but knew how to compensate for these defects by her seductive voice. Blind fortune elevated this woman to such heights and promoted her to a greater intimacy with the king than was proper...[38]

Conversely we see the description of John of Gaunt's affair as highlighting a flaw in his character because not as much condemnation is aimed at Katherine. Perhaps the description of the affair by Walsingham had political motivations and the affair John

---

38 The St Albans Chronicle, p.43, cited from Jeannette Lucraft, *Katherine Swynford: The History of a Medieval Mistress*, (Stroud: The History Press, 2006), p. 76.

of Gaunt had with Katherine Swynford would seem to solidify his argument for the moral unsuitability of John of Gaunt as the royal leader.

> Condemnation then grew for his wicked and disgraceful behaviour, especially because he himself put aside respect for God's dread, deserted his military duties, rode around the country with the abominable temptress, seen as Katherine once called Swynford, holding her bridal in front of his own people, not only in the presence of his wife, but even with all his retainers looking on, in the most honoured town in the kingdom he made himself abominable in the eyes of God...[39]

Overall, the evidence indicates that there was no real opposition from the nobility in general against the Duke of Lancaster for his affair with Katherine Swynford. The main argument against John of Gaunt concerned his political machinations and especially his involvement in the poll tax and the later Peasants' Revolt in 1381.

Katherine Swynford's position as governess in the Duke of Lancaster's household would indicate a convenient arrangement whereby she would be available to John of Gaunt for intimate interludes but also to act as hostess in the absence of the duchess. This was a highly visible position and the 'affair' was probably common knowledge in the household and to the nobility in general after 1372. One can deduce that the relationship may have started earlier with a far more discrete interchanges. I suspect that

---

39 Thomas Walsingham's Chronicon Angliae, ed. Edward Maunde, Thompson (London 1965) 196, cited from Jeannette Lucraft, *Katherine Swynford: The History of a Medieval Mistress* (Stroud: The History Press, 2006), p. 57.

the relationship must have grown over time and that its initiation and evolution cannot be tied only to written records but also to an understanding of human nature and interpersonal interaction in the emotional landscape of sex and love.

The Peasants' Revolt over the summer of 1381 frightened Katherine Swynford into hiding. She took her children and withdrew from public life, probably in a convent. Katherine would've been a target of the peasant mob, a fact of which she was well aware of. Katherine was surely not loved by the typical residents of Kettlethorpe or Lincoln. This was a prudent and smart move by Katherine, indicating her political acumen and understanding of the realm in such a tumultuous period. John of Gaunt went north to Berwick to stay safe, since he would surely have been a target of reprisals by the peasant mob. Luck played a part since his young teenage son, Henry Bolingbroke, was smuggled out during the revolt.

King Richard II was able to quell the revolt with prudent use of rhetoric and the fast action of the nobility when Wat Tyler, the leader of the revolt, was killed during the second day of the negotiations. Richard II declared, 'I will be your leader, you shall have no captain but me,' which produced much confidence in the peasant mob. The rallying of the nobility, and quick and brutal reprisals, led to 200 executions. Order in the realm was restored. This saved the Duke of Lancaster, but he did suffer much loss and destruction to his estates. The Duke of Lancaster repented for his sins and it seemed clear he regretted his actions, but this may have been a good use of political drama. The events of the revolt had impacted all of John of Gaunt's family including his wife, Constance of Castile. The Duke of Lancaster at this juncture put his relationship with Katherine on a temporary hold. This was a prudent move to protect his reputation in public, and a smart political move to protect his estates and reputation among the nobility.

However, John of Gaunt and Katherine maintained a cordial, supportive relationship with one another. The fact that the Duke of Lancaster maintained a platonic friendship with Katherine was to benefit their Beaufort children. John of Gaunt did provide generously for her and she and as a result she and her children enjoyed a comfortable existence at Kettlethorpe. Katherine was a woman of substance and was seen as a capable estate manager. She retained a good reputation with many of her peers, especially with the perceived end of the great love affair. Katherine was well placed in the household of John of Gaunt's son's Henry Bolingbroke. This was a move that may have allowed John of Gaunt to still see Katherine and she also maintained a presence at court. This cooling-off period might have been short-lived, though, and by 1385 the couple may have resumed intimate relations. John of Gaunt tried to press his claim to the Castilian throne during the interim but ultimately he failed. Katherine Swynford must have endeared herself to all in court since she received favour from the king and the Duke of Lancaster and maintained a decent reputation among the nobility.

The Duke of Lancaster threw himself back into the centre of politics and was a key advisor to the young King Richard II. John of Gaunt was instrumental in introducing the new queen to Richard II. He escorted Anne of Bohemia through the streets of London and maintained the dignity of the elder statesman, perhaps even acting as a father figure to the new groom. John of Gaunt was one of the closest living male relatives to the king and may well have been looked upon as a surrogate father figure to Richard II, since the king's father died a year before his grandfather. The Duke of Lancaster invested his efforts into Kenilworth estate as his new Lancaster headquarters and settled into a strong political and diplomatic period of activity. A point of interest outlined in Alison Weir's biography is the suggestion that John of Gaunt issued a quitclaim to Katherine Swynford in 1382. This was a strong move that protected Katherine and the Beaufort children they had together, giving them a sense of financial security and upward social mobility that would ensure an independent wealth base in the future for his bastard children. Weir also points out that St Valentine's Day was chosen by Gaunt to emphasise his deep feelings for them. I may speculate further that this could be a gift for his lady love, with an eye to continue intimate relations in the future. It certainly would inculcate Katherine with hope for her love for John of Gaunt.

Throughout this period the Duke of Lancaster bestowed gifts upon Katherine Swynford that made her life easier and could be perceived as gifts to a friend or something more intimate. Furthermore, Katherine was involved in John of Gaunt's son's household and became close to Mary de Bohun, Henry Bolingbroke's new wife. This would last throughout Mary's life and emphasised a close relationship between Katherine Swynford and the Lancastrian household. She also garnered a close relationship with the Duke of Lancaster's son and this would endure through the upcoming tumultuous period of Richard II's reign.

Katherine's life was closely intertwined with John of Gaunt in many ways and it is hard to ascertain the very nature of their relationship during this period, but intimate contacts cannot be ruled out completely, even if they were somewhat discrete and restrained in nature. Hindsight gives us a unique perspective on these actions and we can engage in some informed speculation of the direction the relationship took due to what happened in the next decade. As we will see there are many distractions and political events that will consume John of Gaunt's attention, so perhaps Katherine was sensitive to this and provided comfort where she could in and out of the bedroom.

The major event of 1387 was the Lords Appellant crisis, which impacted the realm deeply. John of Gaunt was away on campaign in Castile to claim his right to that throne through his wife. The expedition was finally funded by Parliament and the king. There was a juncture between the king and the Duke of Lancaster where the king wanted John of Gaunt out of the kingdom to extend his rule. The king was surrounding himself with favourites that enraged the established nobility. In particular, Robert de Vere supplanted many nobles and created much animosity in the royal court. The machinations of de Vere and the king led to a policy to get the Duke of Lancaster out of the way. There may even have been an attempt to kill John of Gaunt by Robert de Vere at a tournament. The plot, of course, failed, and the Duke of Lancaster did accompany the king into a fruitless invasion of Scotland. The relationship between uncle and nephew did become difficult and this was the trigger for funding for the Duke of Lancaster's venture into Castile.

John of Gaunt's expedition to Castile was fruitless and left his army prostrate. Disease and heat took its toll on his army and it even incapacitated his own person during the campaign. The campaign came to a conclusion in 1387. He was not to become the monarch of the kingdom of Castile and signed a treaty that married his and Constance's daughter to the future monarch of Castile, an unsatisfactory outcome for John of Gaunt. Katherine felt the loss of this venture in a different way, since evidence showed that she lost her sister Philippa during this period.

It is not clear where Philippa died, but she did during this campaign, which would have impacted Katherine greatly. This tragic event may have been the impetus for the reunion with John of Gaunt. Furthermore, John of Gaunt's marriage to Constance had no further political value and John of Gaunt deemed it invalid. The record showed that there was a fissure between John of Gaunt and Constance and they maintained separate households when they returned to England. This fact could have led to a closer relationship with Katherine Swynford. The combination of the empathy John felt for Katherine over the loss of her sister and the dissolving of his marriage probably led to a renewed relationship with Katherine. The question to be asked is, was this a planned trajectory or did the events and circumstances lead to the reunion? The torch for their affair was probably never really extinguished, so we can deduce that any opportunity they had would bring them together.

The Lords Appellant crisis came to a head in late 1387 when the nobles and Parliament forced Robert de Vere out of power. The Lords Appellant confronted de Vere at Radcot Bridge, where he was defeated and banished from the kingdom. The impact on Katherine can be seen in overtures by the king to endear himself to his uncle through her. The political isolation Richard II had found himself in was due to his corrosive rule and resulted in a virtual deposition of his royal authority. Richard II was adroit in the use of his political authority to gain favour with John of Gaunt through Katherine Swynford. The king made her a Lady of the Garter, a position that bestowed great honour on Katherine.

This was to please John of Gaunt and to bring him closer to Richard.

Both the king and Henry, Earl of Derby, the Duke of Lancaster's son, held sentimental appreciation and genuine affection for Katherine Swynford. This can be attributed to her personality, but also to her relationship and influence upon John of Gaunt. Henry, Earl of Derby, did seem to hold true affection for Katherine and confidence in her long relationship with the house of Lancaster. He grew up close to Katherine, and upon the death of his mother Blanche he may have formed a maternal bond of trust and confidence with her. Katherine had been ever present in Henry's life, from his younger formative years and now as an adult, which would have helped foster a true connection with her.

When John of Gaunt returned to England in 1389 he was welcomed by the king with open arms. This was no doubt a politically astute move by Richard II to garner support for his kingship and to regain his power. John of Gaunt was now the richest and most influential member of the nobility in his realm and Richard needed his support to regain royal authority over Parliament. The king's new policy worked well, and John of Gaunt served as an advisor and elder statesman to the young monarch. The old rift had been long forgotten and this would usher in a period of stability for the kingdom. John of Gaunt served as the connecting membrane for a stable regime. The Duke of Lancaster used the new-found royal favour to strengthen the house of Lancaster and his Beaufort offspring with Katherine.

However, the Duke of Lancaster was careful to evenly distribute his largesse between his legitimate heirs of Lancaster and his Beaufort brood. He was prudent in keeping both inheritances mutually separate from one another, a very astute use of resources to avoid future conflicts in inheritance and wealth among his two family lines. However, both lines would inherit the crown in due time, something he would not live to see.

Henry Bolingbroke's wife, Mary de Bohun, delivered their first child, Henry, in 1387. Katherine Swynford was present to help with the child and again made an impact on the future of the Lancastrian line. John of Gaunt now had his past mistress entwined in his family. With John of Gaunt in a secure position, he could now resume his romantic relationship with Katherine in 1391. The evidence suggests that she may have shared residence with John of Gaunt during the early 1390s, which would indicate a level of confidence in the couple's relationship and perhaps a perceived acceptance of their affair. Since the Duke of Lancaster and Constance were not cohabiting, it seemed a safe environment for the couple.

Further evidence of the couple's relationship was displayed in a family reunion during Christmas, for which Katherine was present in the Lancaster household. There was some unrest among the nobility against John of Gaunt but this was due to the shift of power to the house of Lancaster rather than a character flaw of or political mistakes from the Duke of Lancaster. In 1394 John of Gaunt found himself a widow once again and was now free to pursue Katherine Swynford with relative impunity. Richard II lost his wife to the plague during that year, and this seemed to have a profound impact on the king. The queen appears to have stymied the temperamental elements of Richard and his sometimes oppressive behaviour towards his nobles. Historians have surmised that the tragic death of the king's wife probably propelled the shift towards royal absolutism and an oppressive style of kingship that would ultimately violate the bounds of royal authority and

Parliamentary consent. John of Gaunt's son Henry Bolingbroke also lost his wife, Mary de Bohun, in 1394, the last of a trio of important deaths in that year, leaving Henry Bolingbroke as an eligible bachelor and one of the richest heirs (the Lancastrian estate) in England.

John of Gaunt married Katherine Swynford in 1396, although prior to this they had to wait the allotted time to applying for a papal dispensation due to the fact of compaternity – he was the godfather to Katherine's daughter, whom she had with her previous husband, Hugh Swynford, over two decades earlier. It was unprecedented for John of Gaunt to marry his long-term mistress, instead of a politically advantageous marriage. The Duke of Lancaster, even in his later years, was a desirable marriage prospect. The decision to marry for love was uncommon among the nobility. Another point to consider is that John of Gaunt's two previous marriages were based on economic and political gain. The marriage choice of Katherine Swynford can be considered a purely emotional decision; the couple were married in Lincoln Cathedral on 14 January 1396. Katherine Swynford was now officially the Duchess of Lancaster. Another powerful motivation for John of Gaunt to marry his mistress was to legitimise his Beaufort descendants. He also wanted to secure the future of the Beauforts, and the Duke of Lancaster consolidated ties between both families that would endure throughout the fifteenth century and ultimately creates the Tudor dynasty.

The king supported this union and he readily gave his blessing to John of Gaunt to marry Katherine Swynford. Richard II wanted John of Gaunt's support in political matters but not want the Duke of Lancaster to monopolise Parliament. There was a steady decline in John of Gaunt's power in Parliament from 1396 until his death three years later. There was a combination of events that leads to this decline. John of Gaunt's health was declining during this period and no doubt the king took advantage of this to extend his own authority. Furthermore, Richard II never forgot the humiliation of the Lords Appellant crisis (1387) and Henry Bolingbroke's defeat of his royal favourite Robert de Vere at Radcot Bridge. There were rumours also that Richard II had a homosexual relationship with Robert de Vere, although Walsingham was the source of this rumour and so it cannot be taken as historical fact, due to Walsingham's political inclinations and his tendency to be extremely subjective. However, a mutual affectation does seem to have existed between Robert de Vere and Richard II and his defeat and forced banishment served as an impetus for the absolutist policies of 1399.

There was some resentment harboured towards Katherine Swynford by the nobility about her new-found title as Duchess of Lancaster. This sudden elevation of Katherine's status amongst the peerage would engender jealousy and some vitriolic language. Her financial status was elevated to a point where she would never have to worry about estates or manorial security in her lifetime. The nobility must have felt a sense of displacement, since Katherine, a relative commoner, was now married to the most powerful noble in England, and was perhaps the most powerful lady in the realm. This status would be temporary until the king remarried and supplanted her exalted status with a queen. Many thought that John of Gaunt had married below his station and upset the balance of noble families in England. Many of the nobles and their wives snubbed Katherine at first, and wanted nothing to do with her at court. This disapproval and the absence of an official written dispensation from the pope created some insecurity for the couple. However, the king welcomed Katherine and her Beaufort children into the court, which went a long way towards smoothing over discontentment among the peerage in the social and political spheres. Katherine's personality and affinity in dealing with the nobility, using her amicable nature, helped the couple gain acceptance of her new position. Finally, Pope Boniface IX declared their marriage valid in the eyes of God and this, coupled with the king's acceptance, cleared the path for a better relationship with the English nobility, which would have been a great relief for John of Gaunt and Katherine Swynford.

Another event in 1397 that helped pave the way for acceptance was Katherine Swynford's prominent role in the marriage of Richard II to the young Isabella, daughter of the king of France. She had a lot of experience with the Plantagenet royal family and this was useful in welcoming the young queen. Katherine's affinity with children was very advantageous and made the transition for the queen much easier. This obvious advantage to the royal family went a long way towards ingratiating herself with the leading dukes and duchesses of England. The official acceptance of the Beaufort children was a clear indication of the official sanction of the union between Katherine Swynford and John of Gaunt. This also formally and legally declared the Beaufort children legitimate and granted full access to all privileges within the nobility, which included acceptance into the peerage (both secular and within the church), although a later proviso specifically barred them from inheriting the throne.

In the *Excerpta Historica*, Richard is quoted to have proclaimed,

> raised, promoted, elected, assume, and be admitted to all honours, dignities, pre-eminencies, estates, degrees and offices public and

private whatsoever, as well perpetual as temporal, and feudal and noble, by whatsoever names that they may be designated, whether they be duchies, principalities, Earl Jones, baronies or other fees, and whether they depend or are Holden of us, and to receive, retain, bear, mediately or immediately, and exercise the same as freely and lawfully as if ye were born in lawful matrimony...[40]

The Beaufort offspring of John of Gaunt and Katherine Swynford also now had the opportunity to further their status. In 1397 Thomas Beaufort married the daughter of Sir Thomas Neville, one of the richest and influential families from the north. Thomas and Margaret Beaufort would be in-laws as Joan Beaufort married Ralph Neville. This was a strong link with the Nevilles and the Beaufort families, which would have royal implications in the future. The political landscape was about to shift dramatically over the following few years, which would impact the very throne of England.

John of Gaunt was on cordial relations with the king, but Richard II was determined to exact revenge upon the Appellants of 1387. Richard was gunning for Gloucester, Arundel and Warwick and acting with impunity. Richard was ruling with absolutist authority and John of Gaunt was too old and weak to effectively serve as a counter fulcrum to the king's wrath. The Duke of Lancaster's primary concern was to protect the house of Lancaster and especially his son Henry Bolingbroke, who had sided with the Appellants originally. John of Gaunt retreated and

---

40 Excerpta Historica, 154, from cited from Jeannette Lucraft, *Katherine Swynford: The History of a Medieval Mistress* (Stroud: The History Press, 2006), p. 36.

observed a protective stance and also pulled Katherine Swynford from her close association with the royal couple.

It was too late before John of Gaunt realised that the king was pursuing a violent agenda, which resulted in the murder of his brother Gloucester and the beheading of Arundel for treason. This left a bleak landscape in parliament. John of Gaunt was no longer a power player on the political scene. This ultimately led to a despotic and tyrannical rule by Richard II. It seemed that there may have been a plot to kill John of Gaunt and absorb the Lancastrian estate into the crown. Sir Thomas Mowbray revealed to Henry Bolingbroke a potential plot by the king to kill Henry and his father, and then subsequently the king would abscond the Lancastrian estates. Henry immediately told this alarming news to his father and John of Gaunt told this to the king, who rejected the allegations against him. This prompted both Bolingbroke and Mowbray to publicly turn on each other.

All this palace intrigue impacted the Duke of Lancaster's health and he and Katherine Swynford retreated to the one of his estates to reinvigorate his failing health. The king reassured John of Gaunt that he did not have designs on the Lancastrian estates, which we now know was an elaborate ruse to maintain Gaunt's loyalty. The Duke of Lancaster's health continued to deteriorate throughout the summer of 1398, and he would not be effectively involved in politics from this point on until his death. The fissure between Henry Bolingbroke and Sir Thomas Mowbray came to a head, and the king adjudicated over the proceedings and decided on a dual or 'trial by battle'.

The Duke of Lancaster was very distraught over this decision, even though his son was most competent in martial skills. The king was placating John of Gaunt with further granting of offices. On the day of the trial by battle, the chain interceded and declared sentences upon the two combatants. He banished Sir Thomas Mowbray from the kingdom for life and banished Henry Bolingbroke for ten years. This was Richard's plan to eliminate the last two remaining Appellants from 1387, and possibly cleared the path for him to take the Lancastrian estates. John of Gaunt pleaded to the king on behalf of his son, who reduced the sentence to six years from ten. Both John of Gaunt and Katherine went to see off his son to banishment in France. This was a disheartening moment for John of Gaunt and surely contributed to a steady decline in health. This would be the last time John of Gaunt and Henry Bolingbroke, father and son, would see each other. John of Gaunt died on 3 February 1399 at Leicester Castle with Katherine present to mourn him. He was buried forty days later on 13 March and it was a sombre affair, Katherine in full mourning for her husband and lifelong partner of over thirty years.

After John of Gaunt's passing Katherine led a quiet life throughout the tumultuous events of 1399–1400. She was to look for peace while she resided at the Lincoln Cathedral. The king immediately added the Lancastrian estates to the crown and effectively banished Henry Bolingbroke for life. These events would have a profound impact on the English nobility and Parliament. This series of events displayed the king's avarice and willingness to circumvent the law of the land and rule by decree. This was something no monarch of England had done since William the Conqueror, and effectively united many of the nobles under Henry Bolingbroke's banner.

Henry left his banishment in France to reclaim his Lancastrian inheritance. He arrived in England with a small retinue of retainers.

Katherine's Beaufort sons were rather active in the political scene: John Beaufort raised a force that would aid Henry's claim; Joan Beaufort's husband Ralph Neville also rallied forces for Henry Bolingbroke; and while John Beaufort did declare for Richard II, he wrote a private letter to Henry Bolingbroke to declare his support for him – he was obviously playing both sides, but seemed at heart to support Henry Bolingbroke. The balance of forces were in Henry Bolingbroke's favour. He easily swept aside all resistance and forced the surrender of Richard's forces. When Richard returned from Ireland he was subsequently imprisoned in the Tower.

At this juncture, Henry and Thomas Beaufort, and Ralph Neville all publicly declared allegiance to Henry Bolingbroke, who was effectively given the executive authority in England. Parliament and Henry forced Richard II to abdicate his throne on 29 September 1399. Parliament then declared Henry Bolingbroke king. This was unprecedented since the king was effectively created by the consent of Parliament. One could say that he was a usurper, since the great-grandson of Lionel of Antwerp (elder brother to John of Gaunt) would have been closer in line for the throne, but Henry was the blood relative through the male Plantagenet line and had the support of the nobility.

Henry Bolingbroke became King Henry IV on 13 October 1399 and vested the Duchy of Lancaster into the crown. He did, however, honour all of Katherine's inheritance granted by his father. Henry IV also maintained a close relationship with Katherine Swynford throughout the rest of her life. Richard II was sentenced to perpetual imprisonment in Pontefract Castle and he died there. The circumstances of King Richard's death were clouded, but it seemed he was starved to death. This was probably a shrewd decision by Henry IV to quell rebellions to restore Richard as king. An interesting note is that it seemed Katherine's son Thomas Swynford may have been one of the vindictive tormentors of Richard during his captivity. Thomas Swynford was very loyal to his stepbrother Henry and was exacting revenge upon the former king. Fortunately, it seemed Katherine was not aware of her son's rather unchristian and rapacious behaviour. The Lancastrian dynasty was borne of these auspicious events, which would yield further turmoil half a century later.

Katherine Swynford retreated from public life and lived the life of a 'vowess', having taken a vow of chastity. This showed her piety and deep mourning for John of Gaunt. It seemed she would lead a simple, quiet life until her death, and she did not take comfort in the material wealth and possessions that she inherited. Henry IV remarried in 1403 to Joan of Navarre to secure his dynasty with a queen and a substantial dowry. The Beauforts would have a meteoric rise under Henry IV, another legacy of John of Gaunt and Katherine Swynford. A

n interesting note was that Katherine, the dowager Duchess of Lancaster, was not present at Henry IV's marriage ceremony, which was probably due to her declining health. Surely she would have been welcomed with honour among the nobility of England at this royal occasion. Katherine declined rapidly and died on 10 May 1403. She was no doubt overwrought with grief and the subsequent events after her husband's death would have contributed to a state of ill health that would lead to her death. There is no surviving will of Katherine Swynford, but she was buried at Lincoln Cathedral where she spent her last years. Katherine's daughter, Joan Beaufort, sheds some light on Katherine's legacy since she bequeathed in her will a psalter for her older son. This was no doubt a family heirloom that would finds its way into the Neville family. Katherine's legacy was extended by her daughter, which has been outlined by Anthony Goodman:

> The most intriguing provisions in Joan's will is that she was to be buried where her mother was, and that that space was to be enlarged and enclosed, if the assent of the Dean and Chapter of Lincoln could be obtained.
>
> In 1437 she [Joan Beaufort] received a royal license to found a perpetual chantry of two chaplains to celebrate daily at the altar before which Katherine was buried.[41]

The Beaufort Legacy

The affair between Katherine Swynford and John of Gaunt was to last for at least thirty years, and culminated in the bold move of the Duke of Lancaster marrying Katherine in 1396. The marriage yielded four children for John of Gaunt and Katherine and they were subsequently legitimised by the Pope and his nephew the king – Richard II. The importance of these children increased even further when their step-brother Henry Bolingbroke (son of Gaunt and Blanche) ascended to the throne in 1399 by deposing Richard II through the use of force and the consent of the nobility. Katherine Swynford and the Duke of Lancaster had four children: John, Henry, Thomas and Joan. Henry became the powerful Cardinal Beaufort and their daughter, Joan Beaufort, married into the Neville family and became grandmother to Yorkist kings, Edward IV and Richard III. The eldest son, John

---

41 Anthony Goodman, *My Most Illustrious Mother, the Lady Katherine: Katherine Swynford and Her Daughter Joan* (Lincoln: Lincoln Cathedral Publications, 2008), pp. 15–16.

Beaufort, was grandfather to Margaret Beaufort, who was the mother of the then future Tudor king Henry VII. This lineage alone constitutes a significant social mobility in Katherine Swynford's influence upon the royal family of England. In the shadow of Eleanor of Aquitaine we can see the effective ambition and determination that Katherine Swynford displayed and her influence upon the English monarchy in the fifteenth century. The War of the Roses changed the fate of the Beauforts dramatically and it would lead to an eventual Tudor succession. The precedent had been set in 1399 for a cadet line of the Plantagenets to assume the throne.

The Yorks took the throne from Henry VI by force, which displayed an avarice that could be repeated if circumstances would allow such an occasion. Both the York and Tudor lines were direct descendants of Katherine Swynford's blood, and ultimately her offspring would set the stage for the monarchy in the fifteenth and sixteenth centuries. When weakness or conflict reared its head during a reign in the fifteenth century, turmoil followed. Henry VI's weak reign yielded to the violent overthrow of the monarch during the War of the Roses by the Yorks, and subsequently when the York line imploded upon itself in 1483, when Richard III usurped the throne from his nephews, the Tudor dynasty seized the throne through the same violent means that the Yorks employed. The succession was determined by violent means during this era due to the instability of the realm and the many figures that had royal claims to the throne. This was due to a combination of factors, including Edward III's many male descendants, the legitimisation of the Beauforts, the quasi-legal seizure of the throne from Richard II in 1399, which created an inherent instability in the succession, and finally the slow decay of the feudal system. What is rather apparent is that the prodigious offspring of Katherine Swynford and John of Gaunt would eventually see them claim the throne. These were not ideal circumstances, but eventually a successful and stable Tudor dynasty emerged, one that yielded three kings of England, the first regnant Queen of England, Mary Tudor, and then one of the longest-reigning monarchs in English history – Elizabeth I.

6

JOANNA OF NAVARRE

Joanna of Navarre has the distinction of being the only queen of England to be imprisoned for witchcraft, which she suffered during Henry V's reign. Her trial seems to have been a product of the hysteria of the era and the fact that she was a very rich widow. Joan of Navarre was an attractive bride for her wealth and widow status, and Henry IV was in need of cash flow after his usurpation in 1399. She was also of impeccable bloodlines for a royal union, and the combination of these two elements made her an attractive prospect as a queen. If we look back at Joanna of Navarre with twenty-first century eyes we may assume that she was an insignificant figure with little importance to this study, but this would be a hasty judgement. Joanna of Navarre, like Eleanor of Aquitaine, held an attraction to the king because of her rich dowry and what she would bring to the realm. Both queens were independent rulers of royal principalities. They had considerable offspring and experience managing their respective estates. The notoriety surrounding her trial for witchcraft provides a unique perspective on her role as a queen and the environment in which medieval queens operated and survived. As one author succinctly states,

In the long line of the Queens of England, Joan of Navarre, the Queen of Henry IV, is, in most respects, not of outstanding note. In one way, however, she is unique; she is the only Queen of England to be imprisoned for treason by means of witchcraft, yet few queens have had less reason to be discontented with their lot, and fewer have been less malevolent than she.[42]

Henry IV, in the opening years of his reign, was confident of his royal succession. However, the realm that he inherited was financially weak. The new king's primary concern was to secure his position by finding a new queen. He had lost his first wife, Mary de Bohun, in 1397, before he ascended the throne. The king required his bride to have an impeccable royal pedigree, which would augment his newly acquired crown and, of course, come with a considerable dowry to enrich his flagging treasury. In 1402, Henry IV decided upon Joanna of Navarre. She was the daughter of Jean II of France and Charles 'the Bad' of Navarre. Joanna's mother, Jean II, traced her ancestry from the Navarre line which went back to Isabella of France, Edward II's wife. This background had royal lines tied to France and other royal houses on the continent. This pedigree was exactly what Henry IV was looking for and, furthermore, she was a recent widow with a large dowry. As a widow, Joanna of Navarre governed Brittany as regent for her son and exercised a good degree of independence for this era. A result of her first marriage was an exceptionally large dowry which had been shrewdly negotiated by her father. This made her a very wealthy heiress and widow. In addition,

---

42   A.R. Myers, *The Captivity of a Royal Witch: The Household Accounts of Queen Joan of Navarre, 1419-21*, 'Bulletin of the John Rylands Library', vol.24, no.2, October 1940. 263.

Joanna had borne her first husband, Duke Jean, seven children and the eldest son was to inherent the dukedom of Brittany. So Henry IV had decided that Joanna was a perfect candidate to be his future queen. However, there were some obstacles that had to be overcome before he could proceed. Joanna was not permitted to take her sons with her if she was to accept the marriage proposal from the English king. This was determined by the magnates of Britanny and she reluctantly agreed to leave her sons under the care and regency of the Duke of Burgundy. This was, of course, part and parcel of French continental politics. It was important to France to maintain the integrity and independence of its Duchies and its royal authority. This was a protective stance taken by France in general in the wake of recent wars during the reign of Edward III and the constant state of conflict between England and France in general. The biographer of Henry IV, Chris Given-Wilson, outlines the background for the marriage very well:

Anglo-French relations had not been improved by Henry's decision during the winter of 1401-2 to open negotiations for the hand of Joan, Duchess of Brittany, the widow of Duke John IV (d.1399). There were obvious strategic reasons to recommend an Anglo-Breton alliance, and equally obvious reasons for the French government to oppose it. Civil War in Brittany had crucially undermined the French crown between the 1340s and the 1370s, and the prospect of reviving the influence which Edward III had put to such good effect there was tempting. Moreover, Henry and Joan had met on several occasions and seem to have got on well. Joan certainly wrote warmly to Henry in February 1400, and she did not hesitate before accepting his proposal, despite knowing that the French royal family and a fair proportion of the Breton nobility would oppose it. Thus on 2 April 1402, after hasty and secretive negotiations, she and Henry were married by proxy. When news of the match reached Paris the reaction was swift, and by October Duke Philip of Burgundy was in Nantes, where he imposed a settlement on Joan: she was allowed to take her two daughters to England with her, but her sons, including her 13-year-old heir, were removed to Paris, and Philip himself assumed the Regency of the Duchy until the boy came of age. The episode is instructive: Burgundy remained opposed until his death to Orleans's undermining of the Anglo-French truce, but he would not tolerate any attempt by Henry to weaken French authority in what the Valois regarded as their sphere of influence.[43]

This clearly outlines the political position of France and the environment in which this marriage was to take place. Another obstacle was that a papal dispensation was needed, since there was a state of consanguinity between Joan of Navarre and Henry IV. Since this marriage occurred during the Great Schism, there were two popes, one in Rome who supported England and one in Avignon who supported France. This further complicated the situation since Joanna was technically under the Avignon papal authority and had to seek another dispensation to live amongst the 'schismatics' of the Roman pope who supported England. This tangled web was sorted out by Henry IV to expedite his marriage. The motives for Henry IV were readily apparent: besides her pedigree and dowry, Henry was also impressed by her beauty and

---

43   Chris Given-Wilson, *Henry IV*, London: Yale University Press, 2016. 234-235.

the political advantages of a wife with connections and possible influence upon the Bretons. There was also a commercial reason, since this marriage would open up possible trade for English merchants. However, Joanna's motives were a little different. At this juncture I would propose another parallel with Eleanor of Aquitaine, as these two queens shared a distinct vulnerability as rich endowed widows, and they sought a partner who could protect their respective interests. In Eleanor of Aquitaine's case, it was Henry Plantagenet, later Henry II, and in Joanna's case it was to be Henry IV. Being the Queen of England of course brought its own distinct privileges but it also served as a counter-weight to French authority and possible oppression. So Joanna displayed some of the same shrewd characteristics as Eleanor of Aquitaine, and this was a queenly attribute we see throughout her life. As we will see, in the fifteenth century the actual power of the English queen would expand and the Queen's influence upon the realm shifts attitudes towards ultimately accepting the monarchical authority of a woman.

It was to be a winter wedding for Henry IV and Joanna of Navarre. Joanna arrived in England at the end of December, during the Christmas festivities. This was no doubt a joyous time to meet her new husband. The wedding took place on 3 February 1403 at Winchester and she was later crowned queen on the 26th of the same month at Westminster. The coronation ceremony for Joanna of Navarre was resplendent and imbued with political drama. She was seated alone on the throne by the Archbishop of Canterbury and the Abbot of Westminster. She is not depicted in the subservient position below the King, which was typical of this era. This may be due to her independent status and a recognition of her royal pedigree. This deliberate display of Henry's new queen was probably intended to lend a sense of legitimacy to the new Lancastrian dynasty. Joanna was to be a symbol of this idea of legitimacy, one to displace the former Ricardian presence from the English people both in mind and body. It was to usher in the Lancastrian reign with a strong tie to the ideals of the English realm and create a parting from the past, washing away the indiscretions of the monarchy towards Parliament, and re-establishing the very nature of the compact between King and country. Joanna of Navarre was to settle in and balance the monarchy with her heritage, independence and, of course, wealth. Henry displayed a unique understanding of Joanna of Navarre's background and, with wealth to match her status, she gave the monarchy enhanced respect. Asserting the legitimacy of the monarchy was a constant struggle during Henry IV's reign, but the groundwork he carefully laid during his reign paid dividends for his son's reign, which was by far the most successful and celebrated of the Lancastrian dynasty, albeit one of the shortest. As they say, the star that 'burns the brightest, may also burn for the shortest time', and this was true for Henry V.

The dower Henry IV provided for Joanna of Navarre was more than the treasury could realistically afford, but conversely Henry was able to secure a unique source of funds for the Queen and her council. He used the recently absorbed Lancastrian estate to serve as the Queen's source of income, in the form of her dower. This was a new direction that included some semblance of independence for the Queen, who would not have to extract funds from Parliament. This would shield the Queen from economic resentment from both houses in Parliament. It would also serve to give the Queen actual administrative and economic powers over her own estate, and this would contribute to an evolution of queenly authority and power throughout the fifteenth century. A unique precedent was set under Queen Joanna of Navarre that would set in motion an independent queen's council with an independent source of wealth for the queens of England until the Tudor period.

> A major advance in the organization of the queen's council came with the accession of Henry IV. Henry dowered his Queen, Joanna Navarre, with lands from his own inheritance, the Duchy of Lancaster. Hitherto, the administrative framework for the functioning of the queen's household and council had been created anew for each queen, sometimes because there was a queen dowager, sometimes because there had been a period without a queen.[44]

Joanna's independent source of wealth made her a more independent queen, and she shared her wealth with her new husband. This created some resentment from the English Parliament and people. The hoped-for Anglo-Breton alliance never came to fruition and subsequently England and Brittany were in a state of war. Joanna maintained her support for her sons and this of course sparked great resentment amongst the English. In 1404 there was an anti-French petition by Parliament to remove the French influence from the royal court. Joanna was able to keep her daughters and a few close servants, but it was clear they baulked at a queen whose heart was not in England. She also used her influence over Henry IV to negotiate favourable terms in an Anglo-Breton truce, however this would raise suspicion as to her loyalties later in 1417.

---

44   Anne Crawford, 'The Queen's Council in the Middle Ages' in *The English Historical Review*, vol. 116, no. 469, Nov. 2001. 1204.

Henry IV tried to moderate the vitriol heaped upon his queen, with careful use of patronage and influence upon Parliament, however this would change after his death in 1413. Another point of contention, previously mentioned, was the over-abundant dower provided to Queen Joanna by Henry. This was to be the main issue during Henry IV's lifetime and it was further exacerbated after his death.

The Royal union seems to have been a joyous marriage, marked with a closeness akin to a strong friendship. Henry and Joanna shared much time together and she nurtured a friendly atmosphere amongst her stepsons. This was especially true of Henry IV's son John, Duke of Bedford and the Prince of Wales, Henry – the heir apparent. The future King Henry was regent during 1410, when his father was rather sick, and the young Prince worked with Joanna to handle turmoil in France. The internecine warfare between Burgundy and Armagnac flared up during the King of France's mental breakdowns. This mental instability seemed to be hereditary, since it would follow the family line through his daughter and grandson in the next decades, and have dire consequences for the stability of the Lancastrian dynasty in the 1450s. During Henry IV's illness Prince Henry supported the Duke of Burgundy, but when his father recovered he supported Armagnac. Queen Joanna wisely advised a neutral policy to temper any further anti-French feeling among the English. This was a display of obvious political acumen on Joanna's part, since she was inclined to support Armagnac due to her familial ties to Brittany. She saw it prudent to remain neutral in order to instil some loyalty amongst her English peers. However, later toward the end of Henry IV's reign, Joanna supported Prince Henry in his policy of supporting Armagnac, since she would have to establish a working relationship with her stepson when he became king.

The queen's husband died in March 1413 and this made her a widow for the second time. Their union had not been conceived in passion, but was a mutually respectful and loyal marriage. Both Henry IV and Joanna of Navarre were buried at Canterbury and this displayed in death the value that Henry IV put on his marriage to Joanna.

Once Henry V ascended the throne the atmosphere in the court changed. The conciliatory policy towards France became more bellicose. Henry V's wilder days, as evidenced by the historical record and dramatically portrayed in Shakespeare's plays, was a thing of the past. Henry V decided on a course of action that would reawaken the Plantagenet claims from the previous century, which had been initiated by his great-grandfather Edward III. Henry V was aware of the steady erosion of territory in France by alliances, truces and marriages since the death of Edward III. Henry V rallied support through the systematic use of political speeches in Parliament that reinforced his claim to the lost French territories. The French had attacked English control of Aquitaine, which was a treaty violation, and now Henry used this to press his claims. The events that followed in 1415 have become the stuff of legend, with Henry V's invasion of France. The rain of Welsh arrows and the mud at Agincourt have been immortalized in English culture, in both literature and film, bringing this battle to life and elevating it to a legendary status. The victory at Agincourt was a valued conquest for the English court: Henry V was now able to press his claim not only to Aquitaine but to the French throne itself.

Queen Joanna showed support, possibly reluctant, during the elation and celebrations that swept the kingdom when Henry V made his triumphant return to England. Some of Joanna's family members perished during the battle, but it seemed that her son had survived and was a prisoner. There was some suspicion and criticism levelled at Joanna during and after the campaign, since she was close to the rival royal circle. This was the same flavour of discontent that Queen Joanna had felt during Henry IV's lifetime. It would have dire circumstances for the Queen dowager later on in 1419.

The background to the events of 1419 is summed up by A. R. Myers:

The story of Queen Joanna's reputed sorcery has often been told before; but it may be well to recall the main facts. Joan, or Joanna, of Navarre, Duchess of Brittany from 1386 to 1399, became in 1403 the second wife, and the Queen, of Henry IV, King of England. The new Queen was received with great pomp, and the dowry of 10,000 marks (L6,666 13s 4d) per annum was bestowed on her. The Royal favour thus shown to her continued throughout the reign of Henry IV; and not only was she on good terms with the King, but her relations with all her step-sons and step-daughters appear to have been friendly throughout her husband's lifetime. After his death she seems to have continued for several years on very amicable terms with King Henry V; but in 1419 there came a sudden change. On the 27th of September 1419, the royal council made an order depriving her of her dowry and all of her other revenues and possessions; and four days later she was arrested and taken from her own manor house of Havering-atte-Bower in Essex to the royal manor house of Rotherhithe, in Surrey. The reason, so it was stated in parliament, was that her confessor, John Randolph, a Franciscan friar of Shrewsbury, had accused her 'of compassing the death and destruction of our lord the king in the most treasonable and horrible manner that could be devised'. Contemporary chroniclers said more bluntly that she had tried 'by sorcery and necromancy for to have destroyed the king'.[45]

The two major factors that precipitated the accusations of witchcraft upon Queen Joanna of Navarre were firstly the xenophobic reaction to her perceived influence during Henry IV's and especially Henry V's reign, and her obvious ties to France, which made her vulnerable to suspicion. Many in Parliament thought her loyalty was dubious. Joanna did not do enough to endear herself to the nobles or in general to the populace of England. Second, her over-generous dower created much discord amongst the baronage. Joanna of Navarre's independent wealth was contentious and motivated attempts to direct her wealth into the state's coffers; wartime expenditure served as an expedient reason for appropriating it. The cost of the war had grown to a high level due to the resistance France had mustered after Agincourt. The further financial pressure of dower payments for Henry V's incoming Queen Katherine of Valois put undue pressure on the royal treasury. The exceedingly high dower that was to be awarded to Katherine was due to the negotiations around the Treaty of Troyes. Henry V was bartering the wealth of two crowns, England in France, in the dower he was offering, to shore up financial issues within the French royal family. Some historians have proposed that the large dower awarded

---

45   A. R. Myers, 263-264.

to Katherine of Valois was to offset the disinheritance that the dauphin would suffer in the forthcoming treaty. It undoubtedly affected the queens' popularity.

At the same time, witchcraft hysteria had been rampant throughout the fourteenth century and was a constant concern of the realm. Lisa Hilton's recent work outlines how the witchcraft 'anxiety' descended upon Joanna of Navarre:

> In a deeply religious and superstitious culture, witchcraft seemed very real, but it was also invoked as a political weapon. A person accused of 'necromancy' could be easily deprived of his [or her] rights. The archbishop's letter, designed to create an atmosphere of rumour in which the accusation against Joanna would seem more plausible, was followed up on 27 September by an order from the Royal Council depriving the Queen of her dower and possessions on the basis of evidence from John Randolph, a friar in her household... No one appeared to know precisely what form Joanna's magic had taken, and the 'witnesses', Randolph himself and two other members of Joanna's household, Peronell Brocart and Roger Colles, were swiftly imprisoned, but the end had been achieved. Joanna lost not only her dower, but also her servants and property.[46]

The ambiguity of the charges and the incarceration of the two main witnesses undermined the allegations – even for those who believed absolutely in the power of witchcraft. The political motivation for the charge of witchcraft was apparent to many,

---

46   Lisa Hilton, *Queen's Consort: England Medieval Queens*, London: Phoenix, 2008. 368

but Joanna's political and social isolation after the death of Henry IV made her especially vulnerable. She was viewed as an outsider and the English baronage could easily assuage their consciences by vague reference to the biblical model of Eve, the temptress of man.

This unscrupulous process was founded in the inequality that was ever-present in the monarchy. The queen's authority was derived from the king; in other words the queen derived power only with the consent of the king. The queen did not have any true constitutional roots that gave her executive authority. However, as we have seen, in absence of a strong king, the queen could effectively rule through a regency, especially if she was in possession of the heir presumptive – like Isabella of France. But the events of the fifteenth century would start to transform the authority of the queen. One of the key factors that would bar a queen from ruling in her own right was the inability for a woman to lead men on the battlefield. Martial skills were never instilled or trained in a woman of this era. The delegation of military leadership, with the evolution of 'bastard feudalism'[47] in the fifteenth century,

---

47   Bastard Feudalism can be defined thus: 'In every direction the incidents of service were being commuted for money payments or rents. And by the end of the fifteenth century even servile tenures were rapidly disappearing. Feudalism still existed formally intact, but was becoming for all practical purposes a complex network of marketable privileges and duties attached to the ownership of land, with little or no importance as a social force. It was there, and indeed remained so for centuries to come – all pervasive but inactive – in the background, while the new order of patronage, liveries and affinities occupied the front of the stage, as it was to do in England throughout the fourteenth and fifteenth centuries, with an epilogue which far outran so-called medieval times. It is this new order that we call 'bastard feudalism.' Its quintessence was payment for service. The idea of lordship was retained, but because it was divorced from tenure it was a lordship which had undergone a scarcely visible process of transubstantiation, leaving all but a few of its accidents unchanged.' Cited from [ed. G.L.Harriss] *England in the Fifteenth Century: Collected Essays* K. B. McFarland, London: Hambledon Press, 1981. 24.

Above: Eleanor of Provence (far left) and her husband Henry III (far right) as depicted in Matthew Paris' *Historia Anglorum* (Royal MS 14 C VII). (Courtesy of the British Library)

Below: Beaulieu Abbey in Hampshire, where Eleanor rushed to the sickbed of her beloved eldest son, Edward. (Courtesy of Przemyslaw Jahr under Creative Commons 2.0)

Above: The monument to the Battle of Lewes, where Simon de Montfort defeated Henry III and secured powers from the beaten king. De Montfort would be a thorn in Eleanor's side for a long time. (Courtesy of Mintguy under Creative Commons 2.0)

Left: Detail from St George's Palace at Windsor Castle, where Eleanor established her household after Henry's death. (Author's collection/ Ashley Jensen)

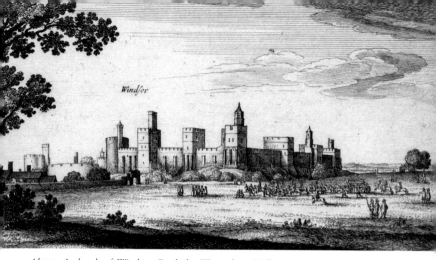

Above: A sketch of Windsor Castle by Wenceslaus Hollar, appearing more as it would have in Eleanor's time. (Courtesy of the Rijksmuseum)

Below: Eleanor died in Amesbury in June 1291 and was buried at the local abbey of St Mary and St Melor. (Courtesy of Matthew Black under Creative Commons 2.0)

The Chateau de Louvre in the fourteenth century. It would have looked similar in the childhood of Isabella of France.

Edward II, Isabella's husband, in British Library manuscript Royal 20 A II. (Courtesy of the British Library)

Above: Pembroke Castle, where Isabella of France had Edward II's alleged lover Piers Gaveston imprisoned. (Courtesy of Reading Tom under Creative Commons 2.0)

Right: The dramatic Tynemouth Priory, where Isabella escaped from the Scots in 1322, having been abandoned by Edward. (Courtesy of Chris McKenna under Creative Commons 2.0)

A manuscript image (Royal MS 14 E IV) of Isabella of France, supposedly with her lover Roger Mortimer. The backdrop purportedly shows the execution of her estranged husband King Edward's new lover, Hugh Despenser. (Courtesy of the British Library)

King Edward's Gate on the way into the grounds of Gloucester Cathedral. Here Edward's body passed after he was alleged to have been murdered on the orders of Isabella's new regime. (Author's collection/Ashley Jensen)

York Minster, where Philippa of Hainault formally married King Edward III in 1328. (Courtesy of Harshil Shah under Creative Commons 2.0)

Two years into his reign, in 1330, Edward III threw off his mother Isabella of France and her lover Roger Mortimer to rule in his own right. Mortimer was summarily executed; Isabella was imprisoned here, at Castle Rising. (Author's collection/ Ashley Jensen)

Left: Sketch of the tomb effigies of Philippa and Edward III from Gardiner's *History of England*.

Above: Joan of Kent's husband Edward 'the Black Prince' from an illuminated manuscript. (Courtesy of the British Library)

Wallingford Castle, Joan's favourite residence. She died here while one of her sons, John Holland, was awaiting a sentence of death handed down by another of her sons, King Edward III. He was reprieved after her death. She is buried with her first husband, Thomas Holland, at Greyfriars in Stamford. (Courtesy of Peter Lawne)

Above: Some Plantagenet men loved by Plantagenet women: Henry IV, Edward the Black Prince and Edward III depicted on Canterbury Cathedral. (Courtesy of Sagesolar under Creative Commons 2.0)

Below: Katherine Swynford's husband, John of Gaunt, had an enormous influence on later events in the Wars of the Roses. He built up a section of Kenilworth Castle, pictured here. (Courtesy of Laura LaRose under Creative Commons 2.0)

Above: Lincoln Cathedral, where
Katherine Swynford rests today.
(Courtesy of Chris Sampson under
Creative Commons 2.0)

Left: Joan of Navarre and her
husband Henry IV from Blore's
Monumental Remains.

Above: Leeds Castle was given to Joan on her marriage to Henry IV. When her step-son Henry V turned against her she was charged with witchcraft and imprisoned in the castle. (Author's collection/Ashley Jensen)

Below: Joan was moved from Leeds Castle to solitary confinement here at Pevensey Castle. However, before his death Henry V returned her to Leeds and relaxed her confinement, eventually freeing her and restoring her property to her. (Courtesy of Prioryman under Creative Commons 2.0)

Above left: Henry V, Joan's stepson and captor, who would go on to marry Katherine of Valois. (Courtesy of the Yale Center for British Art)

Above right: The marriage of Katherine of Valois and Henry V in 1420. Her later liaison with Owen Tudor would bring forth the Lancastrian dynasty in the form of Henry VII. (Courtesy of the British Library)

Below: Bermondsey Abbey, where Katherine died. (Courtesy of Yale Center for British Art)

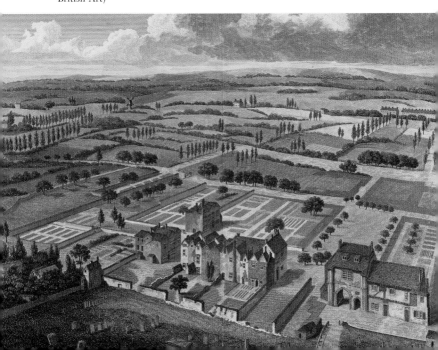

Above: The second
daughter of Rene, King
of Naples and Isabella,
Duchess of Lorraine,
Margaret of Anjou spent
her early life at the castle
of Tarascon on the Rhone
in Provence. (Courtesy of
Αλέξανδρος under Creative
Commons 2.0)

Right: Margaret of
Anjou in a contemporary
depiction from the Books
of the Skinners Company
in 1422, as reproduced
in Wadmore's *Some
Account of the Worshipful
Company of Skinners of
London* (1902).

The Qween Margarete sith
me wyff and Spowse to kyng
harry the sexthe.

Above: Elizabeth Woodville grew up at the manor house of Grafton Regis. She would have been well acquainted with St Mary's Church in the village. (Courtesy of CJ1340 under Creative Commons 2.0)

Left: Elizabeth Woodville, husband to Edward IV and mother to, among others, Elizabeth of York, later Queen of England, and the Princes in the Tower.

Elizabeth's husband Edward IV in an engraving by Hendrick Goltzius. (Courtesy of the Rijksmuseum)

Elizabeth of York, daughter of Elizabeth Woodville. (Courtesy of Ripon Cathedral)

The marriage of Elizabeth of York and Henry VII all but ended the Wars of the Roses, uniting the houses of York and Lancaster. (Courtesy of the Metropolitan Museum of Art)

Richard III and Anne Neville. (Courtesy of Yale University Art Gallery)

effectively changed the martial leadership ideal of the monarch. K. B. McFarland outlines the process succinctly:

> This absence or at least degeneration of the notion of liege homage is as much a feature of bastard feudalism as is the loss of that stability which the tenurial relation may be presumed to have maintained in earlier times. A man was allowed greater freedom of choice at every stage in the pursuit of his own interests.

The delegation of military authority to a professionally trained military was beginning to take shape. This was due to a military revolution of a sort that was transforming the system in Western Europe into professional armies, given the technical and doctrinal changes taking place in warfare. Another factor was the evolution of the political state which began a more centralised approach to governing, something that started in the fifteenth century and came to fruition in the next century during the Tudor era, in the reign of Elizabeth I. The embryonic stages of a modern nation-state were taking shape. Leadership of a nation would no longer be so closely tied to personal martial skills, and the increasing sophistication of warfare required the delegation of authority in battle to a more specialist military leadership.

Queen Joanna of Navarre was never formally tried for witchcraft, which also meant she could not prove her innocence. The ambiguous status and the unofficial social stigma of witchcraft produced the desired result of essentially separating Joanna from her royal and personal wealth. As we have seen in the past, Eleanor of Aquitaine was incarcerated for her political pursuits and her royal status did not afford any protection. Eleanor of Aquitaine may have been tried and executed for treason for her crimes, had she been a man. So this gentler treatment was a mark of the chivalric system. However, the wholesale political manipulation employed to separate manorial wealth from a woman regardless of class or status was used to truncate women's independence and power. Joanna understood the rules of the game and probably did not press for a formal trial on the very sensible grounds that, if convicted, she could have been burned at the stake (though this was unlikely for a royal personage). Henry V was almost certainly reluctant to inflict such a punishment on his stepmother, with whom he had a decent familial relationship until 1419. Perhaps Christian guilt and a sense of morality deterred such ruthless behaviour.

The imprisonment of Joanna was subtly concealed in a veil of legality that covered up its injustice. She was transferred from Havering and shuttled amongst a few strongholds before she was settled into Leeds Castle for the duration of her incarceration. The level of comfort afforded Queen Joanna of Navarre indicated a soft sentence, which reflected the dubious legality of the charges. She was under the watchful but apparently sympathetic eye of Sir John Pelham. Joanna s lived in a gilded cage, since her royal imprisonment was marked with some luxury and freedom, but a cage nonetheless.

The respect for her position as dowager queen and stepmother to the king was still apparent during her forced confinement. There was money for a stable that indicates a relaxed attitude towards the threat of her escape. She was also afforded a wardrobe befitting her status. Queen Joanna was also allowed her personal entourage and physicians to maintain her household, and this would prevail throughout 1420. The condition of Joanna's imprisonment were a little less luxurious after 1420 but she was still provided with luxury goods and a horse and carriage. The expenditure was probably tightened due to the finances needed by Henry V to secure France after 1420. It was the year Henry V concluded the Treaty of Troyes and then married Katherine of Valois. It can be surmised that the financial strain of the war and the need of capital for his new bride's dower precipitated the lower standard for Joanna's upkeep while she was detained.

Queen Joanna did receive guests, which included some prominent royal family members. The historical record indicates that the Duke of Gloucester and Henry Beaufort visited and were subsequently entertained by the imprisoned queen. Her imprisonment did not preclude her from entertaining in style with wine, food and servants to serve her distinguished guests. So we may speculate that Queen Joanna's detainment for witchcraft was not perceived or executed as a true sentence. Leeds Castle was, to all intents and purposes, Queen Joanna's royal court rather than a prison.

The seclusion provided by her imprisonment fostered a close friendship with Lord Thomas Camoys who seems to have stayed with the Queen for nine months. Lisa Hilton's work speculated that, perhaps, this was a more intimate relationship. This informed speculation does carry some weight simply due to the length of his private stay with the Queen:

...and when he [Lord Thomas Camoys] died shortly after leaving Leeds, in March 1421, mourning clothes were ordered for the Queen: seven yards of black cloth at 7s 8d per yard, a satin cape and fur for a collar. It was once assumed that these luxury garments were purchased for the death of Henry V, but that did not take place until the following year. Their richness suggests that Camoys was a very close friend indeed.[48]

The privation the crown was enduring seems to show that Queen Joanna's witchcraft accusations were really a form of royal extortion to ease financial strains. The king was waging war in France during 1421 to 1422 and did not call a Parliament or exact new taxes. The political landscape had changed rapidly as the war became an attritional affair, draining funds and resources from the realm.

Another interesting event occurred before Henry V's untimely death later in 1422. The king reimbursed some of the funds back into Queen Joanna's dower, which could indicate some guilt he felt for his stepmother's predicament. It was a fine gesture but seemed rather overdue.

If financial considerations were a powerful motive for keeping Joanna in captivity for three years, and a continued belief in her guiltiness, it would explain the absence of any trial or formal investigation. If a trial should acquit her as guiltless, there would no longer be any justification for the continuance of her imprisonment and the retention of her property. If, on the other hand, it should result in a condemnation, she would have born henceforth the stigma of being officially pronounced a witch, and might have had to perform a penance as humiliating as that which Eleanor Cobham later had to undergo. Henry would wish to spare her both of these. If, however, no trial were held, all these difficulties would be avoided, and the original charges against her

---

48   Lisa Hilton, 370.

would be a sufficient pretext for keeping her in captivity – a very lenient and comfortable captivity – while the government made use of her dowry.[49]

The precedent had been set to employ the suspicion or allegation of witchcraft to limit the influence of powerfully placed women in English society during the fifteenth century. Since the accusation of witchcraft had been employed as a political tool, either to take the wealth or drain the power from the highest placed noblewomen, such as the queen, this started a trickle-down effect upon lesser noblewomen. The allegations against Queen Joanna were never followed up and there was no real intention to push forward with a formal trial. However, other noblewomen would not be so lucky. The first high profile case of witchcraft after Joanna's precedent was the trial of Eleanor, Duchess of Gloucester, in 1441. Eleanor did not stand accused alone; there was Margery Jourdemayne, Oxford scholar Master Roger Bolingbroke, priest John Home of Hereford, and master Thomas Southwell, a physician at Westminster.

The trial had essentially political motives. However, the results of this witch hunt were gruesome. Margery Jourdemayne was burned at the stake for heresy and the practice of witchcraft. Roger Bolingbroke was found guilty of treason and was subsequently hung, drawn and quartered, which was the grimsentence for this high crime against the state. The others were either acquitted or let off with light sentences. Eleanor, Duchess of Gloucester was found guilty of sorcery and witchcraft, but not of heresy, that carried a death sentence. So Eleanor was sentenced to

---

49   A. R. Myers, 276.

penance and imprisonment for life. The church also convicted her of sorcery because, supposedly, she had tricked the Duke of Gloucester into marrying her. Subsequently the church declared the marriage null and void. Eleanor was afforded some comfort during her imprisonment, which indicated some concessions to her noble rank. The sentence again served political ends; firstly the aim was to dispose of a perceived troublesome and meddling noblewoman in royal circles; and secondly, to eradicate the Duke of Gloucester's influence, especially his pro-war stance with regard to France. These terrible charges of witchcraft in 1441 were far more effective and destructive in their execution than those in 1419 against Queen Joanna. Jessica Freeman sums up the outcome of these later witchcraft trials.

Eleanor's rapid, if inexplicable, rise in status had long been viewed with suspicious envy by courtiers and rivals, who attributed it to magical practices, and contemporaries seem to have accepted Eleanor's guilt in 1441.

But, just as Eleanor believed herself protected by her powerful husband, Margery [Jourdemayne] imagined herself safeguarded by her aristocratic clients and the scholars, clerics and doctors whom she assisted in magical practices. She was not a pathetic, aged figure living in poverty denounced by jealous or frightened neighbours, but probably an able and unvicious woman who met a demand for love potions, folk medicines and charms, in a practice that was usually tolerated by the authorities, and whose customers included the highest in the land.

If Margery had refrained from mingling in high society, and not involved herself in court politics at a time of dynastic uncertainty and intrigue, she might well have died in her own bed, rather than in the smoke and flames of Smithfield.[50]

The spectre of witchcraft would rear its ugly head again in 1469 when Thomas Wake, a servant to the Earl of Warwick, accused the Duchess of Bedford of sorcery. This was an obvious political ploy by the Earl of Warwick to discredit Elizabeth Woodville, the Queen, and her husband, King Edward IV. This did not come to trial since the evidence was withdrawn, but it is another example of the use of witchcraft to discredit prominent women throughout the fifteenth century.

Queen Joanna of Navarre settled into a quiet life after she was released from her imprisonment. She was released about six months after Henry V's death, who had left orders to restore her freedom and her manorial estates. The second order was more difficult to expedite since most of her estates had been redistributed as patronage amongst the baronage. Queen Joanna did, after a delay, have some of her estates compensated for via royal grants. The rest of the queen dowager's life seemed to have been lived in respectable comfort, afforded to her by her step-grandson the King Henry VI. In her twilight years she was granted gifts by the king and, when she died in 1437, Henry VI ensured that she was buried with the honours befitting her status as a queen of England.

Queen Joanna of Navarre is made especially interesting by what she endured rather than any major achievement or advance

---

50   Jessica Freeman 'Sorcery at Court and manor: Margery Jourdemayne, the witch of Eye next Westminster' in *Journal of Medieval History*, 30: 2004. 356-357.

in queenship. However, her short reign shows how important the image of the queen was to the English monarchy and how independence can make a queen vulnerable to political attack. Queen Joanna displays some elements that reflected Eleanor of Aquitaine's example of queenship. She was eventually able to overcome the stigma of accusations of witchcraft and restore her reputation. Her life represents a small step towards regnant power for an English queen to rule with authority – and it foreshadows the next tumultuous era, the War of the Roses.

7

KATHERINE OF VALOIS

You have witchcraft in your lips, Kate: there is more eloquence in a
sugar touch of them than in the tongues of the French Council...

Henry V, Act V, scene 2, line 270

Katherine of Valois is one of the least historically documented of
all the queens in this study, but her vivid portrayal in Shakespeare's
Henry V provides some clues as to how this war-prize queen was
perceived. The standard for the chivalric union of knight and damsel
is present in the imagery of Katherine of Valois and Henry V. Their
marriage was the product of the Treaty of Troyes (1420), and upon
the death of Katherine's father, Charles VI, Henry V and his heirs
were to inherit the throne of France, so this historic union was
symbolic of the chivalric knightly conquest – the conquest being
France, and the prize Katherine of Valois. In Shakespeare's play we
see this in his wooing of Katherine:

No, it is not possible you should love the enemy of France, Kate; but
in loving me you should love the friend of France, for I love France

so well that I will not part with a village of it – I will have it all mine; and Kate, when France is mine, and I am yours, then yours is France, and you are mine.[51]

The contemporary sources viewed this marriage in 1420 as a fairy-tale union, with Katherine as a noble Cinderella and King Henry V the prince. The ceremony was hugely popular; here were two royal symbols for everyone in the realm to heap their adulation upon. But this golden time was cut short due to Henry's war in France and his untimely death in 1422. None of the aspirations of the treaty were to come to fruition, and this left Katherine a widow at twenty-one years old, with an infant son – Henry of Windsor, now Henry VI, King of England and France. The crown was thus thrown into a precarious environment, as was Katherine, a French widow in an England ruled by a regency. The newly gained territories in France were insecure, and this meant an uncertain future for the dowager queen. She would go on to remarry in a clandestine union with Owen Tudor, and from this union another dynasty would spring, resulting in the first ever regnant queen of England.

Henry V inherited the Lancastrian throne from his father, Henry IV, who gained it after the usurpation of Richard II in 1399. Henry IV's reign was precarious since he owed much to Parliament, which granted him his kingship; this put great constraints on his reign and had long-term effects upon England's monarchy. The events that led to Henry IV's kingship set a precedent in the monarchial history of England, opening the throne to a cadet branch of the Plantagenet line – this would have consequences later

---

51   *Henry V*, Act V, scene 2, line 170. William Shakespeare, *Four Histories: Richard II, Henry IV part one & two and Henry V* (New York: Penguin Books, 1994), p. 858.

in the fifteenth century. Henry IV's reign and its precarious nature is well outlined in Chris Given-Wilson's biography of the man:

> The revolution of 1399 brought the best out of Henry. Purposeful and ruthless – as he had to be – he initially secured the throne almost without opposition, but soon discovered that the kingship of a usurper was qualitatively different from that of a legitimate monarch. Even with kings as a manifestly unsuitable as Edward II or Richard the second, it took ten or fifteen years for baronial exasperation to turn to talk of deposition and twenty for the threat to be realized...[52]

When Henry V came to the throne in 1413 it was a different landscape and the single-mindedness and sheer strength of his character pushed forward a policy of war and conquest that swept the nation up into a jingoist fervour. The young Henry V immediately began reasserting the claims of his great-grandfather Edward III to re-establish an Angevin empire.

The circumstances of the French monarchy during this period, combined with Henry V's character, created an opportunity for the young king's meteoric rise. The French throne was occupied by Charles VI, who was a weak and ineffectual king and was overwhelmed on most occasions with a mental illness that denied his reign any stability. The two rival branches of the French royal family that were causing internecine struggle in the kingdom at this time were Armagnac and Burgundy. Theirs became an especially vicious struggle after the murder of a leading member of the Orleans royal family in 1407. These rival factions divided France, drawing the attention of the young Henry V.

---

52   Chris Given-Wilson, *Henry IV* (London: Yale University Press, 2016), p. 526.

A full explanation of Henry V's motivations is not readily apparent. I surmise that it was a combination of two major factors. The first was that the leadership in France, especially the royal leadership, had fractured the nation. This, of course, made it possible for Henry to invade. The second reason is more a matter of domestic policy for Henry V. Henry may have determined that a foreign war would create unity among the barons in England and create popular support for his subjects. Furthermore, the war would divert the English barons' ambitions and restless turmoil away from internal matters and into a foreign channel. The spoils of war would also serve to make the baronage more quiescent to Henry V's policies, foreign and domestic, in Parliament.

Henry's attempts to topple the French and take the kingdom came to a head at the Battle of Agincourt in 1415. The strategy behind the victory at Agincourt is outlined by K. B. McFarland:

Diplomacy does not win victories unsupported by force of arms. As a soldier Henry had two immediate tasks: to persuade the French to fight a pitched battle and to beat them. The danger was that, remembering the strategy of the 1370s, the French would refuse battle. Indeed at the critical moment the old Duke of Berri was in favour of letting Henry return home unmolested. A successor to Crécy and Poitiers was needed to make the English enthusiastic for war and willing to pay for the cost of its early stages and to demoralize the already divided French. Then conquest might be attempted. But the purpose of a carefully prepared expedition of 1415 was not conquest but victorious battle.[53]

---

53 K. B. McFarlane, *Lancastrian Kings and Lollard Knights* (Oxford: Clarendon Press, 1972), p. 126.

Henry's decisive victory at Agincourt secured strong support at home for the war in France. This was important since quick victories provided the morale boost needed to conduct a more lengthy and protracted war. Henry understood that conquering France would require a war of attrition and this did not always draw popular support from the baronage. The victory at Agincourt therefore allowed Henry the freedom he needed to wage the war of conquest he wanted to pursue in France. There followed the conquest of half of the kingdom in 1416 before Rouen was taken in 1419 and finally Normandy in 1420, showing the success Henry V enjoyed. A respite in the fighting occurred in 1420 with the Treaty of Troyes, and the marriage to Katherine of Valois.

Katherine of Valois' family background was chequered with tragedy and corruption and the divisive atmosphere of France. Katherine was the youngest daughter to the mad King Charles VI. She was the baby sister of Richard II's queen, Isabella. We can see an inextricable connection between the French and English thrones throughout this period. In 1409, marriage between Katherine of Valois and Henry V was first considered between the two monarchies, but came to nothing for now. However, the French royal family then suffered a series of tragic events that led to Charles, the youngest of the family, becoming heir apparent in 1417.[54] A regency had been ruling France since 1403 in lieu of Charles VI, who was mentally unfit to rule. His wife, Isabeau of Bavaria, was the head of the regency, but it seemed she was not capable of containing the factionalism that was rampant

---

54 This is an interesting historical anachronism displayed in Shakespeare's play *Henry V*, since Charles is portrayed as the dauphin (heir apparent) on the eve of Agincourt in 1415.

between Orleans and Burgundy. Some unsubstantiated accounts accuse Isabeau of adulterous behaviour with members of both the Orleans and Burgundy factions, claiming that this hindered effective rule, but this would seem to be the typical misogynist historical accounts that detract from an actual analysis of female leadership of this period. Likely the regency was ineffectual due to the factionalism and not due to any supposed sexual transgressions on the part of the queen. The fact remains that France was divided inviolable to Henry's invasion.

Growing up amid this turmoil, Katherine was to be the war prize in the conquest of France. It seemed that Katherine was a political pawn to unify the two kingdoms and her queenship was to be symbolic of the union of France and England. She was to represent the sanctity and piety of Henry's conquest and would provide a legitimate successor to both crowns. Katherine's role was to provide the stability for a succession that would unite two realms at war since 1066. Shakespeare's symbolic display of Henry's sexual potency in conquering France and thus Katherine was a common and misguided trope of male domination of any female independence or power. Katherine and France were bent to the will of the conqueror, which precluded any real romantic notion of love between the king and queen. Love by its very nature denotes consent and, possibly, mutual respect, which is antithesis to a conquering hero. Henry V respects the wealth of the nation of France but does not respect his bride. Katherine is a conduit of conquest and therefore is like the land of France itself – do you ask if the land wants to be conquered?

This was a callous and indifferent approach to marriage and is rather alien to our twenty-first-century notion of love and marriage, though Shakespeare did inject some romantic ideals that were most likely not present in Henry and Katherine's marriage. Lance Wilcox states that 'for whatever reason, Shakespeare has created in Princess Katherine practically the stereotype of an Englishman's fantasy of a French debutante'.[55] The opening quote in this chapter displayed a projected romanticism between Henry and Katherine that Shakespeare surely invented. The marriage was the product of the Treaty of Troyes and this was surely more indicative of a business transaction than a romantic love match. Lisa Hilton sums this notion up well:

> For the English, at least, Troyes was naturally a triumph. Henry kissed Catherine's hand 'joyfully', as well he might, and on 2 June 'the King of the English married lady Catherine and he willed that the ceremony should be carried out entirely according to the custom of the France'. Henry gave 200 nobles to the church of St. John, and the bride and groom were feasted before being ceremonially put to bed, but Henry was in such a hurry to get back to his war that he didn't bother with the tournament to mark the occasion.[56]

The short marriage was marked with war and conquest and the most meaningful product of the marriage was the conception of Katherine and Henry's son. This, of course, was one of the main goals of this marriage. Katherine was paraded through France from Rouen to Amiens and finally Calais as the prize for Henry's conquest of France.

---

55   Lance Wilcox, 'Katherine of France as Victim and Bride', in *Shakespeare Studies* Vol. 17 (1985), p. 62.

56   Lisa Hilton, pp. 376–7.

When Catherine and Henry arrived in England, they were the quintessential medieval royal couple. Katherine was the fair and beautiful blonde queen, which was the face of France to the English people. Henry played his part as the knight in shining armour, who conquered the kingdom and rescued the queen from the clutches of certain doom. The coronation of Queen Katherine of Valois was a grand ceremony with the appropriate pomp and circumstance. The English people were now enthralled with their royal couple and thus would support efforts to further the war in France. It was a carefully played piece of political drama that manipulated the people, blending jingoism and uniformity in a cauldron for war and conquest.

The ceremony and the celebrations were cut short by Henry's obsession with the war in France. He did not even mark the occasion with a tournament, which was traditional for a marriage and especially the coronation of a queen. He had turned his attention to raising money, arms and men for his latest foray into France. Henry travelled through many counties and reunited with Katherine during Easter celebrations, and it seems this was around the time when Katherine was with child. Her gravid state did not deter Henry's further campaigning in the north of England to secure more support for the war.

The couple reunited in London, when Katherine's pregnancy was more apparent, but Henry left for France anyway. The expediency for war and Henry's ambition outweighed any sentimental feeling he may have felt for Katherine. Katherine was in England for less than half a year before she was on campaign with her husband in France. Some of the contemporary sources suggest that Katherine was vain and giddy, but this can be seen as an oversimplification of the relationship.

Another complexity I put forward is Katherine's feelings towards her husband's war. I surmise that perhaps she felt some resentment toward Henry's hostile acts towards her country. If I may speculate, I think perhaps Katherine at first may have felt powerless against the English onslaught and Henry's marriage proposal. As time went on, however, Katherine may have seen France's turmoil and felt that her husband could bring unity to the kingdom, which would have been beneficial to her countrymen.

Since there is little contemporary evidence as to what kind of person Katherine of Valois was, there has been some wild speculation and creative fiction to conjure her character traits. Some of the historical evidence would indicate a sort of affectionate if not passionate relationship between Katherine and Henry; they shared a love of music and both could play the harp. The king had ordered a pair of harps for the two of them. This showed a desire on Henry's part to bond with his wife. King Henry V had ordered many musicians to play at his wedding, and this may have made Katherine more relaxed and joyful. The subjects of the realm of England viewed Henry and Katherine's union as a picture-perfect example of a king and queen. This vision was further promoted when Katherine produced an heir for the heroic Lancastrian king. The zenith of the relationship had been reached by December 1421 when Katherine delivered a healthy boy – the future Henry VI. Eight months later, after hard campaigning, Henry had fallen ill and died. This was a tragedy of momentous impact for England, France and Katherine herself.

The last of the medieval warrior Kings of England, austere in life, single-minded in purpose, a pattern of chivalry, he had lived and conquered by the sword, the greatest of his house; but natural causes laid him low before the walls of Vincennes on 31 August, 1422. His dreams lived on, to bedevil his successor, his House, and his realm for decades thereafter. It was hardly to be expected that the dynasty would indefinitely survive the wreckage of its boldest enterprise.[57]

It seemed Henry was so preoccupied with the war that he did not mention his wife upon his deathbed. Perhaps he had underestimated the severity of his illness and the sudden nature of it caught him off guard for the first time in his life. Some historians have suggested that the couple may have been estranged but there is no contemporary evidence to suggest this. The war was his overwhelming obsession and he may have miscalculated his premature death. Whatever the circumstances were, the outcome was his sudden death. Katherine may have been like a boat against the tide of circumstances; she was in a lonely and precarious situation.

Katherine was present at the very solemn and conclusive funeral of her husband, which closed the chapter on the conquest of France, and her future would be uncertain. England had mourned the loss of its great warrior medieval king; his short life would spark much mythos around his reign.

Katherine's role in the minority regency would be minimal, and her status as dowager queen would be the business of the ruling council. The last dowager queen to serve as regent had been Isabella of France and the circumstances of that regency did not bode well for Katherine. Two major factors excluded her from

---

57   S. B. Chrimes, *Lancastrians, Yorkists and Henry VII* (New York: St. Martin Press, 1964), p. 52.

any participation in the regency. The first was her French lineage; England was at war with her brother, and her loyalty to England could have been deemed dubious. The second was the fact that the history of the previous century may have cast a long shadow on Katherine, since Isabella's regency was marked by corruption and turmoil. Those who would rule in the place of the infant king were John, Duke of Bedford, and Humphrey, Duke of Gloucester, the brothers of Henry V. Meanwhile, his Beaufort relatives were in charge of the upbringing of the young Henry VI. Thomas Beaufort was his first tutor until his death in 1427 and Henry VI's tutelage would reside later with Richard Beauchamp, Earl of Warwick. The Beauforts would remain close to the Lancastrian crown throughout the 1430s and 1440s. Their torch would be passed to Henry Beaufort, Duke of Somerset, after 1447. This generation of Beauforts would be important in the succession through their progeny; young Margaret would ultimately mother Henry VII, the first Tudor king.

The regency government of the king during his minority was rife with discord. Most of the 1420s and early 1430s had been preoccupied with the execution of the war in France. It seemed the war had lacked focus and France was beginning to display elements of unity and nationalism that no military endeavour could overcome. It seemed that without the monolithic drive of Henry V the English campaign lost its impetus. Katherine was left well provided for; the queen's council, which started under Joanna of Navarre, had set a profitable dower for Katherine. This provided an independent source of income for Katherine and an element of freedom which she undoubtedly lacked in France.

Katherine's political involvement was of very little note, but her impact on the succession was of paramount concern to the realm, especially during the minority of Henry VI. The fortunes of war turned against the English in 1429 when Katherine's brother Charles won a stunning victory at Orleans and Joan of Arc presented the possibility of independence to the French people. The tragedy of Joan of Arc served the purpose of Charles VII, who ascended the throne of France in July of 1429. The efforts of the English to purport the illegitimacy of French rule failed, even with attempts to employ Katherine as an avenue for English overlordship to France. The Plantagenet assertion through the Treaty of Troyes held little sway over the French nobility and people, who at this time were intoxicated with national spirit. The English attempted to claim ascendancy over the French throne through the heritage of Edward I and Isabella of France, and to further their claim they employed the symbolism of the Merovingian origins of Clovis. All of this propaganda fell short, and France threw off the yoke of English rule. It is true that Henry VI was coronated king in Paris in 1431, but this was an empty gesture and the tide had turned to a French monarchy with Charles VII as king – a true Valois victory.

The French concluded an alliance between the houses of Burgundy and Armagnac which ended the civil turmoil in 1435. This also coincided with the death of the Duke of Bedford, and with him the hopes of Henry V's Angevin empire in France died. This left the mercurial Duke of Gloucester in charge, and his efforts to maintain the war with France at all costs had done irreparable damage to the English monarchy.

Henry VI came of age in 1437, and his kingship was marked with a passivity and indecision that saw any attempt to extend the war dismissed. The rivalry of the Duke of Gloucester and Cardinal Beaufort had caused much turmoil in the young king's monarchy.

That Henry V's dreams died in the bifurcation of power among the English baronage did not bode well for the future.

While all this was unfolding, after Henry's death Katherine's life went on with little acknowledgement from the English baronage. It seemed she enjoyed a love affair in 1426 with the young Edmund Beaufort, a relative of the Gaunt–Swynford union from the previous century. Katherine was unknowingly thrust into the political spotlight when she lobbied for James of Scotland's release from imprisonment. She had become friends with James, who was married to Joan Beaufort. The connection between Joan and Edmund, with both so close to power, did not escape the attention of Parliament. This prompted Parliament to pass a bill in 1428 to prevent the remarriage of the dowager queen without the consent of the king. It declared any lands of the husband would be forfeit but that any offspring would be acknowledged as part of the royal family. Katherine had lost Edmund Beaufort and was to live in Henry VI's household, which she did until 1432. Katherine showed independence in defiance to these rulings and appears to have been no shrinking violet.

There is no certainty in the date, but somewhere between 1431 and 1432 Katherine of Valois married Owen Tudor. There have been many stories about how Owen and Katherine met. Owen was connected to Katherine's household and had met her in service during this period. They fell in love and married, which indicated a lax attitude to Katherine's behaviour. One of the more creditable stories is that Owen had collapsed in Katherine's lap during a dance and subsequently the two fell madly in love. Another story seems less likely, wherein she lustfully watched young Owen swimming in the nude and disguised herself as a maid to meet the young man. Owen had kissed her, and the rest, as they say, is history. This Tudor folklore is clouded with the passage of time and the true story may never surface.

The marriage between Katherine of Valois and Owen Tudor was a fait accompli, and Parliament gave Owen the rights of an Englishman. This was to counter Henry IV's 1402 law stripping Welshmen of any rights or power. It seemed Parliament accepted the marriage, and was obliged to placate the queen and avoid any further embarrassment to the royal family. Katherine and Owen's marriage seems to have been a blissful one, and they produced four children in a period of six years. A daughter died in infancy, but sons Edmund, Jasper and Owen would live to become influential in the coming years. The historical record sheds a dim light on their life together, but it was seemingly a quiet and apolitical upbringing. The couple resided on Katherine's dower estates and the children grew up in Hertfordshire, Hadham and Hatfield.

Though happy, the marriage was short; Katherine of Valois died in 1437 at a convent in Bermondsey Abbey. The reason for her seclusion before she died may have been the onset of mental illness, which was prevalent in her family; this same mental illness seemed to inflict her father Charles VI and her son Henry VI of England. We can surmise that there was probably hereditary mental illness in the Valois family line. This unfortunate inheritance would be the cause of much uncertainty during Henry VI's reign, as the mental breakdowns and lapses that the king would suffer caused much turmoil and were an underlying cause of the Yorkist rise during the War of the Roses.

Katherine's sons with Owen Tudor would come under the care of Katherine de la Pole, who was the sister of the Earl of Suffolk. This kept the Tudor boys close to the royal family after Katherine's death. The older Owen Tudor had been imprisoned for a short time due to uneasiness among the baronage in 1438, but he was released the next year and remained in Wales thereafter. The Tudor legacy changed under Henry VI, when the king befriended some of the Tudor men. Both Jasper and Edmund joined the king's court in the 1440s. The king had decided to entitle the two Tudor boys in 1453. He made Edmund the Earl of Richmond and Jasper was made Earl of Pembroke. This action was the impetus for the Tudor legacy that was to come to fruition in the next few decades.

The king was keen to surround himself with loyal people, but he was not always aware of the consequences of his actions. In this case he not only ennobled the Tudor boys but also a line of royal succession to the Tudor lineage. However, his own wife, Margaret of Anjou, was pregnant with his child and he must have thought there would be no conflict in the succession to the Lancastrian line. Henry VI had married Margaret of Anjou in 1445 to create some sort of alliance with France, and Margaret proved to be a poor bride in material wealth but a rich bride in spirit, which countered Henry VI's rather soft and genteel personality. In 1453, Henry gave the care of the young Margaret Beaufort to his stepbrother Edmund Tudor. This was an important event that saw the Tudors allied with the Beaufort line, enabling an eventual Tudor succession, albeit a violent one. This was not Henry VI's intention, of course; rather he wanted a tight-knit familial bond surrounding his royal court.

Margaret Beaufort was the Duke of Somerset's sole heir, and the fortune she thus represented made her the most eligible bride in the kingdom. She had married the Earl of Suffolk's son in 1450 but this was an obvious attempt by Suffolk to secure his wealth. The Earl of Suffolk died in late 1450 and the marriage to his son John de la Pole was declared null and void by the king. The king subsequently allowed his half-brother Edmund Tudor to marry the young Margaret Beaufort in 1453. This was a particularly fortuitous event for the Tudor lineage, since it was now tied to another branch of the Plantagenet royal lineage. This strengthened the claim of the Tudors to the English throne, for now there were ties to the royal family from both the Tudor and Beaufort lines. This inevitably linked up with the Lancastrian line, and Henry VI felt this was a good connection to his royal lineage. Henry VI was not aware that this action would put his own succession in so much discord. The complex relationship the Tudors had with the Lancastrian royal line only further complicated the English succession. After 1399 the precedent had been set that a cadet branch of the Plantagenet line could inherit the throne. This, of course, opened the floodgates to all Plantagenet lineage, which was the cause of the War of the Roses. Put simply, there were too many nobles with Plantagenet blood flowing in their veins.

The Tudor line lay in wait like a predatory cat ready to strike from the shadows. In the aftermath of the purges of the bloodlines during the War of the Roses the Tudor claim was a beacon of turmoil. During the conflict Edmund Tudor was imprisoned; he died of plague in 1456, but not before leaving Margaret Beaufort with a son – the future Henry VII. Margaret took shelter with her brother-in-law Jasper Tudor, and put her hopes in her son.

The romanticised image of Katherine of Valois has been immortalised by William Shakespeare, but it is a portrait that sheds little light on her actual life. The vision of the picture-perfect Lancastrian bride who was essentially a means to the French throne is what we see today. Her husband, Henry V, the legendary king and victor of Agincourt, was the monarchial powerhouse who negated any qualities Katherine of Valois had as a queen or even as a person. Her life is an important window to the past and sheds light on queenship during this period.

Unfortunately, much of the historical record of her life is cast in an anecdotal and dubious light, since we do not have any of her papers or even thoughts on the many events during her life. She is portrayed as a mere vehicle for the transmission of property – and in this case a kingdom – to her husband, King Henry V.

This study has tried to portray a woman who was more than the prize won on the fields of Agincourt. Katherine of Valois may have only made an impact as queen in that she delivered France to Henry V, but this was only an ephemeral event. It proved to be rather destructive to her son, and the dream of a renewed Angevin empire was never realised. We may never know how she felt about this role she played, or even her feelings toward her husband's bellicose actions towards her own country. There must have been some conflict in her heart about her culpability during the war in France. Katherine did not flinch from her duty as consort even though it seemed that the choice in this matter was never of her own will. Of all the queens in this study she is by far the most dutiful. She was the product of the Treaty of Troyes, bartered to the conquering king. Shakespeare's play displayed Katherine as perhaps a metaphor for the French populace itself.

To whatever degree we have vicariously enjoyed Henry's conquests, our satisfaction should be complete at the promise of Katherine's gracing the monarch's bed. Our troubled concern for Katherine's welfare, on the other hand, along with that for the French people generally, should be somewhat assuaged by the events of the final act. Katherine accepts Henry as her suitor with no great unwillingness. And Henry, having like Theseus won his love with his sword, nevertheless woos and flatters her as if all rested on her decision alone. From his gallantry towards Katherine, I think we are meant to infer a certain humanity and liberality in his treatment of the vanquished French as well.[58]

We may ask how Katherine of Valois falls under the shadow of Eleanor of Aquitaine. The most obvious is that her dowry, like Eleanor's, was a large portion of the French nation. Both Henry II and Henry V married their respective queens for their dowry. However, Henry II lived to see his Angevin empire come to fruition whereas Henry V never saw this eventuality. Both Eleanor of Aquitaine and Katherine of Valois adopted England as their new home and were model queens for the subjects of their realms. Katherine of Valois was known for her beauty, as was Eleanor of Aquitaine, so the combination of feminine beauty and power was similar. However, Katherine of Valois was overshadowed by Henry V's larger-than-life personality. The last and most impactful element of Katherine's life was her second marriage and the Tudor legacy. The Tudors brought stability to the realm after the tumultuous War of the Roses and this was by far Katherine's most significant contribution as queen. Lisa Hilton concluded with an insightful survey of Katherine of Valois:

One picture of medieval women, now thankfully dismissed, presents them as scarcely more than 'animated title deeds', their existence entirely determined by the transmission of property. Katherine's queenship, more than that of any of her predecessors, might be said to be contained by this very limited concept. She did very little as a consort except to transmit the kingdom of France, a claim whose vanity was to prove devastating for her son...

58   Lance Wilcox, pp. 73–4.

As a woman, however, Katherine was considerably more interesting. She was courageous, independent-minded and astonishingly audacious in the pursuit of her desire. Hers was an extraordinarily vivid life, blighted by war and madness, elevated by marriage to the hero of the age and their love affair really did change the course of history. It is a pity, perhaps, that only hints of the color of that life can be found beyond the stilted, Joule-like radiance of her portraits as the beautiful bride of England's greatest warrior prince.[59]

This was not the legacy Henry V had in mind when he married Katherine of Valois in 1420, but it was what transpired. Katherine's life may seem rather limited in scope as a queen, but as a woman and dowager queen she portrays independence and a steadfast desire to pursue her interests in spite of the conventions of the time. It was sad that her life was immersed in war, mental illness and a dysfunctional family, but she persevered, which displayed a certain strength of character. Katherine of Valois draws admiration and respect. She was more than the beautiful war prize of Henry V, and if he had lived we may have seen a far more active queen and mother who would no doubt have been a fierce defender of the Lancastrian dynasty. Her radiant visage still shines the way forward in our study, but in a rather different direction, to a Tudor rule. Katherine of Valois was the progenitor of that great Tudor queen Elizabeth I; from such small beginnings do great things come.

---

59   Lisa Hilton, p. 389.

8

MARGARET OF ANJOU

Margaret of Anjou's queenship was clouded by a backdrop of the Wars of the Roses, and her legacy has been painted with a tainted brush of partisanship. She was labelled a virago and 'she-wolf' by later writers who were serving a political purpose. Her legacy was of a queen who took control of a prostrate king and a divided kingdom, and she was resented for her behaviour because of her sex due to conventions of the era. Another aspect of her queenship revolved around the fact that the 1399 usurpation set a precedent for possible contenders for the throne who claimed descent from Edward III. This would lead to the Wars of the Roses between Lancastrians and Yorkists. Another contributing factor was the proliferation of nobles who had royal blood in their veins and felt that the country needed a strong and decisive leader. This was the environment that Margaret was plunged into, and she was tied down by her husband, who was an ineffectual king, an anchor dragging down the house of Lancaster founded by his grandfather Henry IV.

Margaret was sixteen when she married Henry VI and did not bring a lucrative dowry to the union, but she had royal blood and was the daughter of Rene of Anjou and Isabelle of Lorraine, and her uncle was Charles VII of France. These connections made her a desirable bride for Henry VI, even though England after the loss of many of its French possessions was in a weak bargaining position for a bride with a more financially attractive dowry. Margaret of Anjou was served by the Duke of Bedford's wife Jacquetta of Luxembourg, who would form a close relationship with the new queen. She escorted the young Margaret from France to England for the marriage ceremony. Jacquetta also was present when Margaret finally gave birth to her son in 1453. These are interesting points of alignment since Jacquetta's daughter Elizabeth Woodville would marry the Yorkist king Edward IV, and this would be a complete reversal in alliances as the events of the Wars of the Roses unfolded a decade later.

Margaret of Anjou represented the truce with France and was considered by Henry VI as a symbolic representation of his peace initiative. Subsequently she would be aligned to the King's Council members who were in favour of peace with France. This was on the surface advantageous to Henry VI but in retrospect it was rather short-sighted. It did not take into consideration the contention that this union would produce among the baronage. Many of the leading nobles in England had profited from the war in France and did not want to see peace at any cost. The war-hawk nobles were to benefit from a lengthy war in France, since they could demand compensation for their outlay. This issue would play itself out in the next decade. Another, more biological reason for Henry VI to marry Margaret was the need of an heir to the throne of England. This would provide the much-needed security for the Lancastrian dynasty. However, it would take another eight and half years for Margaret of Anjou to conceive a child for Henry VI.

Margaret was accepted at court at first, but grew unpopular from 1449 onward. From the beginning Margaret exerted a pubescent charm upon her husband, convincing him to surrender the French province of Maine to the King of France, Charles VII as was stipulated in the Treaty of Tours in 1444. When King Henry VI conceded and relinquished control of Maine to France, he said he could not resist the pleas of his wife, 'our most dear and well-beloved companion the Queen, who has requested us to do this many times'.[60] This was a minor intrusion upon the king's prerogative to rule, but it was a preview of what Margaret would do to influence Henry VI's reign. On the other hand, Margaret had freed herself from another suspicion that previous queens had aroused through their large foreign entourages as she brought only a very small personal contingency with her to England.

As the war in France progressed and peace remained elusive, suspicion arose among the baronage against Margaret. She was not really guilty of the suspicion, but it was a question of guilt assigned to her by association. Her father had joined Charles VII against the English in 1449 and they swept through Normandy and mopped up the rest of the English-controlled provinces in France. This left Calais as the only English stronghold left on the Continent. Another event occurred that threw the war effort into disarray: the death of the Duke of Gloucester in 1449. He was an ardent supporter of the war since the death of Henry V. The loss of Gloucester was the death knell to sustaining the war in France. The loss of the French territory propelled the baronage into split camps on the conclusion of the war. Some felt disenfranchised and others profited, with ministerial positions

60 J. Stevenson (ed.), *Letter and papers illustrative of the wars of the English in France during the reign of Henry the sixth*, etc. (2 vols. In 3, RS, 1861–64), p. 495.

awarded by the king to those who supported the peace initiative. This did not bode well for a weak and indecisive king who could not bring these two factions into agreement with executive authority and force of will, two much-needed attributes lacking in Henry VI.

Margaret was unable to conceive a child during this period, and it seems there was no real reason for that. It may have been due to Henry VI's low libido, but there is not a conclusive historical record of this. The consequences of not having an heir complicated matters further. The major familial split occurred between the Beauforts and the Yorks. The preferential treatment towards Henry VI's Beaufort relatives proved to alienate the Yorks and especially the Duke of York. Margaret of Anjou became close to Edmund Beaufort, the Duke of Somerset, and also the Duke of Suffolk. She naturally rewarded loyalty and allied herself to like-minded barons. Since the Duke of York was the constable of Calais at this time, he would represent a contrary viewpoint to Henry and Margaret. However, it was not that simple since his popularity, especially among the nobles in the north, produced a rather powerful counterweight to the Lancastrian-led barons.

Margaret of Anjou's background was populated by women who had fought for influence for their husbands and did not retire from conflict or political disarray. Her mother and grandmother had in the past provided stalwart support to their husbands' positions. This was a female leadership legacy that Margaret was inheriting. Margaret of Anjou was now to provide her husband with decisive and strong support like her mother and grandmother had before her. It can be inferred that Henry welcomed Margaret's strong presence since he had been told what to do by his advisors throughout his minority as king. Henry VI may have felt better taking advice from Margaret, since she was his wife. This may have felt more like a partnership to Henry VI than his discussions with the ministers of his minority regency council.

Margaret's close relationship with the Duke of Suffolk came to be problematic in 1450. Suffolk was what her husband was not: decisive and a leader. He had also been close to Margaret from the beginning since he was the envoy who brought her to England to marry Henry VI. Margaret was a political neophyte to allow her alliance with Suffolk to appear so open. With the lack of an heir and rumours flying throughout the royal court, many opponents of Suffolk purported rumours of a love affair between himself and the queen. These were never proven, but the damage and factionalism it created grew exponentially. Suffolk and Margaret of Anjou seemed guilty of the Duke of Gloucester's death after she had pleaded with the king to imprison him; when Gloucester died during imprisonment it seemed like skulduggery was at play. There was no conclusive evidence that Gloucester had been murdered, but Suffolk's opponents wasted no time in spreading rumours of their complicity in Gloucester's death. Suffolk and Gloucester had been at odds over the war in France. The Duke of Gloucester was a pro-war proponent and this was contrary to Suffolk and Margaret of Anjou's stance on the war in France. This factionalism made for a suspicious atmosphere in court and Parliament.

The death of Gloucester and the final loss of Rouen in France led to a strong opposition against Suffolk in Parliament. He was deemed responsible for the defeat in France and imprisoned in early 1450, and England was thrown into a state of political chaos. The Duke of Suffolk left England in exile but was intercepted by malcontents; he was murdered and his head delivered to England. The king declared that the death of Suffolk was a crime, unlike that of Gloucester, which was an accident, and it was determined that the 'Kentish contingency' were associated. This sparked a vicious and strong opposition that became Jack Cade's rebellion. This rebellion had shades of the Peasants' Revolt of 1381, when mobs used violence to propel political viewpoints. Ralph Griffiths outlines the impact of Jack Cade's rebellion.

> The events of 1450–51 amounted to the most serious crisis encountered by the house of Lancaster since Henry IV's early days. Not since 1381 had the government in the realm been subjected to such a dangerous popular assault; the disastrous conduct of affairs at home and overseas by the king's ministers had not been condemned so harshly by the king's subject since then. On both occasions the protests were made in the aftermath of military humiliation and scandalous revelations of official corruption and malpractice. Whatever social attitudes or economic grievances may have predisposed Englishmen to assail their masters and rulers in 1450, the King's ministers, servants, and companions must bear a heavy responsibility for creating a situation in which the realm found itself.[61]

Margaret of Anjou did have a minor role to play in the long process of restoring order after Jack Cade's rebellion in the south-east of England. The venue in which Margaret was to display her role was in the form of the royal pardon. This was the traditional role that the queen executed to balance the executive authority of the king. A well-established tradition of the queen's intercession for pardon existed in historical precedent and was also displayed in ceremonial practice. It was more than a symbolic

---

61   Ralph A. Griffiths, *The Reign of King Henry VI: The exercise of royal authority, 1422–1461* (Berkeley: University of California Press, 1981), p. 649.

performance of the queen, executed through her own influence to display power to impact the course of events. However, this intercession was in fact limited for it actually only operated as an enabling device for the public and the political world, bringing mercy and justice into balance within the realm of the queen's authority. Furthermore, this allowed the king's authority a margin of rescission which did not let the king lose face in the public eye. Margaret's offer of a general pardon to Cade's insurgents may have been urged in order to reconcile the bulk of the population of the Kent area and to politically isolate the rebels. Events did leave a power vacuum after the death of the Duke of Suffolk, and this would lead to the ensuing rivalry between the Duke of York and the Duke of Somerset.

After the dust settled from the rebellion, two magnates emerged as powerful personalities who would exert influence over the weak and ineffectual King Henry VI. Edmund Beaufort, Duke of Somerset, descended from the Beaufort line of Gaunt and Swynford and his inheritance was tainted with an illegitimacy that was overturned by Richard II in 1397. It still remained the case that this cadet branch of the Plantagenets was one of association rather than direct lineage. Furthermore, Somerset was directly involved with the loss of power and provinces in France. He was the commanding noble who surrendered at Rouen and lost the Normandy province. Events in France were rapidly leading to a nationalistic policy of a united realm and no military action by the English could overturn this course of events. However, this was not evident to the English nobility and guilt would be assigned to whoever was present at the inevitable defeat. This was the loss of the last vestige of Henry V's legacy, and many in England were not prepared to accept the loss.

Another result of this defeat was scores of battle-hardened soldiers returning from France with little prospect of employment in a country that was in economic distress. This was a recipe for disaster given weak and ineffectual leadership that did not promise a prosperous future. Richard Plantagenet, Duke of York, was a direct descendant in the male line of Edward III through Lionel, Duke of Clarence, and was technically senior to the Lancastrian and Gaunt–Beaufort descendants. He was also one of the wealthiest landowners in the realm. Circumstances also aided the Duke of York as he was not held responsible for the losses in France since he was not present during that catastrophe. York had been appointed the Lord Lieutenant of Ireland in 1449 and this put him out of the firing line of defeat. He became the mouthpiece for the opposition to Lancastrian and Beaufort rule.

However, the Duke of Somerset had closer ties to the royal court and had the confidence of Margaret of Anjou. This put the Duke of York on the outside of the royal court, although he was generating support through Parliament, thus splitting the elite into the two political camps that would push for control of the crown. Somerset, being close to the king, had the support of Margaret of Anjou and this enabled him to take control of the government from 1450 to 1453. Unlike Suffolk before him, he now had to contend with harsh criticism and accusations of treason from the York faction in Parliament. This political landscape was bleak since opposition politics was rapidly approaching violence. Margaret of Anjou was also finding this atmosphere more unsettling, especially since the promises of a truce arising from her marriage were not coming to fruition. She was the obvious target of vitriolic opposition, and her French heritage was now a liability for England. Furthermore, at this juncture Margaret of Anjou had not produced an heir for the Lancastrian dynasty and this further alienated her from the nobility and the subjects of the realm.

The events of 1453 have been well argued by many historians from the male perspective, but I will delve into the female perspective of Margaret of Anjou's actions from 1452 to 1453. Margaret was Queen of England, and with that office comes privileges that need to be understood in the actions of the two main male protagonists. The Duke of Somerset was in a position of power and influence and flouted the authority of the Duke of York. The rising tensions came to a head in 1453 when three major events occurred. First the queen became pregnant with the much-anticipated heir to the throne. This was of course the duty which Margaret of Anjou was to perform to ensure the Lancastrian succession. Second was the final loss of the English forces in France, which imparted a devastating blow to the prestige of the country in general. Blame for this loss was going to be assigned, and the fact that the Duke of Somerset was in power made him vulnerable to this. The final event was the catatonic mental breakdown of the king, which now created a sense of uncertainty for the stability of the realm.

Unfortunately, due to historical circumstances Somerset was now placed at the epicentre of power for the Lancastrian reign. Unrest was breaking out across the country, especially in the Neville–Percy rivalry in the north, which threatened the clouds of war. The first notion that needs to be dispelled is the idea that anybody knew Henry would recover from his mentally and physically debilitating illness. A council was called in 1453, to which York was not invited at first. This was especially troubling in the light of the previous year's confrontation between York and Somerset at Dartford, which forced York from London. This was the beginning of York's seething resentment. Now that the king was completely incapacitated, the question arose as to who would rule the kingdom in his absence. Both York and Somerset felt they were the person for the job. This of course ignored Margaret of Anjou as a claimant, or even as part of the regency council itself. Margaret had also made the Duke of Somerset godfather to the heir apparent. This action further alienated the Duke of York, who was already exasperated by the fact that he had been excluded from the council.

Now let's look at the respective personalities of York and Somerset and how they might have been perceived by the queen. Somerset was in power and worked closely with the queen in what York saw as a sycophantic relationship. York on the other hand was an outsider and approached the queen in a more aggressive and threatening manner. When the council finally met, York was invited due to pressure from Parliament. He was joined by the Duke of Norfolk, and engaged in constant attacks against Somerset. The pendulum swung against Somerset in November 1453, when he was imprisoned in the tower. There were no formal charges against him but he was blamed for the general problems of the realm. This was of course a subjective political and personal allegation towards Somerset. The decision was made that York would lead the council in the king's absence. There was still opposition, but the general consensus was in favour of York.

Margaret's reaction to the events must be viewed through a female perspective to give it a sense of balance in continuity. Up to this point Margaret did not seem to display hatred towards York and in many ways tried to maintain a perspective of neutrality. Margaret now saw this move by York as a direct threat to her family. This was due to the arrogance and avarice York displayed, and he did not try to appeal to Margaret in any way. Somerset was the target of his attacks and Margaret was collateral damage in the assault. York was steamrolling over the authority of the queen, which also must have struck a blow towards Margaret's maternal concerns. This viewpoint is reiterated by Helen Maurer:

> Margaret would have viewed these developments with anxiety, if not alarm. As long as the King remained incompetent, formal arrangements would have to be made to govern the realm in his name. She would not have quibbled at that. Yet the long-term security of the dynasty and the preservation of the crown for her son demanded a reasonable unity of purpose among its lords. Whatever Somerset's intentions may have been – and there is no need to assume that they were anymore high-minded – York's action since his arrival in London guaranteed that personal antagonism and vendetta would not be set aside. Instead, they raised the stakes in the conflict. Margaret would not have had to believe that York aimed for the throne to understand that he had effectively sabotaged any hope of voluntary cooperation in support of the royal 'center'. Although Somerset's removal worked to York's advantage for the moment, it resolved nothing, but left a burning fuse.[62]

The governance of the realm was still in flux since many leading magnates were starting to draw their respective forces into alarming armed camps behind York and Somerset. This was the political maelstrom in which Margaret of Anjou found herself in 1454. In an act unseen since Eleanor of Provence was assigned

---

62   Helen E. Maurer, *Margaret of Anjou: Queenship and Power in Late Medieval England* (Suffolk: Boydell Press, 2003), p. 99.

the regency in 1253, Margaret proposed a bill where she would be regent in the absence of the king. Eleanor of Provence's regency had employed a council to execute her authority and to 'advise', but her position was still a strong step towards a queen as a ruling monarch. Margaret's motivation may not have been just to grab at power but to allay the developing threat of violence between the major magnates. She felt that the monarchy could provide a sense of objectivity above the baronage and perhaps cement a more cohesive policy that would not incite open warfare.

Margaret of Anjou's proposal for the regency suggests a determination to secure her son's interest in the realm for the future. It was an effort to put the monarchy at the epicentre of the crisis and instill a sense of loyalty in the nation, but the leading magnates were not prepared to take orders from the queen – a woman. Her proposal was not summarily dismissed but there were many obstacles present in fifteenth-century English society that pertained to the role of queen. The king could grant offices to a male, but these offices were not transferable to a woman during this time and if the queen was appointed regent it would presuppose a king that had full mental faculties to defer rule to her, which of course Henry VI was not capable at this juncture.

Perhaps the spectre of Isabella's regency rule and its corruptions through Mortimer was another obstacle for Margaret. If Henry VI died and she remained regent, she may have remarried and then this new husband would be a contender who could possibly usurp power through the vehicle of the queen. The queen's authority originated from the king's will and since he did not have that will it seemed antithesis to monarchal power at this time. However, this question will arise again in the next century with a rather different outcome when a queen will rule in her own right.

Parliament was not happy with either York or Margaret in charge of the realm, so many compromises were to be made. Gender is in play here, as a man appointed by the king would have authority and a separate will whereas a queen or wife would be subject to her husband or king's will. These are theoretical ideas in our minds today but during this era these were principles that were practised and believed. It would not be until English government evolved into a more bureaucratic institution that the delegation of power revolved around an office rather than a person. York's appointment is not a full regency either, since he was designated protector of the realm. This was displayed as if this power emanated from the king himself. This was an enabling fact that flew in the face of logic in this particular case. However, it created a sense of security, even though it may seem ridiculous to modern eyes.

The Duke of York was given a position that was rather limited in power and execution; he was to protect the kingdom from threats that were either foreign or domestic, but was not allowed a full regency. York was the first man in the council, which put him on a slightly higher plane than other council members but did not engender executive authority or power. This was a compromise since Parliament was not committed to any particular faction and the queen's authority did not appeal to the majority in Parliament. Margaret did, however, get her son the title Prince of Wales and the position of heir apparent, which may have placated her somewhat. In the end Margaret accepted the council and the Duke of York's role as protector of the realm. The precedent had been made that Margaret was at least a political player.

Margaret of Anjou was prohibited by circumstances in 1453 by the very nature of her husband's illness, which made it difficult for her to secure any legitimate royal authority in his absence due to mental illness. Eleanor of Aquitaine in the twelfth century had exercised informal royal powers during her son Richard's absence from England when he was on crusade in the Levant and during his subsequent ransom. Isabella of France on the other hand had exerted her royal power as queen to overcome the tyrannical reign of Edward II. The circumstances were different and events had taken place with the general consensus of the English nobility. Henry VI was neither physically absent nor was he a tyrant, and subsequently Margaret's abilities and decisive action were compromised by the fact that her husband was present and blameless. Thus we can conclude that if Margaret of Anjou went forward to fill the power vacuum left by the weak and ineffectual king, it would only further cloud the royal authority between her and her husband and emphasising the fact that a woman would be ruling instead of a man – the king. On the other hand, there are limits to what the Duke of York could do since he could only act as a subject and a private individual and not with the anointed power of a king, thus making his abilities to run the state less executive in nature and more oligarchic in practice.

Margaret of Anjou seemed to accept the protectorate under York's leadership, but she did not immediately drop out of sight, instead waiting for circumstances to turn in her favour. This occurred on 20 December 1454 when King Henry VI recovered with his faculties and found that he had a son and subsequently released the Duke of Somerset from the Tower and relieved the Duke of York of the protectorate. King Henry VI's return to power seemed to be clearly of his own prerogative no matter what the queen may have wished. There is no historical evidence that Margaret actively participated in the downfall of the Duke of York. Subsequently this also negated the need for Margaret to be regent, which might have reduced the tension between the Duke of York and Margaret of Anjou. However, this was not to be the case; events only served to further polarise the political factions between Lancaster and York. The release of Somerset lit the fuse; violence was inevitable.

Henry VI's public declaration of his faith in Somerset had ignited York's genuine concerns about any legal arbitration or justice to his position. Subsequently, the Duke of Somerset would not consider himself secure, for the problem of political and physical survival would remain the same, since now political negotiations were off the table. After Richard Neville, Earl of Salisbury, surrendered the chancellorship and the Duke of York fell from grace, a steady build-up of armed retinues began on both sides. Both York and the Earl of Warwick withdrew from court without the permission of the king and began to raise troops to counter the Duke of Somerset's threat, feeling certain they were to be marginalised. This standoff was quickly broken when Somerset summoned the nobility to a great council meeting at Leicester in May 1455. This was perceived by both York and Neville as a threatening manoeuvre intended to eradicate their political presence in Parliament.

The heavy and brooding clouds of war seemed to loom ominously. The Duke of Somerset left London for Leicester with King Henry VI riding happily at his side at the head of a large body of troops. This force of arms would be countered by the Yorkists as they mustered the largest army they could produce to counter the Duke of Somerset's threat. On 22 May 1455 the Duke of York and his forces intercepted the royal party at St Albans, approximately 20 miles north-west of London. At this fateful juncture it became clear that matters between these two factions had evolved from political division to bellicose confrontation.

Trevor Royle accurately and succinctly describes the events at St Albans in 1455 and their gravity for the period:

> As a battle, St Albans occupies a minor place in British military history, but its effects were long-lasting. Great magnates had taken up arms against an anointed king and created their own armies to enforce their will on the country's governance. In so doing, they had executed men loyal to the King – Henry was appalled by the news of Somerset's death, regarding it an illegal act – and the resulting enmity left lasting scars.
>
> Viewed dispassionately as a military action, St Albans was little more than a street brawl with heavy weapons. Once the Yorkists had broken the royalist lines and occupied the marketplace, known enemies, some of them great magnates, were singled out and dispatched with brutal ease. Others received debilitating wounds – Buckingham was wounded in the neck by an arrow, and Somerset's heir, the Earl of Dorset, had to be carried away in a cart, unable to walk. As the fighting died down, the people of St Albans suffered the usual pillaging that follows any battle of this kind, and the surrounding countryside was also subjected to violence by rampaging gangs of Yorkist troops. On that score, it was not very different from similar military actions of that period, but there was a good deal more significance to the battle than the triumph of arms by one side. The fighting in the streets of St Albans was also a bloody coup. As a result of the Yorkist intervention, the court party had been crushed, albeit temporarily, and its principal figurehead, Somerset, had been killed. This was exactly what York wanted – he counted Somerset a traitor and regarded him as a bitter rival whose baleful influence at court had resulted in the creation of wrongheaded policies. All along, that had been his complaint,

and now he had the satisfaction of knowing that his great rival had been permanently removed from the scene. Furthermore, the king was now under the control of the Yorkist faction, and the following day, Henry was escorted back to London. With a symbolism that could not have been misunderstood by anyone watching, the king rode between York and Salisbury while Warwick rode ahead carrying the sword of state. The mystique of kingship remained intact, but it was self-evident that Henry was firmly in hands of those who had defeated him.[63]

Richard, Duke of York, would soon find out that winning a kingdom by force of arms is one thing but ruling a kingdom by force of arms is another, since force, no matter how overwhelming, will always be received with bitter resentment. In the aftermath of St Albans, Margaret would see York as a clear and present danger to her Lancastrian family, and hell hath no fury like a woman scorned. Margaret would have seen that Henry had become a marionette whose strings were pulled by York and his close associates. No matter the nomenclature employed by York, the fact remained that the situation that had arisen was the result of military action and not proper royal ascension. The king's standard and person had been attacked, and this would have been a source of fear and bitter resentment for Margaret. The Duke of York's proclamation of loyalty and official acceptance of his oath to the king and Parliament did little to conceal the fact that the ascendancy they had gained had been through force of arms.

---

63 Trevor Royle, *Lancaster against York: The War of the Roses and the Foundation of Modern Britain* (Hampshire: Macmillan Palgrave, 2008), pp. 150–51.

Margaret of Anjou had now embarked upon a path to remedy the perceived wrongs she had seen perpetrated by the Duke of York, and this would lead to an inevitable confrontation between York and herself. Another, more humane viewpoint would be that Margaret saw herself as the mother of the Lancastrian cause and thus felt her duty was to protect her young son Edward and her husband, who was as vulnerable as her son due to his mental incapacities. The question then arises that challenges the traditional viewpoint of Margaret as the 'She-Wolf of France': was she an aggressor or was she simply protecting her family? Violence begets violence, but perhaps we need to ascertain the origins of this violence and refer to the words of H. G. Wells: 'The man who raises a fist has run out of ideas.' Did the Duke of York raise his fist first to initiate this war? This question still perplexes historians of the period. It could well be that Margaret, being a woman, was merely a victim of gender-based slander through the ages, and in fact was guilty only of responding to events with a passion and conviction – understandable to us today – that was out of character for a woman of her time. Perhaps her actions would not have been judged so harshly if they were carried out by a man.

Margaret's reactions can be seen in the closing days of York's second protectorate. This would be the time for her to take leadership of the Lancastrian cause. The collapse of York's second protectorate came about due to a disagreement over resumption and the levying of taxes that cost York the support of Parliament. The House of Commons took the lead in showing a resolute resistance to York's policies and sought a balance of lords in positions of power, a point that York would not concede. Both sides started to consolidate their respective forces through the years 1457 to 1458, and the balance started to shift towards Margaret. An interesting event occurred in 1458 in which King Henry VI proposed a 'loveday', a traditional ceremonial act to resolve local disputes through mutual cooperation. However, no loveday had ever been proposed for a feud encompassing the whole kingdom of England.

At this 'loveday' ceremony, the Duke of York and the Nevilles were to pay a symbolic financial compensation and offer holy masses for the souls of the lords who had died at St Albans. Subsequently, the fallen nobles were to be recognised as the king's loyal subjects. This was a purely ceremonial device, a political drama to emphasise a sort of placated unity among the nobility in England. This ceremony failed, for it did not alleviate the symptoms nor the causes of the conflict and in fact served only to entrench divisions. No attention was given to the grievances that drove York and his allies to draw their weapons at St Albans in the first place, since this sprang from the difficulty of securing justice and good government in a realm with a prostrate king who was incapable of ruling. In the end, it further polarised both sides and established the Duke of York on one side and the Lancastrian leadership on the other, undoubtedly led by the queen herself.

In 1459, Margaret of Anjou attempted to remove the Earl of Warwick from his position as Captain of Calais. She was unsuccessful, but this further alienated the Yorkist factions. Ralph Griffiths outlines this very concisely:

The earnest measures which the court [Margaret of Anjou/ Lancastrian-led regime] took to humble its enemies and fortify its own position in the realm had their dangers. As far as most of the English aristocracy were concerned, the court managed to retain their loyalty, though with varying degrees of enthusiasm. But the queen and her advisers showed little circumspection and less tact in some of their dealings, and their treatment of the Yorkist lords amounted to victimization. Nothing was done to remove the bitter legacy of St Albans until it was too late, and whatever short-term success the court's administrative, governmental, and military arrangements brought, they signally failed to reconcile the regime's enemies and even alienated other important interests.[64]

A council meeting had been called in late 1458 that was clearly made up of anti-Yorkist lords. This was an attempt by Margaret of Anjou to avert any violence by subduing the Duke of York and the Earl of Warwick. York, Salisbury and Warwick were all summoned and it appeared that only Warwick attended, and only then after receiving an additional summons. If the council intended on taking action against Warwick, whatever form that may have taken, he departed before any action could be officially taken against him. A brawl broke out between Warwick's men and those of the royal household while he was attending the council meeting and may have been viewed as an attempt on the earl's life. The historical record is not clear whether this was a planned attack or a spontaneous outbreak of violence arising from the prevailing atmosphere of factionalism.

Margaret of Anjou does not seem to have been committed to violence at this juncture, but she would see that bloodshed was inevitable in 1460. These instances of political drama were essentially the calm before the storm. Margaret was endeavouring to further isolate York and his allies, and this precipitated an

---

64   Ralph A. Griffiths, p. 799.

escalation of military preparations on both sides. Margaret realised at this point that her case for authority in the royal regime was to be decided on the battlefield and not by any legal or political processes.

The Yorkist forces were gathering in an aggressive, three-pronged offensive formation, with Salisbury raising a substantial army in the north while York raised men at Ludlow and Warwick arrived from Calais with another armed retinue to bolster the Yorkist cause. They were to confront the king in Coventry to make their respective demands at the point of a sword. Margaret was gathering forces to counter this threat, and her leadership was now becoming quite apparent. Margaret's behaviour was a divisive and symbolic display of her partisan leadership, portraying her womanly presence as a commanding element over her husband and her son, and this exposed her distinct vulnerability as a woman in an environment where political leadership still depended on the ability to lead men in battle. Margaret of Anjou did not have the martial ability to actually lead men in battle; she could only delegate such authority. The great magnates would see this, and either accept her authority or reject it wholesale.

The Battle of Blore Heath took place on 23 September 1459, and the outnumbered forces of Salisbury won a stunning victory over a Lancastrian army. This did not have any serious impact, since Margaret then rallied her forces and outmanoeuvred the Yorkist forces at Ludlow, where many deserted, evidently unprepared to fight against the anointed king. The main Yorkist leaders dispersed to Wales and Calais. The Lancastrians, led by Margaret, were able to call a parliament in November 1459 and effectively passed an Act of Attainder against the Yorkists and stripped them of their respective power, titles and lands. Unfortunately for Margaret they were not present to face these charges, and this was a victory on paper only. It also effectively forced all the Yorkists into an all-or-nothing situation.

This Act, which forfeited the Yorkists' lands, served to engender sympathy for the Yorkists among the nobility in general and perhaps mirrored the mistake that Richard II made in 1399 when he tried to absorb the Lancastrian estates. This effectively offered a collective cause to many magnates who were neutral, since they could see this as a violation of the constitutional parliamentarian procedures and a prelude to tyranny, and in this case a tyranny under the leadership of Margaret – a woman. The Yorkist forces flooded in from France spoiling for a fight and overwhelmed the Lancastrians at Northampton in July 1460 and took control of the king. Margaret faced a major upset when her husband was captured and her chief leading military magnates were killed. She was forced to retreat to Wales under the protection of her husband's half-brother and loyal Lancastrian Jasper Tudor.

Margaret would hear news of the defeat while sheltering at Harlech Castle in Wales. Her most feared outcome was to become reality when the Duke of York rode into London, not as defender of the king but symbolically as the king himself, with the appropriate royal standard above his head. York declared himself king in Parliament, expecting to hear cheers of acclamation, but was greeted with stolid silence and horror. It seemed that the Duke of York had overstepped his authority, and Parliament deliberated for about three weeks before coming to a decision. It was a compromise that settled the immediate threat but certainly sealed the fate of Margaret and her son: Henry VI was to remain king until his death, whereupon the Duke of York would accede to the throne. This disinheritance created little discord among the nobles, and it only made yet more warfare inevitable; Margaret was not going to accept her son being squeezed out of the royal line.

This was proof of what Margaret had believed ever since York shed blood at St Albans in 1455 – that this conflict could only be resolved by the total destruction of her enemy, the Duke of York. Margaret's public role was finally transformed in royal importance into that of a queen who would fight for her son's throne and her own power. Henry VI's captivity made Margaret of Anjou the leader of the Lancastrian dynasty, a claim that she would have to push forward with a clash of arms.

The Duke of York underestimated the Lancastrian forces and was caught off guard when he was trapped in his stronghold near Wakefield by the Duke of Somerset and Northumberland. He was massively outnumbered in men and supplies and the battle here saw the death of his son Edmund. Richard, Duke of York, subsequently rode out himself but was captured and summarily executed. The duke's head was mockingly displayed at York on the end of a pike wearing a paper crown, parodying his false pretensions of kingship. Salisbury was also captured and executed at Pontefract Castle, where Richard II died over half a century earlier. These brutal events effectively cemented the surviving Yorkists in a position that would only be remedied with their deaths or that of their enemies. The new Duke of York, Richard's son Edward, united with his cousin Warwick and the pair were now hell-bent on revenge and the supremacy of the Yorkist claim to the throne.

Margaret of Anjou's brutality and swift execution of justice upon York, his son Edmund and Salisbury displayed a viciousness that many in the realm were shocked to see in a queen. However, this is another instance where such actions carried out by a man would have been seen as typically ruthless Plantagenet strength.

Margaret recruited some Scottish soldiers, and the Lancastrian army headed south from York on a rampage of rape and pillage which hurt Margaret's cause and further fed the flames of resentment among the Yorkists. The Scottish contingent in the Lancastrian army, which Margaret and her leading commanders did little to control or restrain, sent London into a fear of a barbarian invasion from the Scottish hinterlands. This was an ancient fear springing from the constant border conflicts between England and Scotland through the centuries. Margaret's failure to follow up on her victory was down to resistance in London to this perceived barbarian horde. Furthermore, Henry's ineffectual rule shook the confidence of many loyal Lancastrians in the capital. The pillaging and raping done by Margaret's army was real, and the accounts spread like wildfire through the realm. This was also coupled with the brutal slaying of the Duke of York and the display of his severed head, which perpetuated the image of a bloodthirsty queen bent on a tyrannical rule. The gates of London were closed to Margaret, and she was denied supplies her army desperately needed. But she did not want to force London to capitulate by threats of violence, since this would erode all confidence in the legitimacy of her cause. She was forced to retreat to the north. On the other hand, Edward, the new Duke of York, displayed many of the desirable characteristics of a Plantagenet king. The gates of London were opened to his forces, and York and Warwick triumphantly entered the city. This was more of a popularity contest than a battle, and Edward was winning by some margin. Helen Castor outlines these actions with the following:

York had been Margaret's greatest enemy but not, it turned out, her greatest threat. At eighteen, Edward was everything her ineffectual and distracted husband was not. Unusually tall, strongly built, and jaw-droppingly handsome, he had irresistible charisma, combining easy bonhomie with an imperious will, and a shrewd political brain that had been honed by early experience as his father's trusted lieutenant. Amid the devastation of the Yorkists' military hopes, his precocious skill as a general had been demonstrated in his victory over Jasper Tudor's army at Mortimer's Cross. He was neither the treason-tainted political maverick that his father had been, nor the limp puppet that Henry now was. He looked more like a king than anyone had seen in years, and he could claim technical justification for the sudden suggestion that the crown might in fact be his, since Henry, so the argument went, in 'deciding' to rejoin Margaret at St Albans, had reneged on his oath to recognise York as his heir and in effect resigned his throne.[65]

The pendulum swung against Margaret due to her failure to unite the north and the south. Another problem was that Margaret represented a failed, ineffectual king, an heir in his minority and a weak ruling government. Conversely, Edward of York represented a fresh start. Eventually it was ruled that Edward of York would be the next king. However, this ephemeral crown, pushed through a factional minority Parliament, was really contingent upon Edward defeating the Lancastrian army in the field.

---

65   Helen Castor, *She-Wolves: The Women who Ruled England before Elizabeth* (New York: Harper/Perennial, 2011), p. 385.

Edward, now calling himself Edward IV, moved rapidly north after obtaining men, supplies and money to bolster his army. The two armies met at Towton on 29 March 1461. King would face 'king' and the battlefield would determine who would rule. It was a lengthy and very bloody battle, and the Yorkists emerged the clear victors. Margaret perhaps had a major handicap in his battle in that she could not be a personal physical presence on the battlefield. This has been argued from the time of Matilda and Eleanor of Aquitaine – an English medieval monarch was expected to lead soldiers in battle, and this was not a skill a medieval woman would be trained for. Edward IV was leading his men at the battle at Towton and could lead by example in a society where actions were more important than words, and this was the essential advantage the Yorkists had.

Henry VI's reign essentially ended on the battlefield of Towton, and Margaret of Anjou could not enact her political authority without a king. The vehicle for her power was removed from her grasp and she was effectively removed from the royal scene. Margaret was exiled to France with her husband and son, where she would garner support and money to support her cause. Unfortunately for Margaret, her uncle and ardent supporter Charles VII, King of France, had died, and she had to negotiate with the new king, the cagey Louis XI. Another setback for Margaret was the later capture and imprisonment of her husband by Warwick in 1465. Margaret lost some of her drive with the capture of her husband, but her son was growing into a young man and therefore held promise for a Lancastrian overthrow of the usurper, Edward IV. This opportunity would come, not through the machinations of Margaret but by the implosion of the Yorkist regime.

The fissure between the Yorkist Edward IV and the Earl of Warwick, precipitated by Edward IV's marriage to Elizabeth Woodville, began in 1464 and led to open betrayal by Warwick in 1471. Warwick, resentful of his loss of authority in the Yorkist regime, appealed to Margaret of Anjou. His sweetener was a marriage contract between his daughter Anne Neville and Margaret's son Prince Edward. This came with a pledge of loyalty and a military alliance to overthrow the Yorkist regime. Margaret did not trust Warwick but she saw this as her only viable option to regain the throne for her son. Their ensuing military actions led to a temporary ousting of Edward IV, but Warwick's death at Barnet in 1471 extinguished the flames of the Lancastrian coup. Margaret was forced back towards the west with the remnant of her army under her son's leadership. The end came at the Battle of Tewkesbury, where her beloved son was killed on the battlefield.

This last straw broke Margaret's resolve, and she was captured by Edward IV. The Yorkist king had killed the heir on the battlefield and captured both Henry and Margaret. Henry died in the Tower in dubious circumstances in 1471, probably on the orders of Edward IV. Margaret was to live in captivity before being ransomed by Louis XI. She would die penniless in France.

Margaret's exercise of power required the appearance of the king's authority, and the more passive, the more a puppet, Henry was perceived to be, the less it appeared that he had any authority that the queen could invoke or represent. The hollowness of the construct was revealed in her 'rescue' of the king at the second battle of St Albans and its aftermath. The striking thing about Margaret's quest for power is not the extent to which she offended gender expectations, but the effort she made to at least appear to live up to them.[66]

In conclusion it seems that Margaret suffered a twofold handicap in that she was a woman and she was French. Her gender and her foreign origins prompted a resentment in the English that could not be easily overcome. However, her perseverance and resolve does suggest a person with leadership qualities that were appropriate for a monarch of this period. She did have the key components to rule as her son's regent, but the ever-present and ineffectual king, her husband Henry VI, was a formidable obstacle for her to overcome, since he was neither a tyrant that created an impetus for overthrow nor a figure of popular hatred like Edward II or Richard II.

Margaret of Anjou was a key step on the path towards a fully-fledged queen with the authority to rule the realm of England. Margaret came too early for the English nation to accept her, a woman, as their executive monarchal leader. Shakespeare was the main culprit in describing Margaret of Anjou as the 'She-Wolf of France', which has coloured our perspective of this woman and queen through the ages. The vitriolic and acidic language employed to describe her character over the centuries has been coloured by subjective and misogynistic sources and Tudor propaganda. Margaret of Anjou ultimately represented a connection originating with Eleanor of Aquitaine and shadowing a long line of authority that evolved over 350 years to create an environment fertile enough to finally support a full regnant queen in 1553.

---

66   Helen E. Maurer, p. 211.

9

ELIZABETH WOODVILLE

Current scholarship of this period provides a nuanced understanding of Elizabeth Woodville's life based on the physical historical evidence and what we know of her contact with the major power players of her day. However, some romantic notions about Elizabeth Woodville and her interaction with Edward IV may be a historical exaggeration. The famous meeting under the oak tree in Whittelwood Forest near Grafton in 1461 was perhaps a 'meeting' place rather than the first place where Edward York met Elizabeth Woodville, as so dramatically depicted in the recent television series *The White Queen* and in literature. Instead, the encounter under the oak tree probably rekindled a long-standing acquaintance between Edward and Elizabeth. The York and Lancastrian camps had been mingling throughout Henry VI's reign and there would have been more than a passing awareness of each other at court. Elizabeth Woodville had known the nineteen-year-old King Edward IV's sexual propensities before that fateful meeting under the oak tree in 1461.

The two families, Woodvilles and Yorks, would both have been involved in political and military activities at the end of the Hundred

Years War in the 1440s. Sir Richard Woodville, Elizabeth's father, and Richard, Duke of York, Edward's father, were knighted by Henry VI at the very same ceremony in 1426. It was before either Elizabeth or Edward were born but indicates their respective family connections. The future Baron Rivers, Sir Richard Woodville, served with the Duke of York's French retinue at Pontoise in July 1441. Only nine months later, in April 1442, Edward was born at Rouen. Mary Clive, in her biography of Edward IV, ruminates that Jacquetta Woodville, former Duchess of Bedford, may have been witness and present in the room of his mother, Cecily Neville, the Duchess of York, when Edward IV was born, which is an intriguing aspect of the York–Woodville connection that would play itself out from 1461 to 1464. The tight-knit circle of the English nobility placed the two families in contiguity, peculiarly so during the Duke of York's first protectorate, during Henry VI's incapacity.

A year before the fateful Battle of St Albans, Richard, Duke of York, brought his son, the heir apparent to the York legacy, to Parliament at Reading for a lesson in power politics. The young Edward, then Earl of March, witnessed the political machinations in the royal court of Henry VI. The queen, Margaret of Anjou, would have had as one of her attendants the young Elizabeth Woodville, who may have made an impression upon the young Edward, perhaps in the form of a burgeoning desire. This could have been the spark that ignited this romance of the hearts of Edward and Elizabeth, and the emotional stirrings in the pubescent Edward. Would Elizabeth become the unattainable lady whom Edward could not resist in 1464? This speculation does follow some logic, based on the events that occurred between 1461 and 1464.

Elizabeth Woodvilles's mother, Jacquetta of Luxembourg, was the eldest child of the French Count of St Pol and Marguerite del Balzo, daughter to the Duke of Andrea in Apulia. This was a family that descended from Charlemagne and were cousins to the Holy Roman Emperor. Jacquetta grew up with war between France and England raging around her. At seventeen, she married John, Duke of Bedford, the youngest son of King Henry V, who had lost his first wife to plague in 1432. But their marriage created animosity between the Duke of Burgundy and England, and had a detrimental impact on the war effort in France. Burgundy at his time began a closer liaison with Charles VII of France.

John and Jacquetta were only married for two years when the duke died in 1435. The two-year marriage did not produce any children but Jacquetta retained her title as Duchess of Bedford and the dower associated with this title, although she was prohibited from re-marrying without the consent of the king, Henry VI. He instructed Jacquetta to come to England and ordered Sir Richard Woodville to escort her. Jacquetta fell for the young, dashing knight, but he was a lowly yeoman knight, far below Jacquetta in social status, a serious hindrance to their union. The couple married secretly, thus thwarting any plans King Henry may have had to marry her off to a wealthy English lord. The issue of their marriage was kept secret for fear of parliamentarian backlash and not obtaining the king's permission. The clandestine marriage probably took place in 1436. The couple's eldest child, Elizabeth, was born around 1437. The matter of the marriage between Jacquetta, dower Duchess of Bedford, and Sir Richard Woodville became a great scandal that year and Sir Richard was imprisoned.

Yet a precedent had been set by the king's mother, Katherine of Valois, who had married Owen Tudor without permission, in a prominent marriage with a squire below the station of the noblewoman. King Henry VI was therefore glad to pardon Jacquetta as a way of displaying the mercy shown to his mother. Subsequently Jacquetta's husband, Sir Richard Woodville, was pardoned and sent home. They settled into a fairly quiet life at Grafton Castle, where they had a large family of handsome sons and beautiful daughters, amongst whom Elizabeth was the brightest star in the brood. The Duchess of Bedford maintained her station as the king's aunt, while Katherine of Valois died in 1437, making the Duchess Jacquetta the first lady in the land until the marriage of the king in 1445. Her daughter, Elizabeth, took rank among the maids of honour of Margaret of Anjou, and was part of her court. Elizabeth Woodville made a match the same year with the heir of Lord Ferrers of Groby, John Grey, who was rich, valiant, and young. He also held military command in the queen's army.

An interesting comparison can be made between Sir Richard Woodville and Sir Thomas Holland in the previous century. Both knights sought matches with wives that had loftier titles than themselves but they both subsequently matched their wives' title and wealth with service to the king in war and on the tournament field. These two knights could also be looked at by their contemporaries as social climbers, but it seems that true affection and love was present in both Sir Thomas Holland and Sir Richard Woodville's marriages.

Elizabeth Woodville's childhood is not well documented and only a piecemeal storyline can be traced. The actual date of her marriage to her first husband, Sir John Grey, is not known, but Elizabeth lived with the Grey family from the age of age seven. It was a common practice during this period, which served to cement bonds between the families of the yeoman gentry, and arrangements were made early to marry Elizabeth Woodville to the Greys' eldest son, John, sometime between 1453 and 1455. The couple probably resided at the manor house at Astley, and had their first son in 1455. The second son may have been born in 1456. This small family experienced tragedy early since Sir John Grey was killed in 1461 in the second Battle of St Albans. The five years together would have given Elizabeth Woodville experience of managing the estates of the manor house while Sir John Grey was away at war. She would have also experienced the various ups and downs of this period, both of the wars in France and the battles between the Lancastrians and the Yorks for control of the crown.

Elizabeth Woodville was firmly attached to the Lancastrian cause, due to her mother and father's connection to the crown and, of course, her husband's service in the Lancastrian army. The Yorkist cause was handed defeat at Wakefield in 1460, where Richard, Duke of York, was killed. His head, along with his second son's, was displayed gruesomely on a pike at York as a future deterrent against Yorkist risings. This, of course, had the opposite impact on the Yorkist cause and further polarized resistance. The subsequent defeat of the Earl of Warwick in 1461 at St Albans was particularly problematic for the Yorkist cause since Lancastrians regained possession of Henry VI. These events led Warwick to crown York's son Edward, Earl of March, as the new king.

The death of the newly knighted Sir John Grey at St Albans in 1461 left Elizabeth Woodville a widow at the age of twenty-four. The great Yorkist victory at Towton effectively put Edward, Earl of March, on the throne as Edward IV, King of England. Both Elizabeth Woodville's father and brother were captured at the battle. Elizabeth retired with her two young boys to the manor at Grafton, to be with her mother Jacquetta. At this juncture in

Elizabeth's life, she was in a legal fight for the lands and estates left by her late husband Sir John Grey. Her mother-in-law claimed the dower lands following a recent marriage into a Yorkist family. It must have created a formidable stumbling block for Elizabeth's dower claim. This dispute was settled in 1463 on fairly amicable terms, for a portion of the dower lands were returned to Elizabeth Woodville through Lord Hastings as chamberlain, a close friend to Edward IV. Nonetheless, the exact status of the relationship between Elizabeth Woodville and Edward IV in this period from 1461 to 1464 remains somewhat clouded:

> No evidence proves that Hastings knew of the impending marriage between Elizabeth and the king, or that Edward IV was aware of this indenture, but it is inconceivable to think that either was uninformed. As Lord Chamberlain and intimate friend to Edward IV, Hastings was the logical man to facilitate the King's visit to Grafton, keeping the larger court ignorant of Edward's *inamorata*. Someone within his court had to explain the King's absences and cover his tracks. Who else but his chamberlain? Similarly, the King surely knew about – perhaps even arranged – the Hastings-Grey indenture. Elizabeth would never have endangered her impending marriage by excluding the King in negotiating such an important bond. It is equally inconceivable that Hastings would have contracted with Elizabeth without the King's approval.[67]

The meetings from 1461 to the official announcement of the marriage (in 1464) between Edward IV and Elizabeth Woodville

---

67 Arlene Okerlund, *Elizabeth: England's Slandered Queen* (Gloucestershire: The History Press, 2006 [2009]), p. 59.

seemed to have been facilitated by Lord Hastings and Lady Jacquetta, Elizabeth's mother. This was a rather sensitive and personal issue. Discretion was necessary to protect both the Woodvilles and the king. The recent book and television series *The White Queen* truncates the events of 1461–64 to a short courtship period. It is, of course, the convention of fiction and movies to keep the narrative rolling, but the real events of history often seem to move more slowly and cautiously. During this period Elizabeth Woodville and her family lived quietly, remaining obscure to the throne and royal court, while she was busy reclaiming her lost lands for her Grey sons.

Meanwhile, Edward IV was consolidating his power base and busy unifying England's political, financial and social structure after the expulsion of the Lancastrians. Edward and Elizabeth's relationship was a secret liaison that was kept from the king's counsellors and, especially, his cousin the Earl of Warwick. The only person who was aware of the relationship and pending marriage was probably Lord William Hastings. The marriage was a private ceremony, if not a secret one. Edward IV made a visit to Stratford on 30 April 1464 while he was on his way to northern territories to meet another threat from the Lancastrians. The next morning, on 1 May, the king rode without his entourage to Grafton where he secretly married Lady Elizabeth Woodville in the presence of Jacquetta, a priest, perhaps two other witnesses and a young boy who helped the priest sing holy mass in celebration of the union. The couple consummated the marriage before Edward IV returned to his counsellors and entourage, declaring he had been hunting in solitude, an excuse that was plausible since Edward had always liked the solitude of hunting and riding since he was boy. Edward found excuses to visit Grafton on several other occasions while he remained in the vicinity, when he presumably made conjugal visits with his new wife Elizabeth.

Edward finally announced his marriage to Lady Elizabeth Woodville in a council meeting in Reading in September 1464. There is no contemporary historical record of this 'official' announcement but we can easily imagine the reaction to this union. There were no doubt concerns and doubts from the royal court and counsellors about the king's bride of choice. The first major objection would arise from the conventions of the time that a king made a marriage for the political benefit of the realm. An advantageous marriage that would bring alliances, a dowry and other considerable financial or political gains would be of paramount importance. Yet this marriage was a personal choice that would effectively bifurcate the major noble houses in the royal court.

The major player who would have felt it as a personal affront would of course have been Richard Neville, the Earl of Warwick. He may have felt a sense of betrayal in not being in the inner circle of Edward's decision on a bride. Warwick would certainly have felt politically and socially humiliated, because the marriage to Elizabeth ran counter to his negotiations for Edward IV to take a French wife, the Princess Bona. This had been a painstakingly long and hard negotiation that Warwick felt would have benefited the young king's realm and was a necessary political marriage to ensure the stability of the English crown. This clandestine marriage was the first major fissure between the cousins, and it undermined the authority and power Warwick had over the young king. Other nobles would have shared this view with Warwick and the sudden surprise of the Woodville marriage would have caused consternation and alarm amongst the baronage. It shows the obvious independence with which Edward wanted to mark his reign. What better way to defy the perceived power that gained him the throne? Edward had already heaped honours and lands upon Warwick and his respective followers, and Edward may have been aware that many perceived him as merely a puppet of Warwick's. Now he would spread his own wings to fly the course he himself had chosen. This was not perceived by Warwick and the some of the nobles as independence, but more of an act of betrayal. However, Edward's decision to marry Elizabeth Woodville needs to be understood from a personal perspective. Many have attributed it to youth and a rather impulsive and impetuous attraction to an unsuitable bride. However, Edward may have seen this as an opportunity to display his own authority in the personal arena, and may have felt he had the right to choose who to marry. It can also be seen as an act of rebellion against overbearing powers that dictated his every move. Now that he was king, he may have felt he had the prerogative to act as he felt best. Another possible motive was that Edward wanted to create a new circle of power around himself, bound to him by marriage and loyalty, through which he could better exert his authority.

The shift of power would have its consequences. It would focus Warwick's anger and vindictive actions against the Woodville family. It would also inflame Warwick into open rebellion against his young cousin. Warwick would not have seen this as treason but as the supplanting of a power group – the Woodvilles. Whatever the exact personal motives behind Edward's decision, it was a fait accompli that had to be digested by his royal court. Elizabeth Woodville was not entirely without any positive attributes to bring to her role. Her family may have been less than perfect in the highly competitive arena of the English nobility, but she herself had the characteristics of a strong, intelligent and independent woman with ability to augment the king's authority, even if it was an authority many resented. Warwick and his allies would have definitely viewed the Woodvilles, and especially Elizabeth, as parvenus seeking power and authority far beyond their birthrights. However, there are some contemporary accounts of Elizabeth that looked at this union in a more positive light, such as Antonio Cornazzano's:

It is worth noting that the chapter on Elizabeth Woodville is one of only two chapters devoted to contemporary women, which seems to indicate that the romantic story of her marriage to Edward IV made some impression on the courtly circles in which Cornazzano moved.

Cornazzano's account of the marriage of Edward and Elizabeth was thus written not more than four years after the event. It is essentially a pleasant tale, not an historian's or chronicler's version. The chapter is entitled ' The Queen of England', and Elizabeth is not mentioned by name. Further, there are some inaccuracies. The scene is set in a city, in which the king has his court, and a palace which is or can be approached by water, i.e. presumably London, whereas Elizabeth was residing at Grafton in Northamptonshire at the time of her marriage. This is a serious error, and in addition it forces Cornazzano to make the king's passion for Elizabeth common knowledge among his courtiers, and renders it difficult to credit that the king was able to keep the actual marriage secret. Elizabeth is also described as pregnant when the marriage was divulged, but in fact her first child, Elizabeth, was not born until February 1466, nearly eighteen months after the ceremony in Reading Abbey, in which she was honoured as queen. Cornazzano, though presenting her as a widow, does not mention her two sons by her first husband, and calls her young, which in the context of fifteenth-century Italy, makes one think of a girl of sixteen rather than of a woman of twenty-six or twenty-seven. These inaccuracies, though serious, do not, however, detract from the interest of this text, which resides in the general lines of Cornazzano's story. For what we are presented with is an account of virtue triumphant: an Elizabeth firmly and courageously resisting the enamoured Edward's attempts to make her his paramour, willing, as Cornazzano says, to risk death rather than dishonour, and gaining the reward for her constancy by finally and dramatically becoming the king's wife. This is a well-known version of the events leading up to the marriage of Edward and Elizabeth, but up till now it has not been supported by any really contemporary testimony. The only fifteenth-century chronicle which in any way reflects this version is *The Fragment Chronicle*.[68]

Edward wanted to overcome the doubts about his choice of bride, so he was determined to make her coronation as queen resplendent with pomp and circumstance, and imbued with regal authority. The coronation of Elizabeth was a grand event and enhanced her qualities in the eyes of the realm through careful use of symbolism.

The king himself began the rituals at the Tower of London on Ascension Day, 23 May 1465, by inducting forty-three men into the Knights of the Bath. Included among the newly designated knights were the queen's brothers, Richard and John Woodville, along with nobles who were already or would be married into the Woodville family. The coronation ceremonies commenced

---

68 Conor Fahey, 'The Marriage of Edward IV and Elizabeth Woodville: A New Italian Source', in *The English Historical Review*, vol. 76, no. 301, (Oct. 1961), pp. 662–4.

with the Duke of Clarence, Edward IV's brother and Steward of England, dramatically riding to Westminster Hall on horseback. This was a careful piece of staged political and social drama to awe the audience. Clarence was followed by the Earl of Arundel, Constable of England, and the royal butler for the feast. The Duke of Norfolk, Marshall of England, also arrived on horseback, richly endowed in golden regalia. Elizabeth's Burgundian royal connections were referenced among her regal attributes. The two saints, her namesakes St Elizabeth, mothers of St John the Baptist and St Mary, were used to make a clear pious connection that would imbue the ceremony with religious legitimacy. All of this would serve to validate her presence as queen and her rightful place as wife to the king. Ultimately the coronation would be seen as a bridge to former Lancastrians and bolster Edward's efforts to unify his royal court. The coronation can be viewed as a rather shrewd and wise political move towards a unified realm. Elizabeth was now queen and she had to execute her duties as consort to the king in a regal manner, no matter the consequences. Warwick's official reaction to the coronation seemed to be a rather tempered one, as outlined in Michael Hicks' biography of Warwick:

Warwick was disappointed, even dismayed, as he himself reported, but he was not humiliated by public promises about Edward's marriage that he could not keep. He was not actually in France as once supposed. He recognized that he must make the best of the King's choice. It was Warwick himself, on Michaelmas Day 1464, who conducted his new Queen into Reading Abbey, who stood godfather to her eldest daughter and presided at her churching. He missed her coronation, where Clarence stood steward, because he was on a mission abroad. He made no recorded objections to the Woodville marriages... [69]

Many aspects of the union caused concern for Warwick but he understood his official role and the proper time and place to stage his objections. However, he would soon find himself overruled in his familiar role, and this would serve to grow his resentment and anger over the next few years.

From 1465 to 1469, tensions would rise steadily between the king and Warwick over the presumptive powers the Woodvilles were exercising over his reign. There was not any one event but rather a gradual build-up of events that would lead to disaster. Marriages between Woodville family members and the aristocracy were to prompt his bitter resolve to act against the queen and her family.

Warwick was especially infuriated since he had two daughters of his own, Isabella and Anne, for whom he wanted politically advantageous unions. In 1465 Warwick had captured the hapless Henry VI and expected accolades and recognition from the king for his swift and decisive actions. Since the aristocratic well of marriages was drying up quickly, due to the Woodvilles' inundation of the marriage market, Warwick proposed to marry his daughter Isabella to the king's brother George, the Duke of Clarence. Warwick was refused this and it no doubt created much turmoil for the Nevilles. It does not seem that Edward IV was intentionally alienating Warwick, but this was the net result of his actions. Some of the Woodville marriages were to close relatives of Warwick's, which further antagonised him. Elizabeth's father, Richard Woodville, was made Lord Treasurer of England

---

69 Michael Hicks, *Warwick the Kingmaker* (Oxford: Blackwell, 1998), pp. 258–9.

in 1466 and subsequently made an earl later that year. This would put him at the same titular level as Warwick, which must have made him keenly resentful of the power shift around the throne. 1466 was also the year in which Elizabeth had her first child with Edward: Elizabeth of York was born on 11 February that year.

It was, of course, the main duty of the queen consort to produce heirs for the Yorkist regime. She would prove to be rather successful in that regard. The royal physicians, employing their study of astrology, assured King Edward IV that his expected child would prove to be a boy – an heir. The king, who was deeply influenced by such myth and lore, had persuaded himself that the infant would wear the crown of England. But the child that was born was a girl, to the dismay of the king and his physicians. In fact, this first-born child of Edward and Elizabeth would further the family line of the Yorks through marriage to the Tudor King Henry VII in 1486. From humble beginnings do great things grow, and this would be the legacy of Elizabeth of York, since all kings and queens of England follow her ancient lineage to this day.

As Elizabeth grew her brood of Yorkist children for Edward, the political landscape would shift in the following year when Edward dismissed Warwick's brother George Neville from the office of Chancellor of England. This was a public affront to the Neville family and especially to the Earl of Warwick. It would lead to open defiance from Warwick in 1468 when he refused a summons by the king to court, due to the fact that Earl Rivers and other Woodvilles were present. He was finally convinced to attend the king but the tensions were rising to a boiling point that would result in a series of bellicose events the following year. Elizabeth started to notice this turmoil, but had no idea how far events would eventually proceed. She had a prodigious period of childbearing from 1467 to 1469, all girls up to the birth of Cecily. The royal princesses were growing in number but there was no male heir to Edward's Yorkist line. This was a source of some trepidation for Elizabeth and Edward, and created an opportunity for Warwick and the Duke of Clarence, Edward's brother.

The Earl of Warwick was senior to Edward IV by fourteen years and harboured the belief that he was more able to rule England than the young king, who had for so long been obsessed with carnal pleasures and courtly games. Warwick was forty years old and felt this was the time to make moves to control the throne and oust the upstart Woodvilles. The earl was full of himself and proud of his royal blood that was traced back to John of Gaunt and Katherine Swynford, a union that was legitimised in 1397 by Richard II but opposed by Henry IV.

In the light of the usurpation of 1399 it was an uncertain environment that created this power struggle for the crown. It seemed a precedent had been set so that any extended cadet branch of Edward III's lineage could assert authority to influence or even usurp a weakened throne. Trouble broke out in Yorkshire in 1469, in reaction to the problems of King Edward IV's reign and local economic issues. It is not clear if Warwick was himself directly responsible for these uprisings, but they did provide him with an opportunity to convince Edward that the Nevilles, and not his favourites the Woodvilles, were the real power behind his throne. The uprisings were led and directed by an obscure individual known as Robin of Redesdale. The true identity of Redesdale was probably Sir John Conyers of Hornby, the Earl of Warwick's cousin by marriage. The events were engineered to bring Edward closer to Warwick but backfired in many ways and led Warwick to commit more extreme acts. While Edward was quelling the rebellion with the help of his brother Richard, the Duke of Gloucester, and Earl Rivers, Warwick and the Duke of Clarence secretly travelled to Calais. This voyage to France had the most defiant objective in mind. Warwick had arranged for the Duke of Clarence to marry his daughter Isabel. There were two obstacles to this union: the first was consanguinity, since Warwick's daughter and the Duke of Clarence were related to a forbidden degree, and a papal dispensation had to be obtained. This was achieved through Warwick's many connections. The other obstacle was that King Edward IV had expressly forbade the marriage, but Warwick defied his authority and went forward with it anyway in France, away from the king's authority. This was a portent that Warwick was ready to put George, Duke of Clarence on the throne over his brother Edward, should he need to. With his daughter married to the heir, he would have greater control over the monarchy.

Warwick now crossed the line into treason by raising an army, with help from Louis XI, which landed and began to gather forces in Kent. This news blindsided both Edward and Elizabeth, for Elizabeth was making a royal visit to Norwich and realised the treachery that the marriage of Warwick's daughter to Edward's brother represented. Since Edward had no male heirs, his brother George, Duke of Clarence, was next in line for the throne and, if he should have a son with Isabela, it would make his claim stronger. In July 1469, Warwick and his men captured, Edward IV and imprisoned him in one of his strongholds. Elizabeth was then devastated to hear that Warwick had captured her father, Earl Rivers, and her brother, Sir John Woodville, and had them summarily executed without a trial. Elizabeth's father and brother were beheaded with no mercy. This brutal act of retribution towards

Elizabeth cemented her hatred for both Warwick and Edward's brother. The vitriolic language now aimed at dishonouring the Woodvilles made an indelible mark on the historic record that would stain its reputation to the present day. Warwick publicly declared his hatred and 'justification' for his acts with the following,

> ... the deceivable, covetous rule and guiding of certain seditious persons: that is to say, the Lord Rivers; the Duchess of Bedford, his wife; Sir William Herbert, Earl of Pembroke; Humphrey Stafford, Earl of Devonshire; the Lords Scales and Audeley; Sir John Wydeville [Woodville], and his brothers; Sir John Fogg, and others of their mischievous rule, opinions, and assent, which have caused our said sovereign Lord and his said realm to fall in great poverty of misery, disturbing the ministrations of the laws, only intending to their own promotions and enriching.[70]

Warwick did not stop there. He now employed a well-known tactic by accusing Elizabeth's mother, Jacquetta, of witchcraft. As we have seen, this had been used in the recent past against Joanna of Navarre and other aristocratic women. It was an open act of treason against the king, but Warwick had the king in custody and was contemplating his next course of action. Warwick might have considered declaring Edward illegitimate and replacing him with the Duke of Clarence but the support was not there for such an outrageous act of sedition. It would rely on the rumour that Cecily Neville, the Duchess of York, had committed adultery with the

---

70   John Warkworth, *A Chronicle of the First Thirteen Years of the Reign of King Edward the Fourth*, ed. James Orchand Halliwell (London, 1839), p. 46. Cited from Arlene Okerlund, *Elizabeth: England's Slandered Queen* (Gloucestershire: The History Press, 2006 [2009]), p. 112.

Welsh archer Blaybourne. It is unlikely that this would have carried much validity unless the Duchess of York would substantiate it herself. This was highly unlikely, but the rumour would resurface again in 1483 when Richard III seized the throne and wove the historical fiction for political reasons, just as Warwick considered doing in 1469. The Earl of Warwick's plan seems to stall at this juncture and, without a clear and precise plan, he was forced to release Edward.

Since her father and brother had been executed by Warwick, Elizabeth herself had been in a very vulnerable position in London, with her three daughters and her mother on trial for witchcraft. Her husband was imprisoned, and it seemed that Warwick was holding all the cards. But the tide of events changed rapidly when her husband was released, after Warwick could not secure the support for his coup from parliament. Edward was able to reassert his authority and regain his throne. Once Edward was secure again he was able to clear the charges of witchcraft against Elizabeth's mother, Jacquetta, but this was still a desperate period for Elizabeth and the Woodvilles with many wounds remaining open that would not be easily healed. The Duchess of York, Edward's mother Cecily Neville, worked hard to secure a reconciliation between Edward, his brother, the Duke of Clarence, and his cousin the Earl of Warwick. Edward, with great resentment from his wife, issued pardons to both his brother and Warwick, in an attempt to reunify his authority. But would Warwick's ambition be satiated or was this just a respite for the next series of tumultuous events? Rebellion broke out almost immediately after the reconciliation and both Warwick and the Duke of Clarence were behind this uprising. They both fled to Calais to escape the wrath of Edward IV, who now accepted that they were never going to acquiesce. Edward immediately ordered Calais to refuse a safe port for Warwick, who had to divert to Honfleur. This was particularly problematic since his daughter Isabel was due to give birth to the Duke of Clarence's child. Unfortunately, she gave birth to a stillborn due to the rough seas and an heir for Warwick and Clarence was not to be.

Warwick began to lay plans for a new scheme. He sought out the King of France. Louis XI began negotiations between Warwick and Margaret of Anjou to restore the Lancastrian monarchy. This was a case in which war and politics made strange bedfellows. It was a very unlikely alliance but it seemed that Warwick had no other recourse and felt that he could still be a maker of kings, even if it was a weak and ineffectual king, in Henry VI. Further, he proposed a marriage between his younger daughter, Anne Neville, and Queen Margaret of Anjou's son, Prince Edward of Lancaster. This would give Warwick a stake in the Lancastrian monarchy through his daughter. Margaret of Anjou was suspicious of Warwick and his motives, and even tested his loyalty by keeping him in a kneeled position at the cathedral at Angers, to clearly assert her higher status. Margaret and Warwick swore fealty to each other and agreed the match. The plan was simple: Warwick was to land a force and gather Lancastrian loyalists to invade south. Once he gained control of the country and Henry VI, Margaret would land in the south near Wales and link up with Jasper Tudor. With her son, Prince Edward of Lancaster, she would consolidate control of England under Lancastrian rule. Warwick was successful in taking London and Henry VI, and he cut off Edward IV with help from his Neville allies. This forced Edward IV to flee the country with his closest retinue: his brother Richard, Duke of Gloucester, together with the young Earl Rivers and his chamberlain, Lord Hastings.

They arrived in Holland where King Edward IV was supported by his wife's relative the Duke of Burgundy, who supplied ships and money to raise a substantial force that would enable Edward to return to England to fight another day.

The period of Edward's exile was particularly hard on Elizabeth Woodville, for she was understandably fearful of her life and any retribution that Warwick would exact upon her and her family. She was also pregnant with her fourth child. Elizabeth Woodville sought sanctuary at Westminster to protect herself, her children and her mother. She delivered her first son, Edward, during this period in sanctuary. This was a gleaming light of hope, for she had delivered the much anticipated heir to the Yorkist throne. It solidified her position as queen, but the circumstances were far from ideal. Under canon law, sanctuary was a right guaranteed by the medieval church to anyone who required protection from secular powers. Criminals could enter a church and subsequently register themselves in the church's sanctuary register book to escape pursuit and arrest. This practise was particularly disturbing to merchants who disliked sanctuary since it protected felons and debtors alike. But this power of canon law over secular law had been supported by kings of England since the time of Edward III. There were only two crimes in which sanctuary would not protect the individual: sacrilege against the Church and high treason.

The series of events that followed tipped fortune in favour of Elizabeth. Margaret of Anjou oversaw the marriage of Anne Neville to Prince Edward of Lancaster in Amboise, France, in December 1470. This secured the alliance between Warwick and Margaret and the ground was laid for the defection of George, Duke of Clarence, to his brother Edward IV. The Duke of Clarence was not a politically astute person but he saw no gain in an alliance with Warwick. Overtures were made through his mother, Cecily Neville, but when Edward IV returned with an army to face Warwick at Barnet, George joined his brother on the Banbury road. The Duke of Clarence also brought about 4,000 men to fight for Edward and his brother Richard, Duke of Gloucester. Edward was also assisted by the Duke of Burgundy due to his rivalry with the King of France. Burgundy was also influenced by the cordial relations enjoyed between the Woodville family and the Burgundians earlier in Edward's reign. Edward IV now sent message to Elizabeth of his arrival in England and pending arrival in London. Edward entered the city in April 1471 with the support of the people. He then restored his crown and went to Westminster to retrieve his queen and newborn son.

Edward's son had been born under inauspicious circumstances while Elizabeth was in sanctuary. The conditions in which she delivered the child were barely above squalor, but at least the family was safe from other dangers. Furthermore, Jacquetta was ever-present, having been released from Warwick's clutches after the failed accusations of witchcraft – a comfort that Elizabeth surely welcomed during this period. Elizabeth and Edward's reunion was a respite from his exile but the threat of Warwick was still looming. Edward prepared his army and went to meet Warwick outside London at Barnet. The Battle of Barnet would be a long and hard-fought battle. It began at dawn on 14 April, 1471 and once again Edward fought valiantly with his brothers. After a long morning of bitter fighting, Warwick was dead and Edward IV was the clear victor. Margaret of Anjou heard of the loss but refused to surrender and marshalled her forces west to link up with Jasper Tudor's forces in Wales. Edward displayed great tactical verve in moving his troops swiftly to intercept Margaret's forces at Tewkesbury. Edward again prevailed by defeating the forces of Margaret led by the Duke of Somerset and her son, Prince Edward. The Lancastrian forces were routed and the Yorkist army claimed victory again. Margaret of Anjou's son, Prince Edward of Lancaster, died at Tewkesbury leaving Anne Neville a widow and no heir for the Lancasters. Somerset had no hope of pardon from Edward IV and sought sanctuary in Tewkesbury Abbey, but Edward forcibly extricated him and had him executed in the marketplace. Edward IV himself and his royal family had been seriously threatened by these stout Lancaster supporters, but did their crimes really justify the violation of sanctuary? These actions may have stained Edward's sterling reputation as a chivalric knight, but these were the fortunes of war. Perhaps, if Elizabeth was present to intercede, there may have been more mercy shown to Somerset. Pribnce Edward of Lancaster was also executed.

In the aftermath of Tewkesbury, Anne Neville and Margaret of Anjou were pardoned. Margaret was imprisoned in the Tower and Anne was given into the custodial care of the Duke of Clarence. Edward entered London triumphantly once again and secured his throne. Henry VI, who was in the Tower, died under dubious circumstances. It was officially declared that he died of depression but it seemed clear he was murdered. This was an act to extinguish the threat of any future Lancaster plots to usurp the crown. It is a matter of speculation who actually committed the deed, but it was ultimately to Edward's advantage to secure his throne and family for the future. Perhaps the circumstances were like Henry II, when he declared someone 'rid me of this wretched priest' with the murder of Thomas Beckett in 1170, where others acted on their own to carry out the king's apparent wishes. Edward consolidated his power by having the all the magnates swear allegiance to his reign, and subsequently created his newborn son the Prince of Wales. Margaret of Anjou was imprisoned for four years and then ransomed to King Louis XI of France, who later absconded her lands in Anjou for his crown. Elizabeth was finally able to feel safe since the period of rebellion and wars seemed to be over.

Elizabeth enjoyed this period of peace from 1472–83 but it was not without its problems. She and Edward were secure on the throne and much loved by their subjects, but internal York family rivalries would rear there ugly head in the aftermath of the destructive battles of 1469–71. Elizabeth experienced a great loss in 1472 when her mother Jacquetta died. We can speculate that the loss of her mother was a tragedy in Elizabeth's life, since her mother's encouragement and influence had helped Elizabeth in times of trouble – and there were many. Jacquetta was instrumental in the courtship and marriage of Edward and Elizabeth, and she was always a steadfast presence and pillar of security for Elizabeth on major royal occasions. Many of Elizabeth and Edward's political opponents, including Warwick, regarded her as a political asset who had to be disarmed, as evidenced by the dubious witchcraft accusations against her. Elizabeth's mother encompassed many qualities of a great medieval noblewoman and, perhaps, without her guidance and example Elizabeth Woodville may not have become queen.

Elizabeth's brothers-in-law would continue to cause problems within the royal family. It would seem natural that Elizabeth harboured deep resentment towards Edward's brother, the Duke of Clarence, for his involvement in the death of her father and brother, even though Edward pardoned the Duke of Clarence and welcomed him back into the family to promote unity amongst his nobles. Edward's brother George was anticipating a large Neville inheritance through his wife Isabel. However, Edward's younger brother wanted to marry the other Neville daughter, Anne.

This would effectively split the vast Warwick estates. Edward IV approved of the marriage between Anne and Richard, his younger brother, but this angered the Duke of Clarence and engendered deceptive and dishonourable behaviour: since he had custodial care of Anne Neville, he attempted to prevent Richard from marrying her. Edward IV was then forced to adjudicate between his two brothers. He did this in a most fair manner by splitting the vast Neville fortune amongst the two sisters, Isabel and Anne. Yet this created resentment in his brother George, who would reveal a covetousness and treachery that would lead to his ultimate downfall.

The degree to which the York boys and Neville girls were related was in fact in complete disregard of canon law. A papal dispensation would have been the proper channel to a lawful union but this was not to be. The marriages violated the laws of consanguinity since the parties were first cousins once removed. But this was the least of the family's worries by the 1470s. The Duke of Clarence had two children with his wife Isabel Neville but she died in 1476, only six weeks after the birth of the couples' second child. He approached the king about a proposed marriage between himself and the daughter of Duke of Burgundy, who had recently died. This would put the Duke of Clarence in a powerful position and possibly threaten Edward's reign. Edward promptly refused, which infuriated his brother and precipitated hatred and resentment that would be aimed at Elizabeth Woodville and her family. However, the decision was clearly Edward IV's and he had every reason not to completely trust his brother, especially in the light of recent events with Warwick. George, Duke of Clarence, began to make a series of challenges to the authority of the king which even implicated him in a possible plot against the king.

After the death of his wife in 1376 he executed his authority at Warwick Castle against persons he claimed poisoned his wife and tried to poison his child. These were clearly false accusations and it was a clear abuse of the duke's authority. If this was not enough George then defended a man, Burdet, who had been accused of sedition, attempting to foment rebellion and plotting the murder of Edward IV and his son. Since Burdet was a close associate of the Duke of Clarence it had thrown suspicion on Edward's brother George. However, he challenged the authority of the court and the king on the execution of Burdet, and this was in a very public forum. Edward was forced to arrest and try his brother on high treason. Parliament found George, Duke of Clarence, guilty and sentenced him to death. He was executed in February 1478, and the means of his execution is subject to lore and myth: was he drown in a vat of Malmsey Madeira wine? The net result was that Edward tried and convicted his brother to death. The emotional tumult this created amongst the York family must have shaken their core. Elizabeth Woodville does not seem to have any direct connection to the Duke of Clarence's death but she, no doubt, felt it justified in light of her personal animosity towards him. Elizabeth would attract blame for the Duke of Clarence's execution five years later, when Richard usurped the throne and spread many rumours and falsehoods to justify his claim to power. This would of course discredit the Woodvilles and Elizabeth would be the prime target of his allegations.

The final years of Edward's reign were marked by prosperity and happiness for Elizabeth. She delivered four more children including a son, Richard, in 1473, and three daughters, Anne in 1475, Katherine in 1479 and Bridget in 1480. The succession of pregnancies Elizabeth endured was evidence that she maintained a conjugal relationship with Edward and retained her husband's affections, notwithstanding his many improprieties and infidelities. His two known mistresses were Elizabeth Jane Shore and Elizabeth Lucy, but they exerted very little influence over court politics. Edward IV did not formally acknowledge his bastards and there was no record of awards and titles, or even a presence at court for the illegitimate offspring.

Edward IV's health, which was marked by corpulence and over indulgence, started to decline by Christmas 1482, but this did not deter the grand, resplendent celebrations at Westminster. Edward corrupted his body after 1471 with a detrimental diet and debauchery, but the rapidity and the acuteness of his illness in early 1483 indicates a disease or virus rather than general poor health. In March 1483, Edward IV became acutely ill and was bedridden. The exact nature of Edward's sicknesses are unknown, and contemporaries attributed it to a variety of causes that mimic symptoms of a wide array of diseases. Diagnostic medicine was primitive during this period and we may never know the main cause. The illness claimed his life and Edward IV died, aged forty, on 9 April 1483. This left Elizabeth Woodville a widow at the age of forty-six and her future was once again uncertain.

The series of events that followed are highly debated amongst historians. Here, the mystery of the princes in the tower and the rise to power of Richard III can be examined from the perspective of Elizabeth Woodville. Cruel as it was, the behaviour of King Richard III was perhaps not so exceptional in a successful medieval English king. Popularity and affability were not always important or necessary qualities for a monarch. Some of the most successful monarchs of England, from the Norman Conquest to this period, were utterly ruthless and displayed an avarice that was fed by greed. Similarly, the behaviour of Elizabeth Woodville was that of a successful medieval queen who exerted influence and power through her relationship with the king and her influence on the succession. This, inevitably, stirred resentment and resulted in an unflattering portrait of Elizabeth Woodville by her opponents. The images of Richard and Elizabeth have both been solidified by partisan historical accounts that have taken on, often unconsciously, some of the slander and vitriol of the original sources.

There were two major groups that controlled power upon the death of Edward IV. Firstly, there were the Woodvilles and Elizabeth, who had raised the princes and influenced Edward V. Their power was resented by the opposition group in Parliament, which grew rapidly after the death of Edward IV. They were led by the Duke of Gloucester, Lord Hastings, Duke of Suffolk, and the Duke of Buckingham. This second group felt that the Woodvilles had too much control of the state and that this should be redressed. However, what transpired was a coup that resulted in Richard, Duke of Gloucester usurping the throne from his nephews. The fate of Edward V and Richard has become one of the most notorious debates in English history. Elizabeth's reaction raises some questions as to who may have killed them: she was willing to reconcile with Richard III, which would have been extraordinarily difficult to do, believing the king murdered her sons, his nephews. A possible answer is that the Duke of Buckingham murdered Elizabeth Woodville's sons, possibly to strengthen a claim to the throne of his own. This claim came through his lineage going back to Thomas Woodstock, youngest son of Edward III. He was a vain and disturbed man who may have thought, in the fog of conflict over succession, that he could prevail over Richard III and blame him for the death of the Yorkist heirs. Richard III may have privately declared this to Elizabeth Woodville but did not want it in the public arena, where it would undermine his authority as king. Elizabeth may have been complicit with Richard III because she had no other options, fearing for the survival of herself and her daughters. Yet Elizabeth arranged the betrothal of her eldest daughter Elizabeth of York to the Earl of Richmond, Henry Tudor. This precipitated a series of events that would force Richard III to the battlefield at Bosworth in 1485. As we will see in the next chapter on Elizabeth of York, there were rumours that she would marry her uncle Richard III, in the aftermath of the king's son and Queen Anne's deaths. But Elizabeth prevailed and, when Richard III fell on the battlefield at Bosworth, her daughter would marry the victorious Henry Tudor. The Woodville bloodline would survive to be a key element in the founding of the Tudor dynasty.

Elizabeth Woodville was restored as the queen dowager by Henry VII in 1485 and maintained a subdued role in the royal court. She was cordially received but kept politically distant from any real power. Henry VII continued to send grants to maintain Elizabeth Woodville at Bermondsey Abbey, which was remote but still present. Elizabeth died there on 8 June 1492. It was a surprisingly modest funeral. Her daughter could not travel to it due to her confinement during pregnancy, and the king and his ministers did not attend. Elizabeth had requested a pious ceremony at her funeral and this was granted. Her burial represents the end of an era and the passing of the last of the medieval queens. Her daughter, Elizabeth of York, was the beneficiary of Elizabeth Woodville's legacy and became the face of a new, more modern renaissance queen.

Elizabeth Woodville set a dramatic precedent for English royalty. When she married Edward IV in 1464, it was the first time that a king had married a member of the gentry. The marriage of John of Gaunt and Katherine Swynford could be a close comparison, but Gaunt was never king and Swynford was his third wife. The York-Woodville marriage was of a different order of importance to the monarchy. It could be concluded that the king's choice of a wife upset the balance of power amongst the aristocracy and created animosity that fed a time of turmoil. However, on a personal level, it was a successful marriage between a husband and wife: Elizabeth and Edward clearly loved one another, despite all the political pressures, family tragedy and the king's infidelities.

The trials and tribulations the couple suffered were overcome by their mutual respect, but the predatory environment of fifteenth-century politics took its toll on Elizabeth and her family, including the loss of her sons. She did live to see, however, a good marriage between her daughter Elizabeth and Henry Tudor, which would usher in a new era, with her offspring on the throne of England. She must be judged, by any measure, to be a remarkable woman who cast a long shadow on queenship in England, particularly in the form of her great-granddaughter, Elizabeth Tudor, one of the greatest monarchs of England.

10

ELIZABETH OF YORK

... she thanked him for his many Curtesies and friendly

... as before ...

in the cause of ...

and then she prayed him to be a mediator for her to the K ...

ge who (as she wrote) was her onely joy and maker in ...

Worlde, and that she was his ... harte, in thoughts, in ... and in all,

and then she intimated that the better halfe of Ffe ... was paste, and

that she feared the Queene would neu ...[71]

When the midst and last of February was past, the Lady Elizabeth, being more impatient and jealous of the success anyone knew or conceived, writes a letter to the Duke of Norfolk, intimating first that he was the man in whom she affied, in respect of that love her father had ever bore him, etc. Then she congratulates his many courtesies and friendly offices, in continuance of which she desires

---

71   Reproduced by A. N. Kincaid, 'Buck and the Elizabeth of York Letter: A Reply to Dr. Hanham' in *The Ricardian*, vol. 8, no. 101 (1988), pp. 46–9.

him, as before, to be a mediator for her to the King in the behalf of
the marriage propounded between them; who, as she wrote, was
her only joy and maker in the world; and that she was his in heart
and thought, withal insinuating that the better part of February
was past, and that she feared the Queen would never die.[72]

The infamous Buck letter quoted above is the surviving actual
text and has been a controversial piece of historical evidence
in the historiography of Elizabeth of York. The second passage
is a heavily revised version written by George Buck's nephew.
We are now dealing with a copy of a copy with revisions. This
can hardly be determined as historical evidence. This being
said, it seems there may be some validity in the Buck letter's
content. I find there was a lot of political subterfuge surrounding
Richard III's reign starting with the *Titulus Regius,* evidence and
accusations of the murder of the princes in the Tower – Edward
and Richard of York – and the relationship between Richard III
and Elizabeth of York. One has to sift through the contemporary
rumours and myths and then shift to the Tudor propaganda and
ultimately to Shakespeare. This is a formidable wall of inexact
historical evidence that needs to be objectively filtered through.

Richard III is perceived by many to be the villain of the
piece and much vitriol has been poured upon him over the
centuries. In 1485 Richard III was in a critical position that
made his kingship a very precarious enterprise and his only
aim would have been to use all the advantages he felt would
continue his monarchy. The contemporary rumours indicated

---

72 Egerton MS. 2216; Bodleian MS. Malone 1; Fisher MS., University of
    Toronto; Additional MS. 27422, Cited from Alison Weir, *Elizabeth of York:
    A Tudor Queen and Her World* (New York: Ballantine Books, 2013), p. 131.

he either murdered or ordered the murder of his nephews, but the rumours were not substantiated at the time (or since). The murder of children would have been an act that would have united a rebellion against the king in and would have been in the historical record. This never happened. Furthermore, Richard was seeking marriages and alliances to secure his throne and may have considered all options to further his cause. There was a record of Richard officially denouncing his intentions of marrying his niece, Elizabeth of York, two weeks after his wife's death. Whether this was a response to the persistent rumours or a paranoid king attempting to pacify his nobles, we cannot determine, but since he made this proclamation there may have been some truth in it, enough to motivate his denunciation. The motivation for Elizabeth of York to write such a letter is a little less clear. Alison Weir states the following is a possible reason for Elizabeth's 'love letter':

> Her becoming Queen would restore their lost prestige; and she would have been in a position to use her influence on their behalf, particularly in regard to finding husbands for her sisters. The advantages of such a marriage were sufficiently powerful considerations to outweigh any propulsion of fear she might have felt, and Elizabeth probably saw it as the only way of ensuring her own and her family's future security.

This does ring true but the incestuous elements of such a union would negate many of the benefits outlined by Weir. Furthermore, damaging rumours against Richard III had been circulating since his ascent to the throne in 1483. This could be another one of those rumours, but one powerful enough to induce an official proclamation in March and April of 1485 by Richard III himself. Another point against such a proposed union between uncle and niece was the fact that Richard III officially denounced the York line from Edward IV as illegitimate in the *Titulus Regius,* which would include Elizabeth of York. What would be the advantage of marrying an illegitimate niece? Elizabeth of York's letter outlined by Buck could be a historical reality, but perhaps one that has been misread through the ages due to its incongruity. I conclude that the Buck letter, if we are to accept its historical providence, was an attempt to play both sides in an outcome that was not certain before the Battle of Bosworth Field. I also think that it may also have been influenced (or even drafted) by Elizabeth Woodville, in an attempt to protect her daughter and family in such an uncertain and deadly environment. This much-debated source starts our last chapter on Elizabeth of York and displays a nuanced and much more complex queen than previously thought.

The whirlwind romance that occurred between Elizabeth of York's parents, Edward IV and Elizabeth Woodville, in 1461–64 was the backdrop against which our future Tudor queen would rise. The environment that young Elizabeth of York was immersed in during the first five years of her life was a tumultuous one. Elizabeth of York would have been surrounded by her Woodville family, including Jacquetta, Richard Woodville, and the many siblings Elizabeth Woodville had as part of a large family. The first child to Edward IV and Elizabeth Woodville was received with great honour within the royal family and court. She was joined by her sister Mary in August 1467 and then Cecily in 1469 and a brother, Edward, in 1470. This was a healthy and strong sibling network for Elizabeth of York to grow up with. However, the events of 1469–71 would create a period of instability for young Elizabeth and she experienced the uncertainty of the royal throne and the uprisings in various rebellions during the Wars of the Roses that her father, the king, had to overcome. At this tender young age, Elizabeth of York would experience the insecurity of the royal court and the general turmoil amongst the nobles in the kingdom. It is impossible to gauge the impact that this trauma would have had on her in 1469, but we can speculate it was most definitely impactful.

We know now through modern science and psychoanalytical theories that the personality of individuals are formed and influenced primarily by experiences as a child, especially between the ages of five to fourteen. Elizabeth of York, at the age of three, experienced the execution of her grandfather and uncle in 1469 and then the uncertain and dangerous circumstances of sanctuary for the queen, her mother Jacquetta, and Elizabeth and her sisters. The dramatic change of environment from the security and splendor of the royal court to the squalor and insecurity of sanctuary in Westminster Abbey was a life-changing event. The secure world Elizabeth of York experienced as a young girl was dramatically ripped from her; however, she did become closer to her mother and sisters and would have drawn on that strength for the future.

After the events of the Warwick revolt and the stabilisation of the royal court Elizabeth of York's duty to her family was to marry a foreign prince to enrich and expand the influence of the dynasty. There were many proposed political marriages for her but none came to fruition during 1471–83. Upon her father's death in 1483, her life was to take a distinctly different path.

Her brothers, Edward and Richard, were taken into 'protective' custody by her uncle Richard, Duke of Gloucester. Now a young woman of sixteen, she understood court politics and power plays made by her family the and the Yorkist contingency led by her uncle. The series of events that saw Richard, Duke of Gloucester, usurp the throne and the heir apparent princes mysteriously disappeared created an uncertain future for Elizabeth York. When Richard became king and started to exert his power throughout the kingdom, he started to destroy and execute the Woodville family members including Elizabeth of York's beloved uncle Anthony Woodville. Elizabeth found herself once again in sanctuary in Westminster Abbey with her mother and sisters. The uncertain fate of her brothers weighed heavily upon her mother and would have affected Elizabeth herself.

The widowed Queen Elizabeth Woodville and her daughters did not have many choices. Elizabeth Woodville and Margaret Beaufort may have been involved in the many plots to overthrow Richard III, which culminated in the failed invasion attempt of Henry Tudor and the execution of Buckingham. After these failed attempts to overthrow Richard III, the parliament of January 1484 passed the statute *Titulus Regius* stating that Edward IV and Elizabeth's secret marriage of twenty years before was invalid and had been of great presumption: 'Without them knowing of the assent of the laws of this land and by sorcery and witchcraft'. The dowager queen herself stood accused of having employed witchcraft and magic to enchant Edward IV. Further evidence supposedly derived, or better yet, manufactured, from two sources that stated Edward IV had been engaged, if not actually already married, to the dame Eleanor

Butler. However, she was dead and so could not confirm or deny these assertions. The end result was a legal confirmation that Edward IV's children with Elizabeth Woodville were prohibited from inheriting the throne. Elizabeth Woodville's position was compromised when Richard III discovered her liaison with Margaret Beaufort and the betrothal of her daughter Elizabeth of York to Beaufort's son Henry Tudor. Elizabeth of York would engage in the dangerous game of playing both sides for the best advantage for herself and her family. This was the best strategy in such a cut-throat environment and she displayed great verve and energy in pursuing this course of action.

Elizabeth Woodville agreed to leave sanctuary in early 1484 on the condition that Richard III swear a public oath to do her no harm and protect her children. This oath suggests that the dowager queen Elizabeth may have believed that Richard III was guilty of having her York sons killed. She was now faced with few options, and there was increasing pressure for her to leave her confinement at Westminster. The dowager queen acted in the best interest of her daughters and realised that sanctuary may not be the safest option due to the incidents of sanctuary violation at Tewkesbury by her very own husband a decade earlier. Events of this turbulent era display the frequency with which people were forced to ally themselveswith even mortal enemies – a good example of this was of course the Earl of Warwick and Margaret of Anjou's alliance in 1469–71. Physical and political survival during this time in the Middle Ages was defined by intense pragmatism and the lack of choice. Appearing to concede to Richard III's demands in early 1484 was the plain and simple politics of survival for Elizabeth Woodville; she could not have predicted that Henry Tudor would successfully invade in 1485. Elizabeth surmised that Richard may retain the throne for decades and the fortunes of herself and her daughters were dependent on his favour. The dowager queen exchanged her sanctuary for another form of imprisonment; however Princess Elizabeth of York was to stay at the royal court of Richard III at Westminster. It is unclear whether this was at the request of Richard III or whether Elizabeth of York went of her own accord. Perhaps Richard III was aware of the oath Henry Tudor had sworn to marry Elizabeth of York the previous year and wanted to keep her away from this dangerous liaison which would threaten his throne. Suffced to say, the events outlined at the beginning of this chapter throw sufficient suspicion on Richard III's motives in keeping young Elizabeth of York close by. She was in a precarious situation by being in her uncle's court and by being betrothed to his arch enemy; she was also to be a pawn in the much larger game of thrones for England.

The Battle of Bosworth Field and the defeat and death of Richard III changed the very landscape of England forever. It also shifted the fortunes of Elizabeth of York to her Tudor future. Henry Tudor was crowned King Henry VII on 30 October 1485 in a splendid coronation at Westminster Abbey. The wedding between Elizabeth of York and Henry VII did not take place for another three months. This is not to suggest Henry was not keen for the match, as some historians have concluded. Henry VII had to consolidate his power and repeal many Acts in Parliament. One of the important acts in parliament that was repealed was the *Titulus Regius*, which restored the dowager queen Elizabeth Woodville's reputation and title. This rescinded Elizabeth York's illegitimacy and created a stable environment for the marriage. Elizabeth of York married Henry VII on 16 January 1486. The political expediency for Henry VII was to display himself as a king in his own right and not through his wife. That was the reason for the delay in the marriage from his coronation. Furthermore, Elizabeth of York was to deliver their first child, Arthur, nine months after the marriage. It was then a full year before Elizabeth was crowned queen, in November 1487. This was to play down the York popularity and to create a new Tudor dynasty with powerful symbols of unity after such divisive wars the previous decades. In February 1487 the royal council was assembled to strip Elizabeth Woodville of all her possessions due to her complicity with Richard III and placing her daughters, specifically Elizabeth of York, in his household. This was done to separate the former dowager queen from an intrigue of court politics that could damage the Tudor throne. It seemed Elizabeth Woodville voluntarily surrendered her lands and decided to follow the tradition of widowed queens by retiring to a life of contemplation. Francis Bacon suggested that Elizabeth Woodville thought her daughter was disparaged by her marriage to Henry and that it did not advance but rather depressed Elizabeth of York's life and that she had therefore collaborated in the Simnel plot. This seems highly unlikely since Elizabeth was far too experienced in political matters to be involved with a plot to overthrow her son-in-law and daughter's throne. Further, why would she have worked so hard to arrange the marriage between her daughter and Henry Tudor just to plot to destroy what she had endeavoured so hard to make happen. This seemed highly unlikely since in February 1487 Henry VII showed the true Earl of Warwick in the streets of London, he was clearly concerned about rumours of an uprising, but why would Elizabeth Woodville involve herself in such a conspiracy? Her loyalties laid with the future of her daughter, the queen. There is strong evidence that Henry VII never seriously doubted Elizabeth Woodville's loyalty either. A Woodville commanded 2,000 troops during Henry VII's reign at the Battle of Stoke Field, which indicated his faith and trust in the Woodville family. Furthermore, Henry proposed a third marriage to Elizabeth Woodville, which was part of the three-year Scottish truce in 1486; why would Henry VII put forth this idea if he felt her intention was to overthrow his reign and thereby her own daughter? The historical evidence suggests that she, like Joanna of Navarre earlier in the century, was simply inconveniently rich and Henry wanted her dower and he put her into a convent to get her out of the way. This may seem insensitive due to what Elizabeth Woodville had endured and his treatment of her was not especially kind, and further it does not reflect well on Elizabeth of York that she apparently acquiesced in his plan to take the lands from her own mother. The last five years of Elizabeth Woodville's life were spent at Bermondsey Abbey and she did not attend her daughter's coronation or the second lying-in of Elizabeth of York's pregnancy in 1489, of her second child. Elizabeth Woodville died at Bermondsey Abbey on 8 June 1492. It was a surprisingly modest funeral. Her daughter did not attend due to her confinement during pregnancy and the king and his ministers did not attend. She requested a pious ceremony, which was granted. The funeral represented the end of an era and the passing of the last of the medieval queens. The funeral of Elizabeth Woodville in 1492 was a pathetic and sad reality of Tudor political expediency and the effective separation of the old Yorkist regime from the new Tudor regime.

Henry VII has always had a reputation as a selfish, calculating and miserly king, and his treatment of his wife's family does nothing to repudiate this. Elizabeth of York's sisters – Bridget, Cecily and Katherine – were entitled by their Yorkist descent to a share of their royal inheritance, but Henry quietly absorbed those estates into his own. Furthermore, he did nothing to provide the princesses with dowries. This could be the reason for the humble matches made by the York daughters of Edward IV, for without substantial dowries, diplomatic foreign matches would not occur. Bridget gave up and entered the convent at Dartmouth priory, from where she corresponded with her sister Elizabeth for the rest of her life. Katherine of York married the Earl of Devon, William Lord Courtney, and Cecily of York married John, Viscount Wells, who was half-brother to Margaret Beaufort. Elizabeth of York rendered financial assistance for each of these marriages with allowances for her sisters and annuities for their respective husbands.

Elizabeth of York's relationship with her ambitious, highly pious and domineering mother-in-law has been described politely as congenial but was historically imbued with ambiguity. In public the relationship was cordial but there seemed to be an undercurrent of control by Margaret Beaufort over her daughter-in-law. Elizabeth of York may have resented this control but the tranquillity of the realm was her overwhelming concern and she would not do anything to jeopardize this. Furthermore, she wanted to maintain the appearance of serenity in court. The Spanish ambassador reported the enmity between the two women in the subjection that Queen Elizabeth of York was to endure from Margaret Beaufort. Elizabeth and Henry had a loving and faithful relationship, but the king's mother was at the forefront of

Henry VII's life in all political concerns of the realm. There was one interesting intellectual pursuit that both women shared: they both had an apparent enthusiasm for cultivated literary pursuits. Elizabeth and Margaret were early supporters of the printing press.

Elizabeth of York was successful in providing a Tudor heir for her husband's reign. Elizabeth was a far different queen than her mother and dispensed her duties in a much more subdued and less tumultuous manner than Elizabeth Woodville. However, both mother and daughter provided their respective husbands with a healthy brood of heirs for the throne. The baby whose birth had prevented Elizabeth from attending her mother's funeral was named for her deceased mother, but the child died in infancy. Elizabeth of York was to lose two more children, Edmund in 1499 and her last child, Katherine, in 1503, but she gave birth to two healthy sons – Arthur in 1486 and Henry in 1491 – and two daughters – Margaret in 1489 and Mary in 1495. Henry VII was determined to control the marriages of his own children and consolidate the Tudor dynasty by connecting them to the greatest royal houses in Europe. The plans for Arthur's marriage began in earnest in 1489 with the Treaty of Medina del Campo, which provided an alliance between England and the recently united Spanish kingdoms of Aragon and Castile. The marriage between Katherine of Aragon, the youngest daughter Ferdinand and Isabella of Spain, and the eldest son of Elizabeth of York and Henry VII was arranged and finalised in 1490. It was to be a very prestigious union that descended from a distant relation with the English royal family going back to John of Gaunt. This was to be the most celebrated marriage and alliance since Katherine of Valois and Henry V in 1420. Alison Weir outlines this in her recent biography:

> In March 1489 the marriage between Prince Arthur and Katherine of Aragon was finally agreed upon with the conclusion of the Treaty of Medina del Campo, which provided for the Infanta to bring to England a dowry of 200,000 crowns (20 million pounds sterling). This treaty, ratified by the king on September 23 1490, was arguably Henry VII's greatest achievement in foreign policy, as it established the Tudor dynasty in the top rank of European monarchies – although it was to be many years before the marriage took place, and at times during those years it would seem as if it might not take place at all.[73]

Elizabeth of York was a willing participant in her husband's plan for the royal family and her queenship displayed a complicity that enlarged and solidified the Tudor monarchy. Her familial and royal duties were the major determining factors in Queen Elizabeth's actions. The dominant presence of Margaret Beaufort was a factor that Queen Elizabeth took in her stride and we can see a marked difference in her attitude towards her royal in-laws versus her mother's, which was more adversarial. The preservation and stability of her royal family was always paramount to Elizabeth and she would ensure her achievements would be determined by her actions as queen, and this could be in contrast to her personal feelings. Hers was a noble and duty-oriented queenship rather than

---

73 Alison Weir, *Elizabeth of York: A Tudor Queen and Her World* (New York: Ballantine Books, 2013), pp. 293–4.

one marked by her own personal and political aspirations. Elizabeth was the model consort and she immersed herself in the education of her children. She distanced herself from her York family background but was sympathetic to some of the Yorkist causes when it did not impact the royal family. It cannot be determined whether Elizabeth's pious and modest lifestyle was a result of her personality or the wishes and desires of her husband. Perhaps moderation was the determining factor in her queenship:

> Impeccably connected, beautiful, ceremonious, fruitful, devout, compassionate, generous, and kind, Elizabeth fulfilled every expectation of her contemporaries. Her goodness shines forth in the sources, and it is not surprising that she was greatly loved. She had overcome severe tragedies and setbacks, and emerged triumphant. We have seen how it is possible to reconcile her much debated actions before her marriage with the gentle Queen who emerges after it. Certainly the sources show that, as Queen, she played a greater political role than that with which most historians have credited her, and that she was active with in her traditional area of influence. It is also clear that, far from being in subjection to Henry VII and Margaret Beaufort, she enjoyed a generally happy relationship with both of them[74]

There were events during her queenship that challenged the Tudor monarchy and her loyalty was unquestionably to her husband. The two major revolts that occurred – Lambert Simnel and Perkin Warbeck – were the most unsettling events of Elizabeth's life.

---

74 Alison Weir, *Elizabeth of York: A Tudor Queen and Her World* (New York: Ballantine Books, 2013), pp. 444–5.

The Lambert Simnel revolt, which resulted in a Tudor victory at Stoke in 1487, was a Yorkist threat to Henry's throne by claiming Simnel was Edward, Earl of Warwick, son of George, Duke of Clarence, and therefore rightful heir to the throne. This was a dubious claim that many diehard Yorkist's rallied behind and was quickly put down by Henry VII. Elizabeth of York never acknowledged the Yorkist pretender and she loyally backed the Tudor cause. This last battle of the Wars of the Roses solidified Elizabeth of York's future with the Tudors and Henry VII. She was the vehicle for the security of the Tudor throne by producing a male heir and this put her future squarely with the Tudor family. The rumours of Elizabeth's mother's involvement in this plot were never proven but her association was something Henry would be suspicious of in this tenuous period of his reign. Henry VII cautiously handled Elizabeth Woodville to secure his throne, but did not want to alienate his wife's family completely – just politically nullify any threat they may pose. Henry VII was generous to Simnel and put him to work in the royal kitchens and eventually he became the royal falconer. This displayed the confidence Henry had in his reign and displayed compassion for his subjects. This event, however, did compel Henry VII to create a network of spies and informants that would serve his kingship well.

The other major threat to the Tudor monarchy and Elizabeth came in 1495–97 and was a little closer to Elizabeth's heart. Perkin Warbeck was claiming to be Richard of York, the brother of Elizabeth of York and a surviving prince in the tower. The identity of this imposter seemed to be confirmed to be false by Henry and most likely this influenced Elizabeth's attitudes towards this claimant. There are two elements that I think would have influenced Elizabeth of York. The first was her mother, who was already dead, and her future was not with her Yorkist past but with her then current Tudor family. The second would be that Elizabeth now had a family and so had a vested interest in the success of the Tudor monarchy, and to see her children ascend the throne. Her position as queen would also be in jeopardy if she embraced the Yorkist pretender. At this juncture Elizabeth would have been more aware of the political wrangling that was occurring to unseat the Tudor monarchy and she would have viewed this as political intrigue rather than any idealist Yorkist monarchal pursuit. Elizabeth was keen to support anyone who helped her family but this was a clear threat to her queenship and her royal family. She may have had some curiosity but the subterfuge that revolved around this uprising seemed to indicate Elizabeth's disbelief in the identity of Perking Warbeck as her brother.

Another point of fact was the support of Sir William Stanley, previously an ardent supporter of the Tudor reign, for the uprising against Henry VII. Stanley's motivation would have thrown doubt on Perkin Warbeck's identity too since it seemed he was motivated by the resentment he harboured because he was not made a peer and the fact that the power of the nobility had been severely truncated by the king's central control on government. Stanley was executed for his part in the plot to overthrow Henry VII and this effectively ended the threat. Warbeck was shown a degree of leniency as he was imprisoned in the tower. However, he escaped and sought sanctuary in 1498 and was subsequently recaptured. This time it had been revealed he plotted with Edward, Earl of Warwick, and this proved to be his end. There is some speculation as to whether the plot with Warwick was a fabrication to eliminate two threats for Henry. It seemed Elizabeth was doubtful of Warbeck's identity but she displayed sensitivity to his plight and this may have been the cause of Henry's initial leniency towards him. However, the later events and political maelstrom that surrounded his revolt would have reinforced Elizabeth's loyalties. Since there are no contemporary records of Elizabeth's reactions and subsequent feelings, we can only speculate on her state of mind. The revolters were seen as political machinations rather than true monarchal claimants, so motivations were not driven by any form of idealism but rather political power plays for executive authority. This Tudor solution was the last vestige of the brutal reality of a political process of bastard feudalism. The Tudor state was clearly heading toward more centralised political authority, where executive power and challenges to that power would endeavor to follow a more legislative process, albeit draconian in nature. We can perceive the early Tudor state to be the embryonic beginnings of true political debate based on a process rather than the execution of raw brute force.

Elizabeth experienced the loss of her grandmother in 1495 when Cecily Neville, the Duchess of York, died. The last matriarch of the old Yorkist regime closed a chapter in that part of Elizabeth's life. She left the last two major estates of York in Elizabeth's hands and her inheritance helped consolidate Henry VII and Elizabeth of York's monarchy and amalgamated the estates of the old regime with the new Tudor state. The future for Elizabeth was to be the legacy of her children and her focus was to ensure the succession of the new monarchy. This was a role she excelled in. She was to be engulfed in the marriage of her son Arthur and in the future of the monarchy through a Tudor heir who would succeed and grow the seeds of a prosperous monarchy. Katherine of Aragon was married to Arthur Tudor in 1501. Arthur and

Katherine stayed for a while at Tickenhill Palace, then departed to Ludlow, the prince's seat of power in Wales, to begin their married life. In early 1502 Elizabeth also saw the marriage of her eldest daughter, Margaret, to James IV of Scotland, which was concluded in a treaty at Richmond. This political marriage, along with her son Arthur's, was the zenith of Henry and Elizabeth's union and displayed the accomplishments of the Tudor monarchy. However, the tide of events would take a dramatic turn.

Elizabeth was to experience the death of her son in April 1502. Henry VII and Elizabeth of York consoled one another over this great loss. It cannot be determined what exactly claimed the life of her beloved son but it does not appear to be plague or another more acute illnesses. Arthur became increasingly ill over a period of seven weeks, which would indicate a more progressive disease or virus. Other theories included testicular tuberculosis, which also may suggest why he did not conceive a child with Katherine. Since there is no clear diagnostic record of the disease and the symptoms mimic many other diseases, we cannot be sure of the cause of death. It seemed he may have been frail and this would indicate a susceptibility to a wide range of diseases including influenza, diabetes and pneumonia, where a strong physical constitution would be key to recovery. Since Katherine also fell ill and recovered perhaps it was a more common respiratory ailment that claimed his fragile body. The loss of Arthur early in 1502 was undoubtedly a terrible blow for Elizabeth personally as well as for the dynasty, but the records show that her life went on and her determination to do her duty did not waver. Her support for her husband behind the scenes shows that Elizabeth of York was not the quiet meek queen some historians have suggested she was, but she provided the charity and humanity that served as an important fulcrum to Henry's cold and calculated reign. Elizabeth's younger son Henry would now be the heir apparent and he was to have his own household in preparation for the kingship. The young Prince Henry would eventually marry his brother's widow, Katherine of Aragon, to honour the alliance with Spain.

Elizabeth was to conceive again for the last time around two months after Arthur's death. This was a clear indication of devotion to her husband and the monarchy. She was thirty-seven years old and still of child-bearing age but it was still risky for her to carry another child. Henry was distant to his wife during this period and we can see a possible fissure in their marriage, most likely due to the grief he felt about the loss of Arthur. Elizabeth's state of mind can only be speculated upon, but it seemed she sought solitude to contemplate her loss, and this could only serve to reinforce the tragedy of her own mother and the loss of her two brothers. Another theory may be that she was bitter towards her husband in the treatment of her sisters and the lack of empathy he had shown towards her family. She had endured many losses in her earlier life and Henry did little to alleviate any of her grief. Henry's paramount concern was the realm and Elizabeth may have felt she was just a pawn in his master plan for the continued success of the Tudor state. There are no records of Elizabeth actively advocating for her sisters but there must have been private conversations between husband and wife that could have been fraught with tension. Another theory that Alison Weir purports involved Henry's interest in the young and beautiful Katherine Gordon, who was at court. There is no indication of any impropriety on Henry's part but the very interest he had in her could spark resentment and jealousy from

Elizabeth. The end result was the fact that Elizabeth and Henry were not sharing a residence together during her last pregnancy and her isolation may have been detrimental to her general health. Elizabeth went into labour early in February 1503 and her husband was present for the birth, but it was a pregnancy marked by illness and the queen was weak. The child was born on 2 February 1503, and was named Katherine. The baby was weak and did not survive, dying only eight days after her birth. It is not clear why the infant Katherine died but a premature birth could lead to many complications. Elizabeth herself fell ill soon after the delivery, dying on 11 February 1503. The cause of death again was not readily apparent and could have been due to many factors. Some of the causes suggested included internal hemorrhaging, childbed fever or puerperal fever, or even unsanitary conditions leading to infection. Elizabeth's death impacted Henry VII greatly and she was mourned by the whole of England. She was a much-loved and cherished 'Queen of Hearts'. Henry VII had organised a great funeral and this displayed his reverence for her qualities as both wife and queen. Henry remained a widower, and his remaining reigning years were as a paranoid and reclusive monarch.

Elizabeth of York's legacy lay in her qualities as the transitional queen born in the twilight of the medieval era but defined England's Tudor era. She produced the flower of the future in her offspring and was the product of the tumultuous era of the Wars of the Roses, which were filled with uncertainty and turmoil. Elizabeth of York was the matriarch of all kings and queens of England to this day. It seemed that her son Henry VIII, who overshadows both his parents in notoriety and grandeur, named his daughter with Anne Boleyn after his mother Elizabeth. This daughter would go on to be known as one of the greatest monarchs of England. Elizabeth of York was the much-needed quiet before the storm of female ascendancy to the throne of England, the grandmother of the first two regnant queens of England: Mary and Elizabeth Tudor.

CONCLUSION

Though the sex to which I belong is considered weak you will
nevertheless find me a rock that bends to no wind.

Elizabeth I

The shadow of Eleanor of Aquitaine's queenship was cast over a
period of over 350 years. The first female claimant to the throne in
the twelfth century, Matilda, created a period of anarchy in England.
There were no laws to bar a woman from ruling as a monarch, but
the fact remained that a successful medieval English king in the
twelfth century had to possess the martial skills to lead men into
battle. Women were not effectively trained for combat or to lead
in war. The traditional biblical role assigned to women was to be
subservient to men, and the Church reinforced this idea. However,
the reality of queenship was that the English monarchy was a
partnership based on two major factors. The first was succession and
the production of an heir. The queen's role was to fulfil this duty and
a failure to do so was considered a fatal flaw. The second duty for
the queen was to temper the brutal and coarse elements of the king's

rule with compassion and humility. These qualities were vital to any kingdom, but they were considered weak characteristics if they came from the king. The queen was the acceptable vessel to dispense these vital elements of Christian law in a monarchy.

Anne Neville was not covered in this study, but her contribution was fairly traditional. She was the daughter of the Kingmaker, the Earl of Warwick, and in her early life was a political pawn for his bid for power in 1469–71. She married Margaret of Anjou's son, Edward, and was to be the new queen when Edward IV was overthrown. This never came to be, but she remained the tool of her father's ambition. After the Lancastrian uprising led by the Earl of Warwick failed and Anne's husband Edward died at the Battle of Tewkesbury, she married Richard, Duke of Gloucester, and was the duchess and heir to the Warwick fortune. When her husband Richard usurped the throne in 1483, she was part of his claim to the throne. She and Richard were a powerful image of king and queen. Anne also produced a male heir for Richard III, which furthered the security of the succession and contributed to the validity of his reign. Unfortunately, their son died in 1484. Anne did not have to overcome the stigma of a low birth, like Elizabeth Woodville, or the xenophobia of a foreign birth, like Margaret of Anjou. She was part of the established English aristocracy and was an acceptable conduit for queenship. The circumstances or Richard III's reign coloured Anne Neville's queenship, since she shared the ambition of her husband. Anne had all the essential ingredients for a successful queen, but she was cursed by her husband's actions.

Margaret Beaufort was the mother of the Tudor dynasty, and her steadfast belief in her son's destiny to be King of England shaped the very landscape of late medieval England, eventually ushering in a new era of dynastic success. Margaret Beaufort was aware that during this period (1450–85) a woman could never have held the throne alone, and she channeled her ambition and transmitted her claims to her son, later Henry VII. She may have accepted the fact that she was passed over in the royal succession, but she was still a political power to be reckoned with. Margaret experienced times of great prosperity and power, but also times of turmoil and terrible despair. These highs and lows were, to a large extent, products of the War of the Roses in which Margaret lived, though she also suffered due to her family connection to the Beauforts. During the Lancastrian rule of Henry VI, Margaret was in a position of power. After the Yorkist victories, her fortunes took a marked change and she was under suspicion. She countered this with careful marriages and alliances to maintain and protect her estates and her son's inheritance. When the Yorkist implosion occurred in 1483 upon the death of Edward IV, she positioned herself close to Elizabeth Woodville and arranged a marriage between her son and Elizabeth Woodville's daughter Elizabeth of York. This union achieved her ultimate goal of putting her son on the throne of England. She ascended to a position of power and influence after Richard III's defeat at Bosworth in 1485 and was one of Henry VII's closest confidants during his reign. Margaret was a steady and able political player who influenced the authority of queenship during this era. She is an example of the long shadow Eleanor of Aquitaine cast over the model of an English medieval queen.

The evolution of the queens and consorts from Eleanor of Aquitaine to Elizabeth of York display a gradual growth in the importance of the English medieval queen. The dower in the lands of Eleanor of Aquitaine defined the very nature of the Angevin empire. Matilda, Eleanor of Aquitaine's mother-in-law, produced the precedent of a valid power base emanating from her male offspring – Henry Plantagenet, or Henry II. This would be seen again in Isabella of France and the successful overthrow of Edward II in the name of her heir, Edward III. Queens were an acceptable vessel through which to effect the change and sometimes overthrow of weak, corrupt and ineffectual kings. Many of the consorts, like Katherine Swynford and Katherine of Valois, are important in the heirs they produced and how this impacted the royal succession. Margaret of Anjou took the reins of power to keep her husband's throne intact and to protect her heir, Edward.

The hostile environment of the Wars of the Roses produced queens who defied convention and were lambasted for it. Margaret Anjou's actions would have been accepted if she was a man, but any failure of her politics was exploited through misogynist slander and rumour. She did lay the groundwork for queenship in its authority to rule. Elizabeth Woodville exerted her influence through Edward IV and furthered her family's ambitions through the royal channels of the aristocracy. The linearity of the growth of queens and consorts from Eleanor to Elizabeth indicated an increasing authority that was not always readily embraced. The anxieties of the times created the impetus for change but both Isabella and Margaret were labeled viragos and she-wolves. They displayed the avarice and ambition of kings but it was their sex for which they were judged. Each queen consort studied contributed to the evolution of an authority that grew out of necessity as medieval life became more sophisticated and the gender barrier became more ambiguous among the aristocracy. The queen's contribution of successors and a dowry could make the king that much more secure in this unstable medieval environment. Eleanor of Aquitaine's dowry was so influential that it shaped the very course of the Hundred Years War, and it would ultimately create the nation states of England and France in the early modern period – coincidentally, the same era saw England's first regnant queens in Mary and Elizabeth Tudor. The queens and consorts who walked in the shadow of Eleanor of Aquitaine in this study created the prototype for the English queen consort. These queens laid the formative groundwork for one of the most successful monarchs in English history, who happened to be a woman – Elizabeth I.

BIBLIOGRAPHY

Allmand, Christopher, *Henry V*, Berkeley: University of California
  Press, 1992.

Annales of Margam [in *Annales Monastici*, ed. H. R. Luard, Rolls
  Series, 1864].

Appleby, John T., *John, King of England*, New York: Knopf, 1959.

Baker, Darren, *Henry III: The Great King England Never Knew
  It Had*, Gloucestershire: The History Press, 2017.

Baldwin, David, *Elizabeth Woodville: Mother of the Princes in the
  Tower*, Gloucestershire: The History Press, 2002 [2010].

Bentley, Samuel, ed. *Excerpta Historica or Illustrations of English
  History*, London: Samuel Bentley, 1833.

Brown, A .L., *The Governance of Late Medieval England 1272–1461*,
  London: Edward Arnold, 1989.

Castor, Helen, *She-Wolves: The Women who Ruled England before
  Elizabeth*, New York: Harper/Perennial, 2011.

Chibnall, Marjorie, *The Empress Mathilda: Queen Consort, Queen
  Mother and the Lady of the English*, Oxford: Blackwell, 1991
  [1993].

Chrimes, S. B., *Lancastrians, Yorkists and Henry VII*, New York: St Martin Press, 1964.

_____, *Henry VII*, Berkeley: University of California Press, 1972.

Church, Stephen, *King John and the Road to Magna Carta*, New York: Basic Books, 2015.

Clive, Mary, *This Sun of York: A Biography of Edward IV*, New York: Knopf Publishing, 1974.

Collette, Carolyn P., 'Joan of Kent and Noble Women's Roles in Chaucer's World', in *The Chaucer Review*, Vol. 33, No. 4, 1999.

Crawford, Anne, 'The Queen's Council in the Middle Ages' in *The English Historical Review*, Vol. 116, No. 469, Nov. 2001: pp. 1193–1211.

Cronne, H. A., *The Reign of Stephen 1135–54: Anarchy in England*, London: Weidenfeld & Nicolson, 1970.

Evans, Michael R., *Inventing Eleanor: The Medieval and Post-Medieval Image of Eleanor of Aquitaine*, London: Bloomsbury, 2014 [2016].

Fahy, Conor, 'The Marriage of Edward IV and Elizabeth Woodville: A New Italian Source', in *The English Historical Review*, Vol. 76, No. 301, Oct. 1961: pp. 660–672.

Foedera, Conventiones, Litterae et Acta Publica, ed. T. Rymer, amended edn by A. Clarke and F. Holbrooke (4 Vols. In 7, Record Commission 1816–69).

Freeman, Jessica, 'Sorcery at Court and manor: Margery Jourdemayne, the witch of Eye next Westminster' in *Journal of Medieval History*, 30: 2004: 343–357.

Galway, Margaret, 'Philippa Pan: Philippa Chaucer', *Modern Language Review*, 55 1960. 481–87.

Gesta Henrici Secondi; The Deeds of Henry II in *English Historical Documents* 1042–1189, trans. and ed. D. C. Douglas & G. W. Greenway, London, 1953.

Given-Wilson, Chris, *Henry IV*, London: Yale University Press, 2016.

Goodman, Anthony, *The War of the Roses: Military Activity and English Society, 1452–97*, New York: Dorset Press, 1990.

_____, '*My most illustrious mother, the lady Katherine*': *Katherine Swynford and her daughter Joan*, Lincoln: The Dean and Chapter of Lincoln, 2008.

Green, David, 'Masculinity and medicine: Thomas Walsingham and the death of the Black Prince', in *Journal of Medieval History*, 35:1, 34–51. 2009.

_____, *Edward the Black Prince: Power in Medieval Europe*, Edinburgh: Pearson, 2007.

Green, Richard Firth, 'John Purvey and John of Gaunt's Third Marriage' in *Mediaeval Studies 66, Pontifical Institute of Mediaeval Studies*, (2004): 363–70.

Greenway, Diana, ed., *Henry of Huntingdon: The History of the English People 1000–1154*, Oxford: Oxford University Press, 2002.

Griffiths, Ralph A., *The Reign of King Henry VI: The Exercise of Royal Authority, 1422–1461*, Berkeley: University of California Press, 1981.

_____, 'Richard, duke of York, and the crisis of Henry VI's household in 1450–1: some further evidence' in *Journal of Medieval History*, Vol. 38:2, June 2012: 244–256.

Hallam, Elizabeth M., and Judith Everard, *Capetian France 987–1328, Second Edition*, Essex: Longman Pearson, 2001.

Hardy, B.C., *Philippa of Hainault and Her Times*, London: John Long Ltd. 1910.

Harriss, G. L., *King, Parliament and Public Finance in Medieval England to 1369*, Oxford: Clarendon Press, 1975.

Hicks, Michael, *Warwick the Kingmaker*, Oxford: Blackwell, 1998 [2002].

Hilton, Lisa, *Queen's Consort: England Medieval Queens*, London: Phoenix, 2008.

Hingst, Amanda Jane, *The Written World: Past and Place in the Work of Orderic Vitalis*, Notre Dame: Univeristy of Notre Dame Press, 2009.

Howell, Margaret, *Eleanor of Provence: Queenship in the Thirteenth-Century England*, Oxford: Wiley-Blackwell, 1998 [2001].

Howlett, Richard ed., William of Newburgh, Etienne de Rouen (moine au Bec), Richard (of Hexham), Anonymous, *Chronicles of the Reigns of Stephen, Henry II, and Richard I: The Gesta Stephani Regis Anglorum*, London: 1886 [reprint Scholars Choice].

Ives, Eric, 'Marrying for Love: The Experience of Edward IV and Henry VIII', in *History Today*, December 2000.

Kelly, Amy, *Eleanor of Aquitaine and the Four Kings*, Cambridge: Harvard University Press, 1950.

Kincaid, A. N., 'Buck and the Elizabeth of York Letter: A Reply to Dr. Hanham' in *The Ricardian*, Vol. 8, No. 101: 1988, 46–49.

Lawne, Penny, *Joan of Kent: The First Princess of Wales*, Gloucestershire: Amberley, 2015.

Lee, Patricia-Ann, 'Reflections of Power: Margaret of Anjou and the Dark Side of Queenship' in *Renaissance Quarterly*, Vol. 39, No. 2, Summer 1986: 183–217.

Licence, Amy, *Anne Neville: Richard III's Tragic Queen*, Gloucestershire: Amberley, 2014.

————, *Elizabeth of York: The Forgotten Tudor Queen*, Gloucestershire: Amberley, 2014.

Lucraft, Jeannette, 'Missing from History: Katherine Swynford', in *History Today*, Vol. 52, No. 5, May 2002.

————, *Katherine Swynford: The History of a Medieval Mistress*, Gloucestershire: The History Press, 2006 [2010].

Maurer, Helen E., *Margaret of Anjou: Queenship and Power in Late Medieval England*, Woodbridge, Suffolk: Boydell Press, 2003.

McFarlane, K. B., *Lancastrian Kings and Lollard Knights*, Oxford: Clarendon Press, 1972.

————, [ed. G.L.Harriss] *England in the Fifteenth Century: Collected Essays K. B. McFarland*, London: Hambledon Press, 1981.

McHardy, Alison K., trans. & annotated., *The Reign of Richard II: From Minority to Tyranny 1377–97*, Manchester: Manchester University Press, 2012.

Meyer, Barbara Hochstetler, 'The First Tomb of Henry VII of England', in *The Art Bulletin*, Vol. 58, No. 3, Sep., 1976: 358–367.

Michael, Michael A., A manuscript wedding gift from Phillippa of Hainault to Edward III' in *The Burlington Magazine*, Vol. 127, No. 990, Sept. 1985: 582–599.

Mitchell, J. Allen, 'Queen Katherine and the Secret of Lydgate's *Temple of Glas*' in *Medium Aevum Journal*, Vol. 77, No. 1: 2008. 54–76.

Mitchell, Mairin, *Berengaria, Enigmatic Queen of England*, London: A. Wright, 1986.

Morris, Marc, *A Great and Terrible King: Edward I and the Forging of Britain*, London: Random House, 2009.

Myers, A.R., *The Captivity of a Royal Witch: The Household Accounts of Queen Joan of Navarre, 1419–21*, 'Bulletin of the John Rylands Library', vol. 24, no. 2, October 1940.

Neillands, Robin, *The War of the Roses*, London: Cassell, 1992.

Norton, Elizabeth, *Margaret Beaufort: Mother of the Tudor Dynasty*, Gloucestershire: Amberley, 2011.

O'Brien, Anne, *The Forbidden Queen*, Ontario: Harlequin MIRA, 2013.

Okerlund, Arlene, *Elizabeth: England's Slandered Queen*, Gloucestershire: The History Press, 2006 [2009].

Ormrod, W. Mark, 'Edward III and his Family' in *Journal of British Studies*, Vol. 26, No. 4 (Oct. 1987). 398–422.

_____, *Edward III*, New Haven: Yale University Press, 2011.

Painter, Sidney, *William Marshal: Knight-errant, Baron, and Regent of England*, Baltimore: The Johns Hopkins Press, 1933 [1967].

Partner, Nancy, ed., *Studying Medieval Women: Sex, Gender and Feminism*, Cambridge, MA: The Medieval Academy of America, 1993.

Phillips, Seymour, *Edward II,* London: Yale university Press, 2011.

Prestwich, Michael, Edward I, New Haven: Yale University Press, 1988 [1997].

Ross, Charles, *Richard III,* Berkeley: University of California Press, 1981.

Royle, Trevor, *Lancaster Against York: The War of the Roses and the Foundation of Modern Britian*, Hampshire: Macmillan Palgrave, 2008.

Salzman, L. F., *Edward I*, London: Constable Press, 1968.

Saul, Nigel, *Richard II*, New Haven: Yale University Press, 1997 [1999].

Shakespeare, William, *Four Histories: Richard II, Henry IV Part I, Part II and Henry V*, New York; Penguin Books, 1994.

Spinks, Stephen, *Edward II The Man: A Doomed Inheritance*, Stroud: Amberley Books, 2017.

Vale, Malcolm, *The Ancient Enemy: England, France and Europe from the Angevins to the Tudors*, London: Hambledon Continuum, 2007.

Warkworth, John, *A Chronicle of the First Thirteen Years of the Reign of King Edward the Fourth*, ed. James Orchard Halliwell, London: 1839.

Warner, Kathryn, *Edward II: The Unconventional King*, Gloucestershire: Amberley, 2014.

Weir, Alison, *Eleanor of Aquitaine: A Life*, New York: Ballantine Books, 1999.

_____, *Queen Isabella: Treachery, Adultery, and Murder in Medieval England*, New York: Ballantine 2007.

_____, *Mistress of the Monarchy: The Life of Katherine Swynford, Duchess of Lancaster*, New York: Ballantine Books, 2009.

_____, *Elizabeth of York: A Tudor Queen and Her World*, New York: Ballantine Books, 2013.

Wenterdorf Karl P., 'The Clandestine marriages of the Fair Maid of Kent', in *Journal of Medieval History* 5, (1979): 203–231.

Wilcox, Lance, 'Katherine of France as Victim and Bride', in Shakespeare Studies: Vol. 17: 61–76. 1985.

Wogan-Browne, Jocelyn, et al, ed., *Medieval Women: Texts and Contexts in Late Medieval Britain: Essays for Felicity Riddy*, Turnhout: Brepols, 2000.

Young, Charles R., *The Royal Forests of Medieval England*, University of Pennsylvania Press, 1979.

ACKNOWLEDGEMENTS

I would like to acknowledge the help and encouragement of Ms. Ashley Jensen, a graduate student of mine who contributed to the research and photographs for this work. I would also like to acknowledge the authors who came before me and inspired me: Helen Castor, Alison Weir, Amy Licence, Lisa Hilton, David Baldwin, and Arlene Okerlund. Thanks also go to Philippa Gregory for her works that inspired films helping to visualise this era so vividly! Keepers of the archives and manuscript collections consulted were unfailingly helpful and without them I would never have been able to write a work of this nature. A final thanks go to everyone at Amberley for making this an enjoyable project. I hope I have provided a small window into the past lives of these amazing women who helped shape modern England.

INDEX